What Others Are Saying about *The Creative Communicator: 399 Tools to Communicate Commitment without Boring People to Death!*

The Creative Communicator is insightful, practical, charming, and the epitome of superb communication. A treasure chest of new ideas and dynamite tools!

Chip Bell, Coauthor of *Managing Knock Your Socks Off Service*

It is so refreshing to read real world case studies of successful companies and their creative use of communications. Now I have years worth of ideas to implement.

Todd Gardner, Market Development Executive, Apple Computer, Inc.

Innovative and creative employee communication is a vital component of your company's commitment to quality. Many quality efforts fail because of a company's inability to convey information freely throughout the organization. Barbara Glanz shows you how to break the mold of unproductive and mundane communication–by putting people first.

Dr. Charles Garfield, Author of *Second to None: How Our Smartest Companies Put People First*

Yesterday you came across a good idea. Something you heard. Something you read. Something you thought about. But you didn't write it down, did you? Me neither. Lucky for us Barbara Glanz has been paying attention—*and* she's been taking notes. Whether you take your ideas one a day or in bunches, *The Creative Communicator* will give you plenty of tools to work with.

Dick Schaaf, Coauthor of *The Service Edge* and *Taking Care of Business*

Barbara Glanz spent a weekend with our management team two years ago and we are still quoting her and using the skills she taught us. Now with *The Creative Communicator* we can have her with us daily. I highly recommend this book to anyone who is committed to commitment without being redundant.

Jay Pettapiece, President, Vision Financial Corporation

THE CREATIVE COMMUNICATOR:
399 Tools to Communicate Commitment without Boring People to Death!

Barbara A. Glanz
Kaset International

IRWIN
Professional Publishing
Burr Ridge, Illinois
New York, New York

This publication is designed to provide accurate and authoritative information in regard to the subject matter covered. It is sold with the understanding that neither the author nor the publisher is engaged in rendering legal, accounting, or other professional service. If legal advice or other expert assistance is required, the services of a competent professional person should be sought.

From a Declaration of Principles jointly adopted by a Committee of the American Bar Association and a Committee of Publishers.

Sponsoring editor:	Cynthia A. Zigmund
Project editor:	Jean Lou Hess
Production manager:	Diane Palmer
Designer:	Larry J. Cope
Compositor:	Publication Services, Inc.
Typeface:	10.5/12 Palatino
Printer:	Book Press, Inc.

Library of Congress Cataloging-in-Publication Data

Glanz, Barbara A.
    The creative communicator: 399 tools to communicate commitment without boring people to death! / Barbara A. Glanz.
      p.   cm.
    Includes bibliographical references and index.
    ISBN 1-55623-832-0
    1. Communication in organizations.   2. Communication in management.
3. Business communication.   I. Title
HD30.3.058   1993
658.4′5—dc20   93–12106

Printed in the United States of America

2 3 4 5 6 7 8 9 0 BP 0 9 8 7 6 5 4 3

To my earthly father, who first taught me a love for books and learning, and to my Heavenly Father, who blessed me with the belief, the opportunity, and the skills to make this dream come true.

Foreword

With the growing understanding of the importance of quality service has come an increasing appreciation for the value of good communication. In nearly every major problem faced in the business world, or society in general, the need for good communication is crucial.

Our individual experiences remind us almost daily that effective communication requires techniques that retain our attention in a positive way. Otherwise we tune out and turn off the message being directed to us.

The Creative Communicator: 399 Tools to Communicate Commitment without Boring People to Death! is packed with ideas for developing positive interaction that keeps the communication circuits open to various audiences.

The book provides examples of creative communications for all types of media and planning aids to help organize communication efforts and pursue them to a successful conclusion.

What helps make the rich variety of resource material in this book especially valuable and credible is the fact that each example is a real case history. I've always had a special appreciation for new ideas that have stood the test of time, and this book provides them in spades.

Our organization has benefited directly from Barbara's personal involvement with us as a consultant. I have had the opportunity to observe the legitimacy of both the ideas and the spirited philosophy underlying the preparation of this book.

Organizational leadership at any level should benefit greatly as well from the myriad of communication tools that make the book interesting, stimulating, and very useful.

John E. Fisher
General Chairman, Nationwide Insurance Companies

If you are at all like me, one of the most difficult things we have to do is communicate—both in our business and personal life. The real challenge is not *just* communicating, it's communicating *clearly, meaningfully,* and *effectively,* and doing it on a consistent basis.

Communicating in business is particularly important, and I'm not just talking about the communication that takes place between the corner offices. Every time a customer or potential customer comes in contact with an employee of your company, some form of communication takes place. This has been dubbed "the moment of truth," and most organizations are judged on these "moments of truth." One of the most important ideas that needs to be communicated in these turbulent times is the absolute priority of giving your customers *extraordinary customer service*.

This is where Barbara Glanz comes in; she shows you how to communicate your commitment to serving customers through the hundreds of excellent ideas she has compiled. I should warn you, however, *The Creative Communicator* is one of those "Why didn't I think of this?" types of books. These are ideas that real people in real companies have used to communicate their commitment to extraordinary customer service. Barbara presents so many good ideas, you may come away feeling as if you've never had a good idea in your life!

However, because I think it is highly likely that you've had many creative ideas, I believe this book will act as an idea-generating resource to help you think of even more ways to communicate your commitment to your customers. At least that's the way I reacted when I read what so many other people had done to get the word out to employees, vendors, and customers. Besides being stimulated and encouraged to become more creative myself, I already have plans to adapt many of the terrific ideas gathered in Barbara's book and to use them throughout Kaset International; I'm sure you will want to do the same with your organization.

Specifically, Barbara has provided us with three important tools:

- First, she shows us how to use the many avenues we have to communicate. Barbara demonstrates that the more avenues we explore, the more we increase our chances to be both creative *and* effective.
- Second, Barbara provides us with 399 real-world examples. The book is chock full of examples of what people have done in hundreds of organizations around the globe, organizations like yours and mine, giving us an international reference guide overflowing with creative ideas.
- Third, Barbara encourages us to simply "just do it!" *The Creative Communicator* is like a kick in the pants to get going, to be straight and bold, to try something—anything—to start communicating with your employees, vendors, and customers about how important extraordinary customer service is to you and your organization.

No matter how you use Barbara's book, it will help you communicate that commitment more clearly, meaningfully, and effectively. The ideas presented in this book will have a lasting impact not only on you, but also on those with whom you communicate. Thanks, Barb!

Dave Erdman
President/CEO, Kaset International

Preface

O ne of the questions I get asked most frequently in my work with executives and managers is, "How can we better communicate our commitment so that our employees will hear us and believe?" My answer: Be creative! Show them and tell them in new and different ways that surprise them, even stun them, and at last get their attention. Along with that kind of communication comes an inherent transmission of the worth and value of each individual employee; it *matters* that they hear and believe so that they, too, can have a sense of mission that their jobs are important.

This book is meant to "whack" your thinking, urging you out of your comfortable cocoon of routine communication to fly free and become aware of all the marvelous, innovative, and creative ideas there are around you. My goal is to encourage you to use these ideas for communicating commitment to plans of action that exemplify your organization's beliefs and values.

For far too long, most business communications have been predictable, boring, and all business (the caterpillar phase). This book shows you how you can escape the cocoon to rise above the dullness of routine communication (the butterfly phenomenon) through real-life, how-to examples. Anthony Robbins, the author of *Unlimited Power*, says that in order for change to occur, you must "break the pattern." The ideas in this book will help you break the pattern of dull, routine business communication so that your employees and your customers will hear and believe what you're saying.

This book is made up of wonderfully creative things other organizations, both public and private, are doing today, both here and abroad. During the process of talking to hundreds of people, it has become apparent that the creative human spirit is thriving in many organizations as they communicate their deepest beliefs and values both internally and externally. Most of the creative communication ideas in this book are related to organizational commitments to customers, to employees, and to society.

Also included are some general guidelines for creative communication specific to each of the categories covered in this book. As a former teacher and a present-day speaker and presenter, I could not resist the urge to include some concepts as well as examples! These ideas come from many sources, but primarily from Kaset International, the very special company that has allowed me to explore and develop my own creative spirit.

My hope is that you will be challenged and stimulated not only to use these ideas, but that this book will be an "idea-generating" resource, one you can turn to whenever you need your thinking jarred. Like the butterfly released from its cocoon, you must not stay on the ground too long! The ideas are listed in numerical order from 1 to 399 so that you can easily communicate with others about specific tools that excite you or seem viable for your organization.

WHO SHOULD USE THIS BOOK

This book is for decision makers and leaders who manage communication in an organization—Training Officers, Marketing Directors and staff, Human Resource Officers, Managers of Customer Service, Corporate Communications Directors, Public Relations Personnel, and other related positions. It is a reference book of ideas for creative communication that can impact both morale and productivity in your organization as both employees and customers begin to pay attention to your communications and believe in their authenticity.

Although many of the examples in the book demonstrate organization-wide programs and decisions that are usually directed by executives and managers, there are also examples that can apply to others in the organization who are either assigned or choose to volunteer for the responsibility of certain kinds of communication. Chapter 3, "Written Communication," is a good example. Ideas #1–23 demonstrate the communication of organizational decisions like mission statements and policies. These ideas are most appropriate for managers and senior executives. Ideas #24–37 and #51–59 have to do with marketing materials, such as newsletters, service guarantees, and brochures. In that same chapter there are also examples that apply to accounting departments (Ideas #43–50) and to those who write memos and reports (Ideas #38–42). In Chapter 7, there are examples for those who have the responsibility for the dissemination of information through signs and posters (Ideas #222–230).

Whereas Chapter 10 is written primarily for senior executives, Chapter 5, "Creatively Communicating Your Appreciation on a Daily Basis," contains ideas for all employees. So, even though the bulk of this book is directed toward supervisors and managers who have direct responsibility for communication and change, no matter what your role is in an organization there is something in this book for you. And again, remember that often it is the idea *outside* your own realm of experience that triggers the most creative responses.

HOW TO USE THIS BOOK _____

This is a right-brained book for left-brained people. (I'll discuss this concept more in Chapter 1.) For now, try to get out of your "mental locks," which can often cause analysis paralysis, and focus on the *ideas* rather than on the logic or the organization of them. Many of the ideas cover several different categories of communication; I've simply tried to place them in the area I think is most appropriate. However, where I've decided to place the ideas really doesn't matter. What does matter is whether or not you can adapt them to your organization or use them to trigger your own creative consciousness. David Armstrong of Armstrong International says, "Innovation is like baseball. The more times at bat, the more hits. The more ideas you try, the more successes you'll have."

Keep in mind that we all see things differently according to some of the rules we have or the tapes we play in our heads. Thus, what might be an innovative idea for you may be routine or even boring for someone else. You may see some of the ideas presented as ho-hum, innovative, or even wacky! Some of the ideas will make perfect sense to you; others may not. And that's O.K.—that's "the way you see it." My hope is that because of the number and breadth of ideas presented, you will find several that will whack your thinking.

I have purposely included ideas from a wide variety of sources. Even though an idea may be from an organization very different from yours, don't automatically discount the idea. The criterion used for inclusion in the book was not the source, but rather the quality, of the idea. All writers on creativity urge you to get out of your discipline and to look for ideas in totally unrelated places. For example, Idea #196, on the "Kindness Campaign" in Kansas City, triggered several wonderful ideas for a reviewer of this book that she could use for a "Customer Care" promotion in her organization. Another reader charged with bringing in three new ideas to boost sales in his large newspaper found five usable ideas, totally unrelated to sales or the newspaper business, in the first 100 pages of the book. When you read about Dr. Jeff Alexander, a pediatric dentist, don't reject the ideas as unrelated to your realm of work or your organization. Rather, think about how he has demonstrated his commitment by looking at situations from his customers' perpective. Stay open and allow your thinking to be stimulated.

Several tools have been included to make this book more immediately actionable:

- Ideas are numbered consecutively, regardless of the category they are in, making them easy to refer to in your own notes as well as in discussions with others.

- The location of each organization is included when it is first mentioned in order for you to get more information if desired.
- At the end of each section, a "Communication Challenge" has been included that contains some questions for you to consider for your organization regarding that category of communication.
- You will find blank "Action Pages" at the end of each chapter to list those ideas that intrigue you and to note your own creative thoughts they've inspired.
- A "12-Month Action Planner" has been included at the end of the book so that you can write down an idea a month to implement in your organization.
- Finally, I've included my address at the end of this preface so that you might send your creative ideas back to me.

As you use this resource and come up with your own unique approaches to creative communications, please feel free to contact me so that I, in turn, can share your ideas with others. If in some way this book is a catalyst for freeing up communication in your organization, I will have reached my goal. I challenge you to begin to communicate your commitment with spirit and passion in innovative, colorful, and unique ways. Many others have done it, as this book testifies; so can you. The result will be happier and more productive employees, more loyal customers, and a better world. May your creative spirit soar!

Barbara Glanz
Kaset International
2001 Spring Road, Suite 390
Oak Brook, Illinois 60521
Phone: 708-954-0020
Fax: 708-954-0053

Acknowledgments

T his book is a compilation of the creative spirits of many wonderful friends and colleagues. I feel deeply blessed that so many of my "heroes" at all levels in my life have participated in creating this manuscript—by sharing their ideas through contributing, writing, endorsing, permitting me to quote them, and creating cartoons; and by sharing their support through gathering names of our customers, helping gather releases, reading the manuscript, sending me clippings and articles, encouraging me when others discouraged, and even making dinner on the days I didn't get dressed from morning until night!

I'd like to thank my heroes:

- *Professional* Heroes—Og Mandino; Michael LeBoeuf; Chip Bell; Ron Zemke; Ned Herrmann; Charles Garfield; Roger von Oech; John Fisher; Jay Pettapiece; Patrick Coggins; Sherry Sweetnam; Deborah Dumaine; Don Baumgart; Juan Gutierrez; Alexandra Lang; the editors of *Executive Female* magazine; Brian McDermott, of "The Service Edge" Newsletter; my editors, Jeffrey Krames and Cindy Zigmund; and each of the individuals and the organizations who were willing to share their ideas.
- *Personal* Heroes—Shannon and Ken Johnston, Dave Erdman, and Milo Paich.
- Special *Supporters*—Bonnie, Sally, Pat, Carey, Charlie, Jean, Deanna, Diane, Becky, and Bill.
- *Family*—Erin, who drew the posters; Gretchen, who took the photographs of the posters; Charlie, who taught me how to use the Mac, proofed the manuscript, wrote the index, and did lots of "odd jobs"; Garrett, who will perhaps be selling this book one day; my mother, Lucille Bauerle; my grandmother, Florence Anderson; and my aunt, Adah Enz; who have always supported me in any endeavor I've ever attempted.

I thank you all from the depths of my being; you have allowed me to "fly free!"

Contents

Chapter One

Introduction
How to Communicate
Your Commitment Creatively—
A Frame

Until one is committed, there is hesitancy, the chance to draw back, always ineffectiveness, concerning all acts of initiative (and creation). There is one elementary truth the ignorance of which kills countless ideas and splendid plans: that the moment one definitely commits oneself, then providence moves too.

Goethe

This is a book about three ideas: *communication, commitment,* and *creativity.* I am using *communication* to mean "the sending of a message." *Commitment* is defined as the "what" of the message—the beliefs and values that are being communicated through some kind of action. And *creativity* is the "how" of the message—those beliefs and values communicated in a new and innovative way.

COMMUNICATION

I have used the following categories of basic communications that occur in most organizations: written, electronic, face-to-face, day-to-day feedback, enhancements and reminders, measurements, rewards and recognition, recoveries, and personal executive actions. The important point to remember with all of these types of communication is that they involve both the sending and the receiving of a message. The more creatively a message is sent, the greater the chances that the message will be noticed and heeded.

Consider these interesting facts shared by Dr. Arthur DeKruyter on communication: 60 percent of the individuals in the United States are in some form of the "information" business. U.S. workers spend an average of 47 hours a week communicating in some way.[1] So most of us are suffering from "communication overload"! Thus, we must communicate creatively if we are going to make our personal and organizational beliefs and values heard.

COMMITMENT LOOKING FOR A CAUSE

Source: © Kaset International.

COMMITMENT

Albert Schweitzer once wrote, "The power of ideals is incalculable. We see no power in a drop of water. But let it get into a crack in the rock and be turned into ice, and it splits the rock; turned into steam, it drives the pistons of the most powerful engines. Something happened to it which makes active and effective power that is latent in it." Commitment is a lot like that. If commitment to an organization's beliefs and values is communicated sincerely, powerfully, and creatively, members of that organization will be inspired in a new way to take action to make those beliefs and values a reality. Creative communication of the organization's commitment can make active and effective the power that is latent in its employees.

Commitment is defined as "being bound emotionally or intellectually to a course of action."[2] Although most of the ideas expressed here have to do with communicating a commitment to customer service, other underlying beliefs and values can be found in various examples throughout the book. These include the value of all human beings, the importance of purpose, recognition of individual differences, a devotion to quality, a desire to serve others, and the need for celebration and fun in the workplace. For example, several ideas from Hal Rosenbluth's book *The Customer Comes Second* have been included. The primary commitment of Rosenbluth Travel is to its employees' happiness. Serving the customer comes second—a result, Rosenbluth believes, of serving employees well.

I have recently been doing lots of speaking on "Communicating Your Organization's Commitment to Service Quality." Each time I give this presentation I am struck by the great gaps in organizations and individuals between what they *say* they believe and value and what they actually *do* to model those beliefs and values. Consider a study done by Louis Harris. When 500 senior level executives from various industries all over the United States were asked, "How important is Quality Customer Service to the ultimate success of your organization?" 98 percent responded "very important," the highest rating possible. In fact, 90 percent mentioned Quality Customer Service in their strategic business plans, and 88 percent mentioned it in their mission statements. However, when these same executives were asked about their actions in the question, "Do you directly link Quality Customer Service to compensation and promotion?" only 63 percent answered "yes."[3]

Therefore, I end every speech with the idea that commitment, very simply, means putting a belief into action. A poster from Great Performance, Inc. says, "COMMITMENT: There's no wavering to commitment, no uncertainty, no hesitation. Your actions are there for all to see. It is only when they match your values that you gain strength and power." I believe that taking the time and effort to creatively and innovatively communicate your organization's beliefs and values is the first step in modeling that you are taking definite action on your commitment.

CREATIVITY

I think of creativity as doing something common in an uncommon way. In his book *A Whack on the Side of the Head*, Roger von Oech says that all of us are bound up in "mental locks" and that we need to have someone or something come along and "whack" our thinking to help us to see things in a new and different way: "Those ideas or situations that cause you to get off your routine paths and 'think something different' are whacks to your thinking."[4]

The attitudes that lock our thinking into the status quo are such things as following rules, finding only one right answer, always being practical, and being afraid to play or make mistakes. Remember my advice in the preface? If you get too hung up on logic and organization, those mental locks will keep you from the joy of innovation.

Consider, for example, the teaching styles represented in two recent movies. In *Ferris Buehler's Day Off*, the teacher portrayed was all business and boring, thus encouraging us to sympathize with Ferris's need for a break. Contrast that teacher with Robin Williams's character in *The Dead Poets Society*, who, through extraordinary creativity and a lot of "whacks on the side of the head," inspired his students to truly love literature and internalize it into their very beings.

Von Oech says, "Mental locks can be opened in one of two ways. The first technique is to become aware of them, and then to temporarily forget them when you are trying to generate new ideas. If that doesn't work, maybe you need a 'whack on the side of the head.' We all need an occasional whack . . . to shake us out of routine patterns, to force us to re-think our problems, and to stimulate us to ask the questions that may lead to other right answers."[5] As you read this book, allow yourself to be "whacked." As a new creative spirit emerges in your organization's communications, so will a new creative spirit appear in all employees' thinking, thus fostering a deeper and more actionable commitment to those values and beliefs for which your organization stands.

There are some very powerful concepts and models that are important to understand in order to successfully appreciate and use this book.

THE HUMAN-BUSINESS MODEL

It is only with the heart that one can see rightly; what is essential is invisible to the eye.

Antoine Saint-Exupery, *The Little Prince*

In Any Interaction

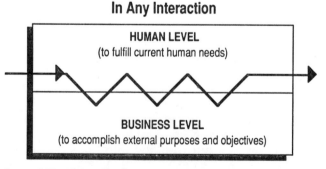

Source: © Kaset International.

Nearly everything in our lives can be related to this model. It is used in Kaset International's Service Quality training to describe what happens in interactions:

> Every interaction includes a Business Level and a Human Level. The Business Level gets the work done; the Human Level satisfies the participant's need for attention, courteous treatment, and acceptance of their viewpoint . . . Human and Business interactions occur simultaneously when people communicate with one another. People get their human needs met while they are doing business or accomplishing objectives. You can always add to the customer's sense of well being by using Human Level interactions. Entering and exiting all customer interactions through the Human Level helps customers to feel cared about and well treated.[6]

When I talk about the Human-Business model to groups of people, I often ask them, "How many of you have gone to a doctor who treated you *only* on the Business level? How did that feel?" Nearly everyone in the room can relate to "feeling like a piece of meat." I then ask them, "How many of you have been managed by someone who managed you only on the Business level? Did you do your best work for that person?" Again, nearly everyone can identify with this situation. We talk about how different those situations can be if we can interact on *both* the Human and the Business levels.

The Doctor, a recent movie based on the life of a real doctor, tells the story of a very successful surgeon who functions almost exclusively on the Business level. He is cold and unemotional, and he cares little for his patients as people. However, the doctor's whole world changes when he discovers he has throat cancer. When the doctor becomes the patient and is treated impersonally and without dignity, he finally begins to understand the importance of the Human level. He even makes the choice to have his critical surgery done by a doctor who is known for his caring rather than the one who is considered the "expert" in this treatment. At the end of the movie, this same doctor requires all his medical residents to put on hospital gowns and become "patients" for several days, thus experiencing many of the tests and procedures their patients endure. He hopes that awakening them to the Human level, in the same way that he became aware of it, will change the way they relate to their patients in the future.

The challenge with this book is to have you begin to apply this model to *all* your interactions and communications. Whereas the Business level accomplishes external purposes and objectives, the Human level is all about how one *feels* about the interaction. Is the person being treated courteously and with respect as a unique, living, breathing human being with his or her own story? After all, the Human level is what all three of the major ideas in this book (*communication, commitment, and creativity*) spring from. Begin, then, to think of both levels in all of your communications.

The Chinese characters that make up the verb "to listen" tell us something significant about this skill. Not only must we listen with our ears, but we must also "listen" from our own personal experience, with our eyes, our undivided attention, and most of all with our hearts. Listening with our hearts as the foundation is the meaning of the Human level.

Ear

You

Eyes

Undivided
Attention

Heart

INTERNAL AND EXTERNAL CUSTOMERS

It is important to define the way I am using the concepts of internal and external customers. Organizations have always been aware of the customers who are external to their organization, because they are the reason the organization exists. However, there is a new awareness of the people you may serve within your organization. These people are called your *internal customers*; an internal customer is defined as "someone who is dependent upon the timeliness, quality, and accuracy of someone else's work. You are a customer of others within the organization. You also have internal customers."[7]

It is helpful in reading this book to consider that you will be communicating with *both* internal and external customers. In some places in the book, I've used these two categories as delineators in listing the ideas to clarify the recipient of the communication. Regardless of whether you're communicating with an internal or an external customer, though, they each want to be treated on the Human level as well as the Business level. Several years ago a British Airways study indicated that there are four things all customers want:

"Friendly, caring service; Flexibility (jiggling the system for them); Problem Solving; and Recovery when the organization has made a mistake."[8] These are the kinds of treatment both internal and external customers want, and many of them fall on the Human level.

USING THE WAY IT IS MODEL

What is innovation? One person's innovation is another person's harebrained idea.
Casey Corr, *The Seattle Times*

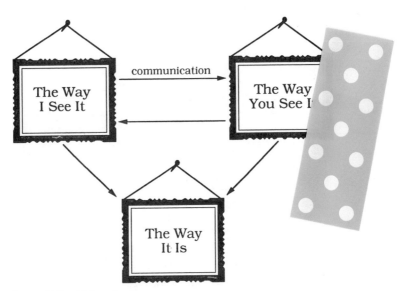

Source: © Kaset International.

As you read this book, another important frame to keep in mind is the phenomenon of everyone seeing the world differently.

Each of us has a different frame of reference—a different way to perceive what is going on around us. Another way to put it is that we each wear a different set of eye glasses, filtering out some things and adding others. It is certainly apparent that there is not always complete agreement between two people on the same situation. In any situation between two people there is always "the way I see it," "the way you see it," and "the way it is." The whole idea that others have a different frame of reference from yours, and that you accept their "frames" as okay for them, makes living in a society with so much cultural diversity a lot easier. It doesn't make one person right and another wrong, only different.[9]

Remember The Way It Is model—what may appear to be an innovative idea to some may be routine or even outrageous to others. In collecting information for this book, I asked hundreds of people,

"What is your organization doing that is different from others to communicate your commitment creatively?" Whatever they answered was "the way they saw it."

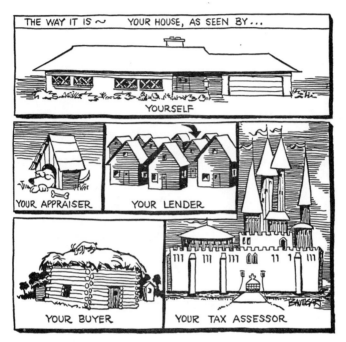

Source: © 1989 Kaset, Inc. Tampa, FL.

Keep coming back to this book to have your thinking stimulated. I hope the book will begin to affect "the way you see it," and then you, as the innovator in your organization, trying new and different ways of expressing your organization's commitment, will greatly affect "the way it is."

CHOICES

Charles Garfield, in his book *Peak Performers*, quotes Abraham Maslow on choices:

> Let us think of life as a process of choices, one after another. At each point there is a progression choice and a regression choice. There may be a movement toward defense, toward safety, toward being afraid, but over on the other side there is the growth choice. To make the growth choice instead of the fear choice a dozen times a day...is a movement toward self-actualization.[10]

Several years ago I created a visual model that illustrates the choices we have in each individual interaction:

Achieving Extraordinary Customer Relations

Discounts (-)	Business Only (0)	AAAA's (+) PMCE's
	c h o i c e	c h o i c e

Source: © Kaset International.

This model shows that in *every single interaction* we have with any-one, we have the *choice* to create either a negative (−) experience for that person by making him or her feel less important than ourselves or our organization, a neutral (0) experience by taking care of his or her business needs only, or a positive (+) experience by considering the person's human needs (the "Four A's," special skills to help us create positive interactions, will be discussed in Chapter 5).

Although this model represents interactive choices, this book also offers you lots of choices in each category of communication I've included. If you don't ever try to communicate your commitment or if you're not committed to anything except the bottom line, that's a minus. To stick to dull, boring, routine business communications is a zero. You can, however, *choose* to communicate your commitment in an innovative, creative, Human way to make the experience a plus for both your internal and your external customers.

If you choose to take the risk to become more innovative and free in your communications, *you will make a difference* in your organiza-tion. You will see a new spirit, a new generation of the Human level as others begin to realize that you can "fly free" by adding heart to all interactions.

RIGHT BRAIN THINKING
VERSUS LEFT BRAIN THINKING

In the preface, I described this book as "a right-brained book for left-brained people." According to the definitions in Ned Herrmann's book *The Creative Brain*, most of this book comes from the right quadrants of the brain. The four quadrants of the brain are illustrated and described in the Whole Brain Model.[11]

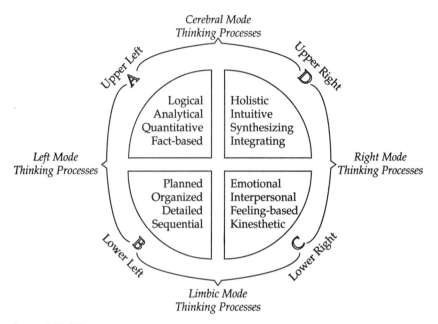

Source: © Ned Herrmann.

What does all this mean to the readers of this book? Can you recognize your preferent quadrant or quadrants? These preferences for different thinking modes will initially affect how you perceive the information in this book. Herrmann suggests the importance of keeping the following ideas in mind as you read *The Creative Communicator*:

> First, we are not a single individual quadrant but rather a coalition of the four quadrants; therefore, most of us have preferences in more than one quadrant. Second, a given profile is neither good nor bad, right nor wrong, and although profiles tend to remain constant if there is no reason for change, they can and do change in response to life situations. So, those of you with left mode preferences may, because of this experience and a conscious choice to change your communication style, find yourself changing your preferences to more right mode methods of communication as this book suggests.

The important point to remember is that no matter whether you're predominantly right-brained or left-brained, you *can* choose to express your ideas in innovative and creative ways. You only need a few "whacks" and a little practice.

> *Creativity may express itself in one's dealing with children, in making love, in carrying on a business, in formulating physical theory, in painting a picture.*
>
> Jerome Bruner

Chapter Two

Guidelines for Communicating Your Organization's Commitment

L et me share with you some guidelines for communicating your commitment. These guidelines become especially important when you are just beginning to communicate a cultural change in your organization, a change in beliefs and values, such as a new commitment to Service Quality:

1. Use the "quiet splash." Especially when you are just beginning a cultural change, it is important that it not be viewed as "just another flash in the pan" or program of the month. To build credibility, begin the effort rather quietly. For example, rather than using bells and whistles and a huge promotion, begin with meetings of employees and senior management to explain the new philosophy. The huge promotions are more appropriate later as celebrations or ways to keep the changes alive.

2. Avoid setting high employee expectations. When you set high employee expectations (e.g., "this change will take place overnight"), they will probably be disappointed with the results—no matter what *actual* changes you make. However, if you set low expectations (e.g., "this is a slow process and will take us 5 years or more to achieve"), they will probably be pleased with whatever changes they perceive. (See figure at top of following page.)

3. Expect varying levels of commitment. I like to use the metaphor of a train pulling out of the station to explain employees' reaction to a new organizational direction. Hopefully the CEO and most senior managers are in the engine! Now, many of your employees will readily jump on board; however, there are those who will watch and wait for the train to get up to speed before they decide to climb on. Others will wait until the very end and grab the caboose just before it leaves the station. Some others may even wait for the "next" train. Finally, there are a few who will get in front of the train and in one way or another try to halt the progress, even rip up the rails—they

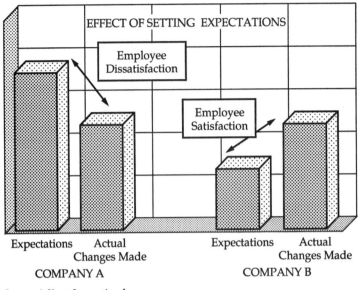

Source: © Kaset International.

are the ones to be concerned about. At some point, after training, coaching, retraining, coaching, and sometimes even "banishment" (giving them a job where they interact with few or no customers), if there is not buy-in to the new cultural values, senior management must model its commitment through action and terminate these employees.

4. Begin the initial announcement with the employees' input:

> These are the things you've told us . . . and here are some ideas of how we are going to deal with those issues and concerns. However, we can't do it without your ideas, support, and help. You are the ones who truly know our customers, and your ideas are critical to this change occurring. Perhaps we haven't listened very well to your input in the past, and that was our loss. Now we are going to try very hard to listen to what you tell us.

Let them know that you are listening to them and that their ideas and concerns count.

5. Get employee buy-in by involving them. Ask them to be on task forces, teams, and committees to actively work on changing the culture. Hold interviews, focus groups, and informal meetings with senior management to allow employees arenas to share their thoughts and ideas. Involve them in planning social events and fun campaigns to keep the spirit of change alive. Kaset International asked over 300 senior executives to list the three factors that most contributed to the overall success of their Service Quality initiative. The number three factor for success was "employee input and involvement," right behind "extensive employee training" and "observable commitment and involvement of management."[1]

6. Acknowledge and appreciate what employees have already done. Instead of focusing on what they haven't done, focus on the positive things they *have* done, adding encouragement that as this cultural change occurs, barriers disappear, and policies and procedures change, it will become even easier to model the beliefs and values of the organization. You should also involve employees in setting up programs to recognize and appreciate *one another* on a daily basis. I have included many ideas for this in Chapter 6—"Day-to-Day Feedback." In a study that has been conducted each year since 1948, one of the top three things people want from their job is "full appreciation for the work done."[2]

7. Stress that this is a long term project. Ken Johnston, author of *Busting Bureaucracy*, says that in most organizations a cultural change will take at least five years to complete, so the changes will be gradual. Emphasize the importance of a long term commitment from each member of the organization.

8. Recognize that mistakes will occur and that taking risks is acceptable within the culture. In applying "The Way It Is" model, we are often asking people to "reframe"—to choose to see something through a different lens or frame. I often ask people what the word *mistake* connotes to them. Most of them will say things like "negative," "bad," or "failure." I then ask them to hyphenate the same word— *mis-take*—and I ask them if that doesn't have a different feel for them. I point out that in the movies it might take hundreds of "takes" to get a final print; just so, a "mis-take" is simply trying something that didn't work and learning from it. By reframing the word, they can have a new understanding of the importance of sharing their "mis-takes," not as failures, but rather as approaches that didn't work. In fact, I encourage you to publicize goofs and what you learn from them as much as successes. This sends a message to your employees that you are being honest with them, that mistakes are O.K., and that you are "practicing what you preach" by sharing the mistakes (especially those of managers) and helping everyone to learn.

9. Focus on management *actions*, not on talk. Remember that commitment without action is hollow, so to truly prove to your employees that you are committed, you must share with them what you have actually *done*, not simply future goals and expectations.

10. Stress teamwork. By giving employees a sense of mission in the importance of what they are doing, you are creating a new team spirit.

11. Promise to keep them informed and then *do* it. When employees have been asked what they want from their jobs in the annual study that I mentioned in guideline six, one of the top three things they say they want, even before money, is "a feeling of being in on things."[3] We also suggest that you keep announcements on an organization-wide basis, so each employee feels equally included.

This book is filled with creative ways you can keep your employees informed. Communicate often, keeping the process fresh and different, and emphasize the Human.

12. Tell specific stories about good Service Quality performance or whatever beliefs and values you are trying to communicate. Begin to collect company legends, tell them at company meetings and functions, and write them in your communications. This, too, will add a new sense of pride and humanness to your organization. Give credit as much as possible to the frontline and support people, not to management. They are the real "warriors" of the cause.

13. Encourage the following specific executive actions:

a. Manage the transition or cultural change; don't just "let it happen." Mutually set goals, involving employees in the process. Monitor the progress by including specific measurements of the beliefs and values you are communicating. And keep those beliefs and values visible in every communication, every company meeting, and in your own personal actions. Chapter 11, "Personal Executive Actions," will share with you some of the ways other executives are creatively communicating their commitment, and Chapter 8 presents ideas on "Measurement."

b. Provide skills training to support the beliefs and values to which your organization is committed. In the study I mentioned earlier, the number two response of senior level executives to the question "What are the top three factors contributing to the success of your Service Quality initiative?" was "extensive employee training."[4] Again, Chapter 11 will give you some creative ideas of how other executives have communicated their commitment specifically to this training effort.

c. Make the beliefs and values matter—reward and recognize those employees who exemplify them. Chapter 9, "Creative Rewards and Recognition," contains many powerful, unusual, and fun ideas for recognizing and rewarding employees. If we want people to demonstrate particular behaviors, we must reward them for doing so. Michael LeBoeuf calls reward "The Greatest Management Principle in the World!"

d. Revise policies, practices, and procedures to reflect the beliefs and values of the organization. If your focus is on Service Quality, then your policies, practices, and procedures must be customer-friendly, existing to make it easier for the *customer* rather than easier for the organization. In Chapter 3 you'll see some examples of creative ways other organizations have made their policies customer-friendly.

I encourage you to keep these guidelines in mind as you plan your communications. They incorporate in an actionable way many of the models and concepts I have presented as a frame for this book.

Chapter Three

Written Communications
*How to Make
Your Written Communications
Express Your Commitment
in a Creative
and Customer-Friendly Way*

The difference between the right word and the almost right word is the difference between lightning and the lightning bug.

Mark Twain

T he written pieces sent out from your organization and your policies and procedures all project an "image" of your organization—is it a friendly place that cares about its employees and its customers or is it cold and bureaucratic, concerned only with rules and systems? Is it a "formal" organization or does it have an informal, flexible feel to it? Is it most concerned about customers or about the internal organization? And finally, do these written pieces give the customers confidence and make them *want* to do business with your organization?

In order to manage what you communicate through your organization's written documents, you must first be very clear on what kind of image represents your organizational vision. How do you want to be perceived by your customers? Then it becomes exceedingly important to carefully scan each written document sent out by your company and each policy and procedure *from the customer's perspective* to determine if you are communicating the beliefs and values you want to communicate. As you add a new creative spirit to these communications, the impact on customers, both internal and external, will significantly increase.

GUIDELINES FOR CREATIVE BUSINESS WRITING

Creative business writing might seem like a contradiction in terms. After all, "creative" suggests unlimited, fresh, and non-routine. "Business" suggests "bottom line," "top line," or numbers. Being able to communicate from both these worlds simultaneously results in a "double power" communication because it is integrating the functions of both the left and the right sides of the brain. The "logical left" brain provides the facts, details, and analytical thinking for writing, and the "creative right" provides the innovative, big-view, fresh outlook on a situation.

Unfortunately, many people believe that when they write for business they should write in a very formal business style, strictly from the logical viewpoint. The result is usually boring, routine, ho-hum writing that doesn't get read.

The reason bringing creativity to the page is so important is that it is the source of our enthusiasm, passion, and humanness. It is that very creative side that readers find most interesting, personal, and real. The only way to tap that creativity is to learn to manage ourselves during the difficult phases of the writing process. Creativity can only be tapped when we are writing without judging or criticizing ourselves. Most of us are masters at criticizing our own writing; we haven't learned how to master non-self-criticism.

There are two tools recommended for learning to write more creatively and without self-judgment and self-criticism. They are:

1. Mindmapping. This technique was introduced by Tony Buzan. There are a few basic guidelines: start with a blank piece of paper, and in the center, write down the subject of the business writing task you are going to write about. Draw a circle around that subject and then just let the ideas flow out of the center. Don't write in full sentences or be logical, just put down the key thoughts. Every mindmap looks different and depends on the mood, enthusiasm, and experience of the writer.

   Many people say that mindmapping is one of the most easy and useful creative thinking and planning tools they have ever used.

2. Freewriting. This technique has been formally described by Gabriele Lusser Rico, Peter Elbow, Brenda Ueland, and Natalie Goldberg. The guideline is to write in sentences about what comes from your heart—again, no editing, no criticizing. The idea is to focus 100 percent of your energies on writing. The focus on editing comes after the first freewritten draft.

After practicing both of these tools over a period of time, people find that their confidence level and creative thinking expand. And most important, the power of their personal voice starts to emerge. In that personal voice is found a directness, a clarity and depth of thought, a conviction that far surpasses the traditional ho-hum business writing style that is

continued

filled with the "as pers," and "in reference tos." Creative business writing means finding your own voice, your own path, your own style, within your unique business environment.

The great communicators in our society—whether in business, government, academia, or the arts, are those that are able to tap into the creative, unique, personal voice inside themselves and therefore bring their whole self to the page. And what that voice does is touch the reader—your customer, your manager, your peer. And in doing so, you are much more likely to meet your business goals because you have communicated as a whole, real person.[1]

Source: Sherry Sweetnam.

STATEMENTS OF PURPOSE

Every organization needs a statement of purpose in order to focus its efforts and to align all its employees. Generally, we think of a mission statement as an expression of organizational purpose, service strategies as the framework for implementation of service standards, and the vision as a statement of "what it can be like," the ideal for that organization. James J. Mapes defines a mission statement as one which "comes from the head; a Vision comes from the heart." Incorporated into and underlying all of these statements are the philosophies and values of that organization. Chapter 10 will address in more detail how senior management can effectively and creatively communicate the organizational vision.

Let's first look at some interesting ideas and guidelines for mission statements and service strategies. Juan Gutierrez suggests asking the following questions to determine how customer-focused your organization is:

- Is there a current written mission statement?
- To what extent does the mission statement focus on serving customer needs versus the needs of the stockholders/investors?
- Do employees and managers know and use the mission statement in their daily work?
- How many employees and managers can quote the mission statement?[2]

So, if your organization has as its vision becoming a customer-focused or customer-driven organization, then your mission statement, properly written and utilized, can drive this cultural change.

A service strategy can be defined as

a tool to communicate what central service theme is critical to your unit. As a communication vehicle, it insures all service people in your unit are aligned and directing their energies toward the exact same end. It is the theme, the story, and the explanation which makes sense out of your service standards and measures. In other words, it provides the "why" for all the service actions expected of your front-line service people. A Service Strategy is a serious statement of commitment that:

- Makes you different.
- Has value to your customer.
- Has value to the employees.
- Can be delivered to your customer.[3]

One of the challenges that occurs in writing unit service strategies is including the Human level as well as the Business level. You will see some creative ways of accomplishing this task in the examples that follow.

Mission Statements

Let's first look at several different kinds of mission statements. Keep the Human/Business model in mind as you read Ideas #1–#13. You will find several more examples of mission statements and statements of purpose in the appendix.

#1.   Kaset International's mission is

to help organizations achieve extraordinary customer relations. Kaset International's service strategy is to provide the full spectrum of industry-specific consulting, training and measurement services that organizations need to achieve and maintain extraordinary customer relations. We fulfill this strategy through friendly, caring people who give responsive and flexible service to our customers and to each other.

#2.   Wisconsin Power and Light in Madison, Wisconsin, has an *employee mission statement*:

- Employees are experts at their jobs;
- Because of their expertise, employees are in a unique position to identify improvements that will save time and money, assist co-workers and better serve customers;
- A part of every employee's job is to think creatively, make suggestions, investigate opportunities and implement solutions;
- It is management's responsibility to encourage teamwork, to listen and be supportive of employee ideas, and recognize employees for their efforts.

#3.   The Florida Division of Forestry has its mission statement printed on the back of every employee's business card. A framed copy of the mission statement is prominently displayed in each of the Division's 16 field units. A standard question to every internal applicant for a promotion during their interview is, "What's the Division's mission?"

#4. The mission of Moore Business Communication Services (MBCS) is to be the leader in profitably providing products, services, and systems solutions for vital business communication needs that result in increased efficiencies and/or effectiveness for customers.

MBCS Strategy

FOCUS IS THE KEY WORD FOR OUR GROWTH STRATEGY.
DEVELOP THE HIGHEST QUALITY PRODUCTS AND
SERVICING.
INVEST IN NEW SUPPORT SYSTEMS.
INVEST IN TECHNOLOGY.
INVEST IN PEOPLE.

Vision Statements and Philosophies and Values

#5. The Division of Rehabilitation Services of the Georgia Department of Human Resources recently created a document that they call P-V-P, which stands for Purpose, Values, and Philosophy. It is the culmination of over 130 brainstorming sessions over 20 days that included 1,740 employees to ensure that all staff would have input; hundreds of hours of work by the P-V-P group sorting and analyzing the data (over 1,300 flip charts of information were generated); several long sessions with the division's leadership team; and finally a statewide conference in order to continue the P-V-P refinement at the strategic level, truly making this a "shared process." The division decided to substitute the word "purpose" for "mission" and to commit to using *employees'* words, not bureaucratic ones.

This is the pledge the Director, Yvonne Johnson, made at its unveiling:

> I am personally committed to making this more than something we hang on the wall. Along with the leadership team, I pledge to each of you that this will be a "living document," one that directs how we will behave and on what we will base our decisions. I challenge each of you to make a similar commitment. There is not a stronger message that we could send than living up to our stated values.

> *Purpose:* Our purpose is to provide opportunities to improve the quality of life for Georgians with disabilities.
> *Philosophy:* We celebrate a belief that all people deserve the best we have to offer.

1. We value persons with disabilities.
2. We value quality.
3. We value our people.
4. We value an organization of honest, sensitive, and responsible people.
5. We value leadership that is committed to integrity, trust, teamwork, and open communication.

#6. Cuyahoga Savings in Cleveland, Ohio, uses an acronym for its Cornerstone Beliefs:

S = Strength is paramount

E = Exceptional customer service

R = Responsive to customers

V = Value is what we sell

I = Integrity is essential

C = Community involvement

E = Employee Dedication

#7. Zenger-Miller of San Jose, California, has created a philosophy statement that incorporates their philosophy regarding their Clients, Quality, their Associates, and their Products and Services:

CLIENT PHILOSOPHY

Our clients are our colleagues. We will demonstrate our personal respect for their professionalism, dignity, competency, uniqueness and intelligence. They deserve extraordinary service, support and concern from us. Our dealings should be ethical, honest, straightforward, and with an uncommon desire to do what is right. Our clients should feel that we are with them for the long run as collaborators in finding practical solutions to organizational change and training needs. . . .

#8. "We create products and services that treat all people involved with dignity." This is the Statement of Values and Philosophy adopted by city employees of the City of Gillette, Wyoming, in 1985 as a statement of the principles and values to be followed by city employees in their interaction with citizens, vendors, and people the city does business with:

1. We value a quality, well-planned living environment for all Gillette citizens.
2. We value fiscal responsibility.
3. We value excellent public services and high-quality facilities.
4. We value a clean and beautiful community.
5. We value the opinions of our citizens.
6. We value a high level of education and training in City employees.

7. We value a free and healthy economy.
8. We value a safe living and working environment.
9. We value a positive and realistic image of Gillette, both within and outside of the City.
10. We value courteous, competent and responsive employees and public officials.

#9.   The Savings Bank of Rockville, Connecticut, has a document that states:

WE PROMISE:

- To answer all phone calls on or before the third ring and return all calls on the same day.
- You'll get approval on consumer loans within 24 hours, plus five day mortgage approval and construction advances. We'll respond to customer letters within 24 hours.
- To keep the customer lines moving with peak period tellers. You'll always be greeted with a smile and be on your way quickly and without delay.

Our employees have agreed in writing to make sure that you get the best customer service possible. Our officers and staff are ready to take the extra step necessary to give you prompt, efficient, courteous, and personal service. *The sincerest desire to serve is what makes The Savings Bank of Rockville so special.*

#10.   Standard Insurance in Portland, Oregon, uses this statement as their Quality Service Vision:

EXCELLENCE
Dedication to excellence is emphasized in Standard's mission statement. Excellence is encouraged by building and maintaining quality relationships with customers, employees, field representatives, and suppliers.
RELATIONSHIPS
Long-term relationships are nurtured by asking customers, employees, and field representatives what they need, listening carefully, and exceeding their expectations. This continuous process adds value and builds lasting relationships.
ENVIRONMENT
Relationships with employees and field representatives are strengthened by an environment that fosters trust and teamwork. Employees and field representatives receive training, tools, support, and necessary authority to respond to customers' needs. Customer satisfaction is the basis for recognizing and rewarding individual and team performance and excellence.
DEDICATION
Standard encourages company-wide dedication to being the best. We take pride in our leadership in our industry and our communities.

#11.   The corporate vision statement of PSI Energy of Plainfield, Indiana, is printed on the back of employees' business cards: "OUR VISION: We will be a leader in the emerging energy services industry by challenging conventional wisdom and creating superior value in a safe and environmentally responsible manner." The vision statement is also printed on 5 × 7 posters for employees to have at their work stations as a touchstone for what is important to the organization.

#12. The City of Scottsdale, Arizona, has the following vision—"Scottsdale...Simply Better Service!"

On our way to the year 2000, City of Scottsdale employees will be recognized as innovative, environmentally sensitive and committed to quality service; members of an organization in which leadership, teamwork, and respect for the individual are valued, and employees take pride in everything they do.

OUR VALUES

- Respect the Individual
- Be a Team Player
- Commit to Quality
- Risk, Create, Innovate
- Listen, Communicate, Listen
- Take Ownership!

Service Strategies

#13. These service strategies were created by different departments of Vision Financial Corporation in Keene, New Hampshire, to support the organization's purpose—"Our business is to provide quality payroll deduction administrative services to our customer insurance companies, our most important assets":

Case Coordination Department
  To provide our customers with the education and resources to establish and maintain a successful list bill client. We will approach each encounter with our customers with a positive, cooperative and understanding attitude.
Customer Service Department
  To actively search for and achieve methods of delivering thorough personalized service that consistently and positively surprises our policyholders, agents, and ourselves.
Premium Accounting Department
  To provide our customers with easy-to-follow, timely premium notices as well as useful and personalized information. We process payments in an accurate and timely fashion and respond to customer inquiries in a friendly and satisfying manner.
Claims Department
  To provide courteous and prompt acknowledgment, investigation, objective evaluations and fair claim settlements. All claimants will be treated as we would want to be treated if we were in the claimant's position.

COMMUNICATION CHALLENGE. Does your organization have a mission statement or a statement of purpose? If not, get started! If it has a statement of purpose, does it focus on the customer? Does it have a Human level? Do your employees know it? Do they believe in it? Peter Lichtgarn of The Times Mirror Company says, "The benefit of a mission statement is its undisputed definition of a corporate culture. Its weakness is the (usually) pompous and grandiose tone. They are often so far removed from the employees as to be laughed at and ignored. . . . [However, a good mission statement] allows management to show that the company does have a soul. At the same time, mission statements allow employees to see the larger scheme of company activities beyond their individual jobs."[4] These are some excellent thoughts to consider as you either write or re-examine the statement of purpose of your organization.

LETTERS AND POLICIES, PRACTICES, PROCEDURES

Each letter or written communication your organization sends creates an experience for your customers. It is important to consider each piece of communication from the customer's perspective, always thinking about what kind of image your organization is presenting. Look carefully at the words you choose to state policies and procedures in your organization—are they controlling, punishing, fear-inducing words? Or are they reasoning, flexible, and friendly? Look at whether or not you've included the Human level in your written communications—remember the creative ways you can do this with graphics, cartoons, quotations, pictures, and words of appreciation and acknowledgment. Use active, not passive, voice; change negative language into positive; and use the customer's name in the body of the letter.

Letters

#14. A letter from the president of the company is sent to each new customer of Buckner Corporation, Fresno, California, to welcome them and to inform them of Buckner's "total customer satisfaction."

#15. Customer service representatives of The Savings Bank of Rockville, Connecticut, send letters to "out of area" customers who want to open accounts by mail. William J. McGurk, the bank's CEO, says, "Opening accounts in this manner is not conducive to community banking, and we have had excellent success with this letter. It has eliminated difficult accounts and allowed us to form strong relationships with those actually relocating to our area. One such customer relocated from England and was instrumental in my college-age daughter obtaining summer employment in the mall where he is employed." Note the customer-friendly wording:

Dear _____:
Thank you for your interest in opening an account at The Savings Bank of Rockville by mail.

As a community bank, we pride ourselves on PERSONALIZED superior customer service. While many of our services ARE available by mail, and we encourage use of mail for such transactions as payments, deposits, etc., we prefer to open accounts in person. We build our business on relationships and referrals, and this first personal meeting will give you an opportunity to sample our quality service.

On your next visit to our area, I invite you to stop in, meet us in person and open your account. We appreciate your inquiry and look forward to an opportunity of being "your bank" when you've relocated to our market area.

Very truly yours,
William J. McGurk
President
Chief Executive Officer

#16. SouthTrust Corporation has listened to its customers and created more customer-friendly envelopes. Customers had been complaining that when they tried to open the self-sealing envelopes or their Certificate of Deposit statements, they ripped their statements. As a result of customer surveys, completed lobby cards, and unsolicited feedback, a Service Improvement Team was formed to find a solution. Although the design they came up with was more expensive, the bank was very pleased with the positive customer response.

#17. This is a pamphlet that is enclosed with Disconnection Notices by Clark Public Utilities in Vancouver, Washington. Usually, when your service has been or is close to being disconnected, the letters are threatening and humiliating. However, this note is supportive and friendly, and allows people to keep their dignity. (A Guarantee of Service Plan is discussed in this Idea, as well as in Idea #60.)

Having trouble paying your electric bill?
Let us try to assist you.
If you are having trouble paying your utility bill, Clark Public Utilities may be able to assist you. Through a network of energy assistance sources, you may find that your past due bill can be resolved without an additional hardship on you, and without the necessity of disconnection. If you have already been disconnected, it may be possible to have service restored without payment.

Maybe our new payment plan will work for you.
You may find that you qualify for our Guarantee of Service Plan, which requires only a minimal payment each month—one that you can afford. The plan would also exempt you from paying a security deposit or late charges.

Give us a call.
Why not call our Customer Service office and inquire about what may be available for you. Simply tell the representative that you are behind on your payments and are unable to pay. They will take it from there and tell you what to do.

Our Com/Care representative can work for you.
If you are really unsure about your future ability to pay your utility bills and feel you could use some professional guidance at no cost to you, feel free to ask for one of your Com/Care representatives. They are our employees, but they work for you and will do everything they can to assist you.

There may be an alternative to disconnection.
Don't allow your service to be disconnected needlessly. A simple phone call could be all that is necessary.

#18.   In their book *The Joy of Service* Ron McCann and Joe Vitale talk about the idea of "Personal Signature." They say, "There is a way to increase service recognition while increasing your ability to give extraordinary service. It is *so* simple. All you have to do is start signing everything you do."[5] Here are some examples they give:

- Let's assume that you are a payroll clerk. What if the check read "Prepared by (your name)"?
- What if you bought an airline ticket and right there beside your flight number was "The pilot responsible for this flight is (his or her name)"?
- If you are a nurse, perhaps you can put a sign by your patient's bed that says something like "Cared for by (your name)."[6]

Your personal signature is a declaration of your commitment to the quality of your work and to your customers. I would also add that the Human touch—these signatures being handwritten rather than typed—would be even more effective.

#19.   Dr. Jeff Alexander, owner of a children's dental practice in California called The Youthful Tooth, believes that every piece of literature and even the words you speak in your business should be an extension of the culture aligned with your organizational vision. Because his vision is that the children are the stars and they should discover the powers of healing in a fun and friendly place, every new patient gets a letter describing what will happen when they come to his office. He says, "Imagine how important a 5-year-old feels getting a personal letter!" Instead of appointment cards, the children get tickets—"there is a seat reserved for _____"—with the time and date. (Earlier I discussed the importance of choosing customer-friendly words. All of the dentists are called by "Dr." and their first names, and they do not use words like "needles," "pain," "pull," and "blood." For example, a "drill" is called "the fastest toothbrush in the world." Rather than the dentist "deadening" a tooth, he puts the tooth "to sleep and it wakes up refreshed.")

Policies, Practices, and Procedures

#20. In an issue of *Exceptional Times,* the in-house newsletter produced by Hydro-Electric, one of the two Scottish electricity companies, to support its Customer Focus Initiative, employees were invited to "indulge yourself in some healthy, satisfying Bureaucracy Bashing!" Every employee has an opportunity to nominate that policy, practice, or procedure that gets in the way of providing extraordinary customer service. To date, Ray Smethhurst, Customer Focus Manager, has received over 600 nominations from employees. This information is gathered from the staff in two ways:

1. It is solicited by the Customer Focus Team members at each customer service training session.
2. It is gathered through staff workshops.

The information is collected and managed through a database that organizes the information. It is then passed on to Service and Corrective Action Teams for suggested revisions.

#21. In one of the exercises in Kaset International's customer service training, participants are asked to focus on two policies or procedures relating to their jobs that always seem to get either internal or external customers upset. At the beginning of the program they are asked to write the *exact words* they would use with the customer to explain this policy or procedure. At the end of the program, they come back to the same exercise, and this time, with all their new learnings about service, they write what they would say *now.* Here are some real life examples:

Problem: An employee wants an expense that has been refused reimbursed.

First answer: It isn't that I wouldn't approve it if I could. It is an IRS regulation and out of my control.

Second answer: I understand your desire to have the expense approved. I would want the company to reimburse me for it, too. If it was within my power to do so, I certainly would. Perhaps if I explained why it isn't reimbursable, that might help.

Problem: An agent complains that our disability income premiums are too high.

First answer: Our premium rates are based on assumptions we have made about expenses and expected claims.

Second answer: You're right, our premium rates are high. Many people find disability income coverage is quite expensive. Let's look at some possible ideas to reduce your premiums.

Problem: An agent has complained that we would not issue a disability income contract to his client without income documentation that his client refuses to provide. The agent argues that income has nothing to do with health.

First answer: Proper underwriting of disability income requires that we verify the proposed insured's current income to avoid anti-selection.

Second answer: I can understand how you might feel that way. I'd be upset and frustrated, too, if I hadn't gotten the result I had expected. You've been with _____ a long time, and I want to do what I can to help. I'll personally discuss this with the underwriter. There may be some additional information the client could provide or some changes to the benefits that we could make that would allow us to issue this coverage. I'll call you at 3:30 tomorrow.

The interesting thing about this exercise is that nothing about the policy or procedure has changed—only the way the employee responds to the customer. He or she has answered with much more human concern and empathy as well as creativity when thinking of other options to help the customer. This is an idea to use in examining how your organization states its policies and procedures.

#22.   Armstrong International has two policies that are rather unusual:

- Instead of causing people anxiety trying to figure out all the unstated, between-the-lines issues on travel, they now have one policy for travel: "When you travel for the company, live the way you do at home." David Armstrong says it is always consistent: "Do you always go to first-class restaurants when you go out to dinner? Then please do that when you're on the road for us. Do you always eat at fast-food places for lunch? Then do that while you are traveling for the company. If you drive a luxury car, then rent a luxury car. Common sense makes the best sense."

- Another policy has to do with the Armstrong cafeteria—the vending machines are unlocked and there is no cash register. The cafeteria is completely run on the honor system! The employees pay for their food or cigarettes by putting money in a box. Armstrong says, "Either you trust your employees or you don't. If you trust them, you don't need locked cash registers, time clocks, and scores of supervisors. If you don't trust them, get rid of them."[7]

#23. Ron Chapman, Manager of Corporate Services, told me how Alberta Power Limited, Edmonton, Alberta, Canada, rewrote their Electric Service Regulations (ESRs):

ESRs are the basic rules and regulations (policies) established to ensure fair handling of all customers. They are formal, legal rules—approved by the Public Utilities Board (government regulatory agency). For years these had been written by and modified by lawyers. They certainly were not customer or employee friendly. In fact, it had gotten to the point where they were almost uninterpretable by the front-line staff.

We completely rewrote the ESRs based on input from our front-line staff. After they were approved by the regulators (one of them complimented the company on clearly making the rules more understandable and obviously more focused on providing good service to customers), we took it one step further. We prepared an annotated version to be used by the front-line staff. This version included the exact wording of the approved ESRs *plus* two additional parts to each regulation. We added a section called "Intent" and one called "Procedural Guidelines." In the formal ESRs we frequently used the term "the company may . . ." The "interpretation" provided for the empowerment of the local front-line staff and gave the philosophy of the company as a guide. The "Procedural Guidelines" gave important information on responsibilities, necessary documentation, and the like.

COMMUNICATION CHALLENGE. Have you ever taken time to look at your organization's written documents from the perspective of the customer? If so, are you communicating the commitment your vision suggests? If not, begin some changes immediately, particularly with your form letters. Be aware of how they look (poor photocopies, outdated versions) as well as what they say. Be creative as you rewrite them and remember to include the Human level. Also look at your policies and procedures and determine ways to make them more customer-friendly. This will probably take a task force and many months or even years to do; however it is of the utmost importance in communicating clearly your beliefs and values as an organization, particularly if you are striving to become customer-focused. Fix the past and create the future—you can start now with the next policy you write!

PUBLICATIONS, BROCHURES, AND INVITATIONS

Look carefully at marketing pieces, packaging, and other promotional material your company produces—are you communicating your organizational beliefs and values or are you simply communicating words? How creative are the pieces you're using? How often do you change them? If customers receive the same kinds of materials time after time, will they remember your company and more importantly, know what you stand for?

#24. Hawaiian Electric Company publishes a booklet called "Energy Tips and Choices—A Guide to an Energy-Efficient Home." They demonstrate their commitment to energy as well as to their customers in the introduction:

> Aloha. Electricity is vital to our quality of life. It's our cleanest, safest, cheapest and most flexible form of energy. At Hawaiian Electric and its subsidiaries, our motto is "People with a powerful commitment." In other words, we're here to help. We're partners with you in the use of electricity. We want to help you, our customers, use electricity more efficiently, to get the most value for your money. In this booklet, you'll find dozens of money-saving tips. Keep it handy. Energy is precious. We all need to use it wisely. Mahalo.

#25. Clark Public Utilities in Vancouver, Washington, has an "Owner's Manual" that it gives to new customers. It says inside, "When you became a customer of Clark Public Utilities you also became an owner. We hope this manual will answer your questions about your new utility." The piece is very customer-friendly, with lots of pictures and coupons—one was for a free night light and the other was for 10 percent off an appliance repair service call.

#26. Alberta Power produced a special book called *Portraits of Power* for its 65th anniversary that profiles 65 employees as full, three-dimensional human beings. The text contains frank quotes, colorful stories, and black and white photographs that focus on expression and manner rather than task and equipment. A reader said, "It's one of the most relaxed and personable corporate publications I've seen." Why the complete emphasis on people rather than history? "It's been a tough couple of years," says Barb Kuester, supervisor of internal communication. "We saw this as an opportunity to show that the company has the same spirit, that it's built on people. It's a morale builder, and it works because it speaks to employees in their own modest language. There are no inflated claims here, no company line—just the satisfaction of people who know they do their jobs well." The album was a two-person job, with one writer and one photographer criss-crossing the territory over four weeks, looking for a representative sample. The special issue was sent to employees' homes, for families to enjoy; reader reaction has been overwhelmingly positive.

#27. The First Interstate Center for Services Marketing, Arizona State University, produced a very unassuming brochure that contained a small drawstring bag with something in it! The brochure read on the outside: "CAN YOU TELL THE DIFFERENCE? YOUR CUSTOMERS CAN. . . . " Inside it said, "Even though iron pyrite looks like gold on the surface . . . it isn't. Today's demanding customers quickly cut below the surface of an organization to see who does...and who doesn't...treat them with a 24-carat touch. Customers recognize and reward organizations that have a true service and quality orientation." The brochure then announced the symposium "Activating Your Firm's Service Culture—a solution that goes beyond the surface." (What was in the little bag? Iron pyrite, of course!)

#28. Campbell Soup Company uses a brochure that looks exactly like a Campbell soup can for their "C3" brochures, which introduce the "Campbell Customer Care" program. The brochure lists key Customer Care Managers, presents their direct dial numbers on detachable rolodex cards, as well as information about the Customer Care program in Question and Answer format.[8]

#29. American Express uses the picture of a dollar bill on the outside of an invitation to a program called "Collection Skills that Work," a workshop for Credit Analysts. It contains the What, Where, When and the Why: "You have many experiences to share. You are a valuable contributor to AMEX's success. You will collect more $$$$."

COMMUNICATION CHALLENGE. Think of simple things like announcements and invitations that could be more creative, and then later take a hard look at all your organization's promotional material. Document how often marketing pieces are changed and see if these materials are communicating the beliefs and values of your organizational vision and mission.

NEWSLETTERS

Internal Newsletters

Juan Gutierrez developed the following sample editorial plan for an internal newsletter that communicates a commitment to service quality. He suggested that the newspaper include:

- Internal and external "good deed" stories.
- A monthly column on how to create extraordinary customer relations.
- Results of corporate-wide customer satisfaction scores.
- Examples of top management activities that support service quality.
- Changes in policies, practices, and procedures that are improving customer satisfaction.
- What departments are doing for internal customers.
- Progress on reaching customer satisfaction goals.
- Stories of management doing things that support the effort, not just preaching the importance of good customer relations.

#30. At Cuyahoga Savings in Cleveland, Ohio, a weekly one-page newsletter called *Sales and Service Success Stories* is routed to all employees "to build and enhance an organization-wide sales and service culture." According to the President, Chet Kermode, "This publication is designed to recognize employees and share success stories involving superior customer service and outstanding sales performance. All employees are urged to submit ideas for publication (written or verbal) to anyone in Senior Management."

#31. Oliver Carter of the United States Postal Service Training Academy has created a newsletter called DID YOU KNOW. The DYK is a communication tool used by the Field Programs Training & Development Department since 1988. Its purpose is to keep the Postal Employee Development Center network of training professionals informed about the development of new *field* training programs.

#32. While Bank Mart was experiencing financial trouble, Dick Freeman, their former President, inserted a column called "Dear Gabby" in the company newsletter. This allowed employees to send in anonymous questions that he ensured received candid and frank answers. He felt this was one of the most important things he did to enhance good staff communications during the period of turmoil.

#33. Names of newsletters can enhance the organization's commitment: J.C. Penney Credit Services has called its newsletter *Creditlines*. It recognizes employees who have submitted workable project proposals. The Limited Credit Services calls its internal newsletter *The Rapporter*. Commercebank in Coral Gables, Florida, has a monthly newsletter called the *Dazzler Express*. It is full of hints for improving customer relations, service reminders, accomplishments of employees in the bank's branch offices, and recognition of service stars.

#34. In their service quality newsletter UPDATE, SouthTrust Corporation recognizes its employees who are the winners of "Out of the Blue" awards. These awards are presented by the CEO, and anyone can be nominated for creating exceptional service. Here are two examples of stories about the winners:

Tricia Cyr, an employee of SouthTrust of Central Florida, recently showed extraordinary friendly, caring service and problem solving for a customer. When leaving the bank after closing one day, Tricia noticed that a customer had a flat tire. She brought this to the customer's attention, and the customer became upset because she didn't know how to change the tire. Tricia offered to help and had the tire changed in about ten minutes. The customer was amazed and commented, "This *really is* a full-service bank, and I love this bank!

Vicki Amos works as a teller at the Westgate branch in Enterprise. One Thursday, a very good customer of the Elba branch stopped at the Westgate branch to cash a check before she left to go out of town. The Westgate branch closes early on Thursday; however, the customer was not aware of this. Vicki was leaving the branch and met the customer outside. In talking with her, Vicki discovered she did not have an ATM card. Since the branch doesn't have an ATM, Vicki went to a competitor's ATM, withdrew $50 from her personal account and gave it to the customer. The personal attention, problem solving, and flexibility displayed by Vicki created a positive memorable experience for the customer.

#35. Joe Hopkins, Media Relations Manager for United Airlines, Chicago, Illinois, shared several of their internal newsletters. One of them is called *Management Insight* and is the newsletter for United management. Another is called *Employee Newsline* and is a one or two page sheet published daily for all employees. The third is called *United Times*, a monthly newsletter designed like a tabloid size newspaper that is published for "the People of United Airlines." I noticed the following note on the front of the paper: "Please read and recycle this paper. (This reminder of environmental responsibility comes from an ACT team in San Francisco)." A feature at the bottom of the last page of every issue of the Times is called "Employee Ideas at Work." It features a picture of an employee team that has come up with a good idea for the company and a brief description of that idea.

External Newsletters

#36. The City of Goodyear, Arizona, publishes a newsletter called *City Report* that is mailed to each resident and business each month. They have also established a separate mailing list for individuals and businesses outside of Goodyear to receive the newsletter at no cost. The *City Report* features a local business each month and a column outlining major Council actions for the month, entitled "Your Mayor and City Council at Work." Harvey Krauss, the Assistant City Manager, said, "It has proven to be a very effective tool for communicating to our citizens." Of particular interest is a column on the back page of every newsletter titled "Your calls and letters DO count—DO make our laws better." It contains the names and phone numbers of all Federal, State, and County elected representatives.

#37. Republic Mortgage Insurance Company in Winston-Salem, North Carolina, has a special program they call STEP (Service, Teamwork, Efficiency, Performance). The Underwriting offices have recently been participating in a newsletter contest called "STEP Challenge." Each month each of the offices writes a newsletter on how they have exemplified the four functions of STEP during the past 30 days. These newsletters contain such things as how they've handled a difficult customer experience to how they've changed systems in their offices. They are creative, seasonal, have a Human touch, and are often even 3-dimensional with a "surprise" attached. Different people in the office work on these newsletters each month. Each of the 14 offices as well as the Home office judges the newsletters, and a winner is selected every month. At the end of the year the office that has won the most months is the overall winner, and each person in the office receives a cash award. This contest has added fun to the workplace, friendly competition among offices, a chance for creative energies to blossom, and is a wonderful tool for internal communication and keeping the customer service skills alive!

COMMUNICATION CHALLENGE. Because most organizations already have internal newsletters, I would ask you to consider if the publication itself communicates what you value as an organization. Does it have a customer service component, for example? Look at the percentage of the publication devoted to customer service issues—what does that tell you about the *real* importance of customer service to your organization? Is there a Human element in the newsletter? Is it fun? Are there lots of people stories and pictures or is it all "Business"? And most importantly, do employees look forward to reading it or does it lie on their desks untouched for days? Then I would ask you to think about an external customer newsletter if you don't have one. This becomes an extraordinarily powerful way to creatively communicate your organization's beliefs and values as well as sharing what other customers are doing to better communicate theirs. It can be informative, educational, create networking, and help to keep customer service skills alive if you have sent your employees through training.

QUOTATIONS AND ARTICLES

Some of our customers "humanize" their memos and reports by adding a graphic (sometimes seasonal, sometimes pertaining to the content) or a relevant quotation at the top or bottom. By adding the Human level to even the most boring material, you are enhancing the experience as well as contributing to a greater possibility of adult learning occurring.

I am a great lover of the written word, and one of my "signatures" has always been my use of quotations in whatever I do. These are some of the ways I have found to use quotations:

Whenever I speak or conduct training programs, I line the room with brightly colored flip charts of quotations that relate to the topic I'm presenting. This not only creates an atmosphere of excitement and challenge, but it also enhances learning. My hope is that each person present will find one or two quotations that are meaningful and will write them down. These, then, become a connection to the material that is being presented. I always write the quotations in my own handwriting in bright colors, usually with a symbol or picture that relates to the words used—all of this to add more of the Human level. From the earliest point in the presentation participants are aware of what is important to me because of the quotations I've chosen to use. Thus, I also use this tool to communicate my beliefs and values in a way that is related to my topic.

When I speak, I read or share many of the quotations that have been meaningful in my life, again as they are related to the topic.

Some of them are intellectual:

Far better is it to dare mighty things, to win great triumphs, even though checkered by failure, than to rank with those poor spirits who neither enjoy much nor suffer much, because they live in the gray twilight that knows neither victory nor defeat.

Theodore Roosevelt

Some are spiritual:

Years wrinkle the skin, but to give up enthusiasm wrinkles the soul.

Samuel Ullman

Some are just practical wisdom:

Why is it that people who need love and understanding the most usually deserve it the least!

Lou Holtz

And some are funny:

If you plan to swallow a frog, it is best not to look at it too long. If you have a number of frogs to swallow, swallow the big one first!

Bruce Larsen, *The One and Only You*

In order to appeal to the wide variety of personalities and interests present in any group, I share thoughts from many different sources—writers, teachers, politicians, heroes, saints, sports figures, and TV and cartoon characters, as well as just ordinary folks. I have compiled collections of my favorite quotations, poems, and funny things as a handout at the end of a presentation. Then it makes it easy for people to begin using quotations in their own workplaces.

#38. At the PEMCO Financial Center in Seattle, Washington, as part of their Quality Quest process, copies of quality, courtesy-focused articles and quotations are sent to each manager and supervisor. These go out every other week and are gleaned from various publications received by the Quality Quest coordinator. Length, subject, and appropriateness to company philosophy are all considered. This flow of information allows for sharing and helps to give gentle reminders of quality principles.

#39. Donna Kovaleski, Manager of Customer Caring at PSI Energy in Plainfield, Indiana, has prepared a calendar of customer service reminders and quotations that is given to employees.

#40. The Virginia Department of Motor Vehicles puts up a new set of customer service quotations every month in the elevators and on the tables in the cafeteria. These quotes serve as reminders to their employees of the value of customer service.

#41. Mary Trowbridge, Ohio Bureau of Employment Services, plans to do a weekly distribution to each office in the organization of the imprinted message on one of the cards from Roger von Oech's *Whack Pack*, a collection of challenges and questions to encourage innovative thinking. She feels this will encourage conversation and stimulate a feeling of amused anticipation for the "next edition." She says, "Who knows where that would lead? Competitions could develop for the best response to the Whack of the Week—that is, creative ideas that could improve communication within the organization or better procedures for the business in general."

#42. Steve Carter, Assistant Vice President of Service Quality at Standard Insurance, has prepared a Quality Service handout for their employee annual meeting that includes the following:

- Essays on Quality by employees.
- A few children's drawings of quality interpretations.
- Some of the "best" window panes from Kaset's *Achieving Extraordinary Customer Relations* training. (He is referring to an exercise in which groups of three or four people divide a large piece of flip chart paper in quarters and creatively illustrate their ideas of the four A's of customer service—Acknowledgment, Appreciation, Affirmation, and Assurance.)
- Stories of extraordinary service provided by Standard employees.

COMMUNICATION CHALLENGE. Begin to collect your favorite quotations, particularly those that support your organizational beliefs and values. Include quotations in your letters and other information that you send to customers, both internal and external. Also think of creative ways you can "humanize" boring memos and reports.

PAYROLL, BILL, AND STATEMENT INSERTS

This category is a relatively untouched and unrecognized resource for creative communication. Since *all* employees receive a paycheck and *all* customers receive bills and statements, why not use these vehicles to communicate with them? Particularly with customer bills—any way you can make them more customer-friendly will certainly help to "ease the pain"! Remember, however, that customers, both internal and external, will come to look forward to this addition and will probably be disappointed if you stop, so be prepared to meet their ongoing expectations if you begin this new communication effort. Show your commitment on a long term basis.

Internal Customer Examples

#43. The Department of Natural Resources in Minnesota inserts a nominating blank for co-workers who are good with customers in each payroll check as a reminder of what is important to the organization.

#44. We at Kaset International often have a printed message on our paycheck stubs with a human element: holiday messages ("Only 7 days of shopping left!"), reminders of things happening in the company, and funny things such as cultural puns.

#45. Commercebank in Coral Gables, Florida, uses a special technique to remember the concept "Don't get hooked" (by a difficult customer). They had a rubber stamp made to put this reminder on all envelopes used internally for checks.

#46. The employees of Great Western Bank in Chatsworth, California, recently got their paychecks in an envelope that said, "This paycheck brought to you courtesy of our customers." This envelope will be used for all of 1993!

External Customer Examples

#47. Virginia Power includes a publication called *Customer Connection* in each customer's quarterly bill. They publish current and topical articles as well as addressing "the big S's—safety, savings, and service." P.A. Bhagchandani, former director of demand-side technology/market research—Customer Service & Marketing, discussed a recent customer survey that indicated a need for better communication from the company, and the publication is designed toward that end. "Customers want the company to tell them more," he said. Also, residential customers indicated an interest in more ways to save money on their electric bills and service tailored to their individual needs—thus, the "big S's"!

#48. Gary Wheaton/First Chicago Bank in Wheaton, Illinois, is currently perfecting an imaging system especially for personal and relationship bankers. This system allows them to write a personal message on their customers' monthly statements as well as add their picture, a cartoon, or a graphic. These are changeable every month.

#49. At Carolina Telephone in Tarborough, North Carolina, they have created an insert to place with the customer's bill. It thanks them for being a customer and also provides them with a number to call to give suggestions on how the company can serve them in even better ways.

#50. I recently heard about a plumber whose service charges were higher than most other plumbers in the area. However, when the man of the house was paying the bill and asked his wife about the exorbitant fee, she replied, "It's O.K. He wrote a *great* recipe on the receipt!" Several weeks later, at his business, he again had a bill from the same plumber. When he asked his office manager about the high charges, he had the same reply! By including a recipe on his bills, the plumber was able to charge 20 percent more *and* make his customers happy—all because he was a gourmet cook and wanted to share his expertise in another area with his clientele.

COMMUNICATION CHALLENGE. Think of a creative way you can use employee paychecks to communicate what's important to your organization or for fun reminders. Then tackle customer bills and statements.

CUSTOMER GUARANTEES

This is a relatively new concept for service organizations. It has come from manufacturing companies, and unfortunately, many service organizations are afraid to issue a guarantee. It has been interesting, though, to see how relatively little these guarantees have cost the organizations who use them compared to the goodwill, publicity, and customer loyalty that has resulted. Another result has been the jolt these guarantees have given to employees as well as to the organization—they are a constant reminder of what is important to the organization and to the customer. The organization is "forced" to fix inefficient systems and procedures, whereas the employee is "forced" to perform effectively. And the customers are the prime beneficiaries.

External Customer Guarantees

#51. At Seafirst Bank, if a customer has to wait in line more than five minutes, the customer gets $5 cash. If the bank makes an error on an account statement, the customer gets a $5 account credit. These are "guarantees" of good service or "your money back . . . !"

#52. Apple Computers has a one year *worldwide* warranty on parts and labor for all new computers. What this means is that your computer will be repaired at no charge, wherever you happen to be in the world!

#53. Workshops by Thiagi, Bloomington, Indiana, advertises a special three-way guarantee:

1. NO BAIT AND SWITCH. Thiagi will personally conduct the workshop.
2. NO CANCELLATION. There is a maximum number of participants, but there is no minimum. The workshop will *not* be cancelled—even if you are the only registrant.
3. NOTHING TO LOSE. If you are not satisfied with this workshop for any reason whatsoever, let us know. We will return your entire registration fee.

#54. SouthTrust Corporation, headquartered in Birmingham, Alabama, has a Customer Satisfaction Guarantee that says:

SOUTHTRUST PAYS MORE THAN LIP SERVICE TO SERVICE.
SouthTrust's customers rely on us for the very best service. And we put our money where our mouth is. If you happen to get less than our best, we'll pay you for your trouble. The guarantee covers Accuracy, Response, Promptness, Reliability, and Convenience:

1. Guaranteed Accuracy: If you find a mistake we've made in your SouthTrust statement, let us know. We'll fix the error and credit your account with $10.00.
2. Guaranteed Response: If you have a question or problem with your SouthTrust account, call or come by. If we can't answer immediately, we'll get back to you by the end of the day—or credit your account $5.00.
3. Guaranteed Promptness: If you have to wait longer than 5 minutes in a teller line in our lobby for service on your SouthTrust account, just tell the teller. You'll get $1.00 right then and there.
4. Guaranteed Reliability: If a SouthTrust Anytime Teller atm is out of service when you try to access your SouthTrust account, just tell us when and where and we'll credit your account $2.00.
5. Guaranteed Convenience: SouthTrust has MORE OFFICES IN ALABAMA THAN ANY OTHER BANK. So no matter where you are, we're not far away. And with the other service guarantees that only SouthTrust offers, it just might be worth each short trip. ©1989 SouthTrust Corporation.

#55. Andy Fischer, a professional colleague, tells this story about the service guarantee on his new Saturn car:

> I was driving from Tampa to Chicago straight through with a friend. We stopped for gas around 2 1/2 hours out of Chicago; I locked the doors as I got out of the passenger seat (a habit of mine from years of downtown driving). Joe got out of the passenger's seat and threw the keys on the driver's seat since he had no pockets on his shorts. He closed the door as I went to the washroom, sealing our fate.
>
> Once we realized the keys were locked in the car, we tried in vain to get in the car with a "slim-jim," the tool preferred by all good car thiefs! I decided then to call Saturn's (800) Roadside Assistance number, just to see if they could help at all.
>
> The woman on the phone informed me that "lock-ins" aren't covered in Saturn's Roadside Assistance Program. She then paused, asked for the number from which I was calling, and said that she would call me back.
>
> Sure enough, not five minutes had passed, and she called back to inform me that a locksmith was on his way. She said that Saturn would take care of it for a special one-time-only service. I thanked her for all her help and was feeling quite dazzled.
>
> One detail I had forgotten until now that struck me funny at the time was that she asked me if I felt physically safe where I was waiting. I told her "Yes," but later I realized what an important question this was. Had I been in a bad part of town, I felt as if she would have done her best to make sure I was safe.

#56. The outside marquee of Suburban Hospital in Hinsdale, Illinois, announces their amazing new Emergency Room Service Guarantee: "If you are not seen by a professional in 15 minutes, your visit is free."

#57. A. W. Dahlberg, the President of Georgia Power, writes about his company's new service guarantee:

> While I've always thought of Georgia Power as a first-class company, we've never offered our customers any sort of guarantee. The reason is fairly obvious. The electricity that we sell is no better and no worse than the electricity sold by any other company.
>
> But electricity is only part of what we provide for our customers. The other part—a major part—is service. What separates us from others who make and sell electricity is how we deliver that electricity to our customers. Excellent service is the factor that will make us an extraordinary company. . . .
>
> After talking with hundreds of our customers and employees, we've decided to do something that to our knowledge no electric utility has ever done before—adopt a policy of guaranteeing our customer service. . . .

This is their Customer Service Guarantee Policy:

- **We will provide timely, courteous service.** We are committed to giving you extraordinary, world-class service. If we are ever discourteous or if your inquiry was not handled in a timely manner, please take time to let us know. Your comments will help us serve you better. (Customer service guarantee numbers listed.)

- **We will connect your service by the date promised.** We will do everything in our power to connect your service on the date promised. If we fail, our customer service reps are authorized to credit your account $100 per day for every day late (maximum of $500) or pay reasonable expenses up to $500.

- **We will install your outdoor light or street light by the date promised. We will repair a broken light within three calendar days.** We will do everything possible to install or repair your outdoor light as promised. If we fail, our customer service reps are authorized to credit your account an amount equal to one month's service, on the light, plus prorate the bill on a broken light. If we fail to provide service on a street light as promised, a credit of $5 per lamp will be provided to the appropriate governmental account.

- **We will provide you with an accurate bill.** We always strive to give our customers 100% accurate bills. If you are ever over billed, we will correct it plus credit your account an amount equal to 10% of the corrected bill. If you ever are under billed, we will correct it plus credit your account an amount equal to 10% of the corrected bill, up to 6 months. Any credit will be a minimum of $5 and a maximum of $500, not to exceed the amount of the error.

- **We will respect your property.** We know how important it is to have respect for the property of others. If our employees damage your property, they are expected to initiate prompt resolution of the problem.

#58. Fringe Benefits Management, Tallahassee, Florida, a firm that administers benefits plans, was experiencing service problems. Faced with the loss of a customer because of bad service, CEO Michael Sheridan took risky steps to save the contract and, in the process, created a guarantee that puts his company's money where its mouth is! Sheridan and his client drew up a detailed list of performance standards that were backed by cash guarantees. For example, Sheridan promised an average hold time of less than 40 seconds on customer service calls or the company would pay a $1,000 monthly penalty. Although the company had been terribly inconsistent in the past, sending out claims in anywhere from 5 to 20 days, they now guarantee payment in 10 days and currently the average is three. Phone hold time has improved from a minute to 15 to 30 seconds. Sheridan plans to include guarantees in every contract. In the first six months of 1991, the company paid out $1,200 in penalties on $4.3 million in revenue. He is also tying a greater part of employee compensation to the guarantees to keep mistakes down. His 200 employees help set the 40-plus standards in the contracts, and cash penalties come out of their bonus pools.[9]

Internal Customer Guarantees

#59. GTE's Management Education and Training Department at GTE Service Corporation in Norwalk, Connecticut, has an internal "Service Guarantee." It says "GTE Management Education and Training guarantees that you will be satisfied with any GTE Management Education and Training sponsored course or we will refund your expense." This guarantee has been particularly helpful in communicating to senior management as well as course attendees that they are committed to providing the best possible learning experience.

#60. This is not a service guarantee like the rest of the examples; rather, it is an important guarantee of electric services for low-income customers. The "Guarantee of Service Program" began in November of 1988 at Clark Public Utilities in Vancouver, Washington. Since its inception, it has focused on three goals: to provide affordable service to low-income customers, to reduce delinquent payments, and to encourage responsible payment practices among low-income customers. The Guarantee of Service Plan is open to customers whose gross yearly income is at or below 125 percent of the federally established poverty level. Once accepted, participants are obligated to pay 9 percent of their adjusted gross income toward their electric bills. An Energy Assistance grant covers the shortfall between the actual billings and the participant contributions. The "guarantee of service" means just that—no disconnects as long as payments are made.

"Not only are we giving these customers a payment plan they can live with, but also an incentive to pay regularly and on time," says Customer Service Manager Jerry Watkins. "We are preventing disconnects and increasing payments through incentives like no late charges, no security deposits, and energy assistance suited to specific needs." It's working! There are currently over 2,000 GOSP participants. Prior to GOSP, most of these customers were consistently late with payments; now only 15 percent are late. Customer disconnections have been reduced by 74 percent since 1986. Write-offs and losses, now at a fraction of 1 percent of total revenues, are at their lowest point ever. Watkins credits the program's success in Clark County to close working relationships between the utility and several agencies. He stresses the need for a foundation of excellent interagency relationships, which are essential for success. Another bonus for the program is customer response. "This program promotes goodwill and regular payment habits which allow customers to feel better about their utility," says Watkins. "It means better service to our customers and lets us be part of the solution rather than part of the problem."

COMMUNICATION CHALLENGE. Could your organization offer any kind of service guarantee? What does this say about how trustful you really are of your services and products and how capable you are of delivering them?

BUSINESS CARDS

This is another little-used idea for creative communication of commitment. We all have business cards, yet how few of us use them creatively! The figure above shows some of the ways others have chosen to use these time-honored symbols as true communicators of what they stand for.

#61. At a regional conference where I was speaking, Vincent Engelke gave me a unique business card. It is made up of two magnetized pieces of metal with DSM's name and logo on the front. When you separate the two pieces of metal, an address book of 12 two-sided sheets opens out accordion style, and the top piece is a personal identification sheet. In order to "demonstrate" what this is, the cards are not preprinted with the employee's address and phone; rather, when a card is requested, he or she takes a few moments to open and write in the information. What a memorable idea and unique gift!

#62. Mark Thompson of Jacksonville, Florida, has named his company "Mark of Excellence," and he has his mission statement printed on the card: "Our Mission is to encourage and facilitate the personal and professional growth of others."

#63. HML Alane Perrigo, Educational Services Division, Naval School of Health Sciences, has a business card with the following on the back: "COMMAND MISSION: Our mission is to conduct training for officer and enlisted personnel in basic, advanced and specialized subjects to perform such other functions as may be directed by higher authority. OUR VISION: Is to attain national recognition as a leader and pacesetter in Military Medical Education."

#64. Joseph and Janet Newland of PARTNERS FOR SUCCESS, in Upper Arlington, Ohio, have included a quotation from Ralph Waldo Emerson on their card: "Our chief want in life is someone who will help us do what we can."

#65. Diane L. Maher, the Manager of Customer Order Services for Henkel Corporation in Ambler, Pennsylvania, has written on the back of her card:

OUR QUALITY POLICY—WE ARE DEDICATED TO ACHIEVING TOTAL CUSTOMER SATISFACTION BY PROVIDING PRODUCTS AND RELATED SERVICES MEETING OR EXCEEDING ALL REQUIREMENTS.

#66. Wayne Anderson, President of Southern California Machinery Company in Irwindale, California, has an interesting and strategic business card. His company logo is a log, because most of his work involves selling large pieces of machinery for woodworking, and his card features the logo and a green and white striped border around the entire card. When I asked him about the border, he explained that it makes his card really stand out on the bulletin board out in the mill where his customers keep business cards for easy reference.

#67. Dr. Bruce Bauerle, a lecturer/author, marine ecologist, mountaineering and survival instructor, and a professor of Biological Sciences at Mesa State College in Grand Junction, Colorado, has an extremely creative and representative business card. On the front the information is printed on a background of pine trees and mountains, and the back shows a photograph of Dr. Bruce in his wet-suit holding a spiny puffer fish.

#68. Employees of H_2O Plus, quality bath and skincare stores, have a business card that looks like a wave. This wave motif is used throughout the stores in the decorating (glass wave shelving, wave ceilings) as well as in the packaging. It emphasizes the store's commitment to natural, water-based products and hydrogels and the concept of being "your skin fitness center." Healthy skin requires staying out of the sun and drinking lots of water (H_2O)!

#69. Kathy Koontz is a Marketing/Training specialist for TOOLS for LIFE, "Options Using Assistive Technology," which is a service of the Division of Rehabilitation Services of the Department of Human Resources for the state of Georgia. Her business card has the "O's" in the word "TOOLS" presented as screws and gears, symbolizing real tools. The toll-free number is even 800-497-TOOL.

#70. Bob McDonald, a consultant, has a very striking business card. It is cream and black with a large circle drawn in yellow, black, red, and cream, which contains a spinner. The spinner is pointing to a space that says "Call Bob" with his phone number. Under the dial are the words "Management's Quest for Excellence."

#71. At the end of customer service training, First Vermont Bank gives participants specially printed business cards. One side contains bank information and the other says "We put you first" with a place for a short handwritten message. These are to be given by employees to customers as a way to show their appreciation for them and their business.

#72. An article in *Executive Female* magazine November/December 1990 tells of some very interesting business cards:

- Agnes Hodges, office manager of Label Service, Inc., in Charlotte, North Carolina, prints her company's business cards on the fabric the company uses to manufacture labels for the garment industry.
- Idaho Circuit Technology in Glenns Ferry manufactures the printed circuit boards used in electronic products. Debbie Nugent, sales and marketing manager, sent us her card printed on fiberglass—the base material of the circuit boards. Nugent's card is also die cut to fit a Rolodex telephone directory.
- Harriet Drummond of Anchorage, Alaska, is a graphic designer, and her clients range from "the one person shop" to the large corporation. She hands out a navy-and-tan card in a corporate setting and an orange-and-blue card in a more lighthearted situation. Although the type and design of both cards are identical, they impart entirely different impressions.
- Melanti A. Skindzier, a massage therapist, uses the back of her card to explain her service in more detail than would be possible by printing on one side only and to promote her gift certificates and group rates.[10]

COMMUNICATION CHALLENGE. How might you redesign your business card to differentiate you or your organization and to better communicate your beliefs and values?

ACTION PAGE

Chapter Four

Electronic Communication
Using Technology to Creatively Communicate Your Commitment

The more high technology around us, the more the need for human touch.

John Naisbitt, *Megatrends*

VIDEO-AUDIO MESSAGES

As the expense of video equipment has diminished, more and more organizations are using this amazing and simple technology to communicate the actions they have taken to demonstrate a commitment to their beliefs and values. Videotapes are much more effective than audio tapes because a higher percentage of adults are visual rather than auditory learners. Communication is enhanced, because one sees the expressions and body language of the speakers. Also, viewers feel more "a part of the action" with videotapes. They can be relatively inexpensive to produce, easy to disseminate, and easy to view, because most offices and homes today possess a video cassette recorder and a TV. They are particularly valuable in helping off-site offices stay abreast of what's happening at Headquarters as well as share learning experiences. And they promote creativity with the possibilities of the technology and the recording of special performances and events "for posterity."

There are several reasons to choose video to communicate:

- Audiences are familiar with video.
- More people will watch corporate information than will read it.
- Video can be cost effective, depending on the size of your audience and the expected use of the video.
- Video production costs are often competitive with print costs.

The advantages of video are:

- Consistency of the message—video's standardized delivery ensures that every viewer will receive the same amount of information, presented exactly as you intended.
- Scheduling convenience—employee training sessions or customer viewings may be held at pre-arranged times (such as at assemblies or trade shows) or at individual convenience (for home or office viewing). Also, your on-screen instructor or host will never be late or sick!
- Visual impact—effective videos utilize the many visual tools available to the videographer: moving camera, talent in action, eye-pleasing composition, lighting, editing, and effects. Add to that the audience acceptance factor. Almost everyone is accustomed to viewing images on a television screen, being entertained, or passively receiving information from the ubiquitous glowing box.[1]

Here are some creative possibilities for the use of video in an informal way:

- To share support from senior executives.
- To gather success stories from employees.
- To tape interviews with customers.
- For testimonials from class participants.
- To share meetings and educational experiences.
- To record special performances or other events, including celebrations.

#73. When the State of Minnesota began customer service training, Governor Rudy Perpich did a three minute videotape encouraging the participants and pledging his support for this new service initiative.

#74. Tampa Electric produced a videotape called "Join the Winners" which contains powerful individual success stories told by actual employees. This tape is used in new employee orientation to emphasize "You are now a part of this caring, customer focused team. You, too, can go the extra mile for customers."

#75. McDonnell Douglas Corporation produces an internal quarterly news videotape program entitled "90 Days" that is mailed directly to every employee's home.

It features a review of the company's quarterly financial reports, along with two or three stories that discuss quality themes and recent company news. In one video, for instance, employees saw how manufacturing and production personnel worked together to solve a quality problem involving hinges on the wings of an F-18 fighter plane. Employee reaction to the 2 year old plan has been positive: 93% of employees responding to an initial survey said they wanted to keep receiving the video and 62% said the program taught them something they could use on the job.[2]

#76. Kansas City Power and Light produced a videotape of customer interviews to use in their training. They went to a local shopping mall and asked customers what they thought about their company and its service. These tapes are used in all customer service training classes.

#77. A facilitator training class at Comerica Bank (formerly Manufacturer's Bank) in Detroit, Michigan, wrote and filmed a skit titled "Creating Satisfied Students." It's about their customer service training experience and has become a legend in the company. It is often shown at the beginning of company meetings. A large utilities organization also invited participants in their customer relations training classes to create short video vignettes of program concepts. These vignettes were used to get the attention of other employees and interest them in the training.

#78. Barbara Boxer, while running for the senate in California, sent out a 30 second videotape to the homes of constituents instead of written literature. Her reasons: 80 percent of the public have VCRs, they could watch the tape over and over and share with friends, and the cost was considerably less than TV advertising. Although you might question whether she was communicating a commitment unless you had seen the tape, this is still a valid idea for communicating your beliefs and values.

#79. SaskPower in Regina, Saskatchewan, Canada, saw the vast geographical separations that employees in Saskatchewan face as an opportunity. They not only scheduled many employees for training in locations other than their usual workplace and then arranged electric power plant tours, but they have also developed a series of videos to keep employees informed and involved. The videos feature introductions by the president, other executives, and union leaders. One of them, called "Take-10," approximately 10 minutes in length, is shown bi-monthly to update employees on current events, the progress of current projects, and allows employees to visually identify other SaskPower employees, departments, and locations.

#80. Puget Power has an electronic newsletter called *The Circuit*. When they piloted a training program on customer relations, they sent in a crew to film a portion of the training to include in this newsletter to inform and excite other employees.

#81. Centura Bank of Rocky Mount, North Carolina, produced a video to introduce its Service Quality Initiative to employees. It begins with an introduction by Dick Futrell, the Chairman and CEO. He gives his assurance that this Service Quality Initiative is a long term commitment, and he asks for their help in making it happen. The video is filled with testimonials from employees at all levels sharing their ideas about the importance of customer service and putting the customer first. Their goal is exceptional customer service—to go "ABOVE AND BEYOND" (the company's motto) what the customer expects. The video states that they have written the Centura commitment, they have spoken it, and now they must *live* it! That commitment is CARE:

Care about the customer.
Always do what's right.
Respect and empower people.
Expect excellence in everything.

#82. At the end of each year Guest Quarters Suites holds an employee appreciation ceremony. The top corporate management brings a videotape of what the other hotels are doing, and there is a general theme for the year. In 1991 the theme was "The Way You Do the Things You Do." The Columbus, Ohio, hotel created teams of different people from different departments to do videos, putting words to the background music of the Motown song. Their videos were also presented at the appreciation ceremony and were judged on the creativity and enthusiasm of the teams. An employee told me how much that experience helped create company spirit and high morale.

#83. SouthTrust Corporation in Birmingham, Alabama, includes a closing video at the end of all of their customer service training. This video presents the Chairman/CEO and the president communicating their views of and commitment to quality service.

#84. Electronic Realty Associates, headquartered in Shawnee Mission, Kansas, has a new videotape that shows home sellers how to market their current house to their best advantage as well as find a new home. The video, titled "Answers for a Faster Sale," was created by ERA Real Estate, L.P., to educate consumers while it supports the marketing efforts of ERA Sales Associates.

The convenience of the video format permits an ERA Sales Associate to cover many customer service questions in the client's home. "The tape lets us meet consumers in the relaxed environment of their home," said Mac Heavener, Jr., president, ERA ServiCenter Division. "It's an easier way for them to get an understanding of what ERA has to offer."

#85. Videotape used creatively can provide employees with valuable customer service lessons and insights:

At Motorola's plant in Sequin, Texas, for instance, managers videotape their product flow from the point when it leaves the production area to the point where a customer installs the component in his or her own product. Viewed later, Motorola workers see their product move through the customer's receiving, inspection, and stockroom areas, and finally to the shop floor. Production manager Keli Witteried says it gives Motorola operators a "vision of the fact that there really is a person who deals with our product.... They start thinking about ways to make processes easier for customers."

NYNEX Information Resources Co. (NIRC) in Middleton, Massachusetts, helped employees to see the company through its customers' eyes by videotaping customer focus groups.

Subaru of America videotapes problems found in its cars when they're unloaded on the docks. If a car has a dead battery, for instance, a Subaru staff member explains the problem on the videotape—in English and Japanese—and the camera operator flashes the car's serial number. The videotape is then duplicated and immediately air freighted back to Japan. There, the technicians who worked on the cars see the tapes. Supervisors believe that employees are less likely to forget mistakes communicated in this fashion.[3]

COMMUNICATION CHALLENGE. Do you have a video camcorder available in your organization? How difficult is it to procure? How efficiently are you using this equipment? Are employees encouraged to use the camcorder for "fun" projects as well as for more serious communication? Think seriously about what events in your organization you want to capture to be viewed over and over and what areas of communication might be enhanced by using video.

CLOSED CIRCUIT TV

If your organization possesses the equipment to use this medium of communication, there are some really creative ways to enhance what you might already be doing. Remember some of the creative uses for video and then look at some of the suggestions below.

#86. Some banks use closed circuit TV for internal communication in branches to share company information or talks with senior management. Other banks use closed circuit TV to "entertain" customers while they are waiting. The programs include new products, investment information, and community messages.

#87. At the Nationwide Insurance Training Center in Columbus, Ohio, there are several closed circuit TVs positioned around the buildings. These have continuous messages for employees who are there for training such as: "Chris, Thanks for taking the time. Ed" "Steve, call your wife at work ASAP!" "You really did a great job, Sharon. Thanks! Bill." It also lists information about the center such as the pool hours, cable movies and times, as well as all the menus for the day.

#88. Six Flags Great America Theme Park in Gurnee, Illinois, uses closed circuit TV to entertain its customers while they wait in long lines for rides. At various places in the line there are monitors which continuously show Warner Brothers cartoons interspersed with some commercials and information about the park. Not only are the customers entertained while they wait in line, but also their perception of the time involved is minimized. So the result is happier customers!

COMMUNICATION CHALLENGE. If you have the equipment available to use closed circuit TV, you are fortunate. Brainstorm with your colleagues, and come up with one new, creative way to communicate something important to the organization. What about a series of motivating quotations or weekly skits on customer service or a "candid camera" segment for fun with customers?

TELEVISION COMMERCIALS

Although this method of communication is costly, it certainly communicates an organization's commitment to a wide audience. Creativity becomes of the utmost importance here, however, to gain people's attention in just a few seconds. Most experts say you have about 2–3 seconds to capture them or they switch!

#89. Robert Peltier, an automobile dealer in Tyler, Texas, has done an exemplary job of conducting customer surveys and then responding to customer needs. In a TV commercial Mr. Peltier personally says to the audience, "You asked for a 24 hour number for whenever your car breaks down, and now you have it. " He then gives the number. Then he says, "You asked for a loaner whenever your car is being repaired. Now you have it." He also tells them that because of their input, whenever their car is being repaired, they will be given a pager when they come into the shop so that no matter where they are, they can be immediately paged when their car is ready. He truly exemplifies what it means to listen to customers and then to take action on their needs, and the commercial is a powerful testimonial to his personal commitment.

#90. Guest Quarters Suites calls itself "an Empowerment Hotel." All employees are encouraged to both go out of their way and to jiggle the system for their customers. The national sales office of Guest Quarters is currently preparing a commercial on the best empowerment actions of the year. Each hotel was asked to send in one example from their staff, and several will be picked for the commercial. In the Columbus, Ohio, hotel, Judy Myers told me about the recent winners of the "Best Empowerment of the Week": The night auditor received a call that a customer needed a special disk for his computer. The auditor knew that his roommate had the disk the customer needed, so he called, the roommate brought it over to the hotel, and the guest was dazzled! Another employee got a call that a customer coming to check into the hotel was lost, so he quickly made a sign that read "Guest Quarters" and had an arrow, then ran down to the next street, where he stood until the customer drove by. When a guest forgot her baby's hat, a waiter ran down to the street level and into the parking garage to return it to her. An executive housekeeper even gave her shoes to a customer whose shoes had gotten lost in travel!

COMMUNICATION CHALLENGE. If your organization can afford a TV commercial, remember the Human level. If it cannot afford one, why not have a contest with video equipment and have your employees create their own commercials for your organization?

COMPUTER NETWORKS AND E-MAIL

Electronic mail seems to be the "technology of the day" as evidenced by the many creative ideas in this section. However, because it is such advanced technology, it becomes extremely important to add the Human touch to our messages in any way we can. It only takes awareness and sometimes a little extra time.

IT'S SORT OF A TRADITION THING... SOMETHING TO DO WITH
MESSENGERS BEARING BAD NEWS.

Source: ©Kaset International.

I recently was doing a pilot session of our foundational customer service training program with a group of senior level executives, and in that program we talk a lot about the Human level and the importance of empathy and other listening skills with your customers, both internal and external. At lunch on the second day, many of them went back to their offices to answer messages and calls. When one of them returned, he was grinning like a little kid, and he told this story: "When I began to answer my E-mail messages, I, as usual, got right to the point of the business. Then, all of a sudden, everything you had been saying clicked, and I went back and *rewrote* my messages, always responding to the human needs of the internal customer first. Boy, did it feel good!" He then proceeded to share a couple of his "before" and "after" answers. I could not have set up a more dramatic learning experience for that whole group!

Some suggestions for ways to "humanize" your E-mail system as well as to communicate a commitment to organizational beliefs and values are: If your organization has gone through any Service Quality training, have a "skill du jour" (or week or month) that comes up on their screens when they turn on their computer. This serves as a constant reminder of what the organization is committed to. Another idea is to have a "quote of the day" (or week or month) that comes up on their screens. These can be chosen for their relevance to company values. Don't forget to use quotations or thoughts from your senior managers as well as from employees. This becomes a wonderful vehicle for frustrated writers to have their thoughts in print—as long as they're short! You might also use the first access on the screens for reminders about service trainings or other events important to the organization. Remember, everyone must turn on their machines in order to get their mail, so for a few seconds, you have a captive audience, and if you are creative, people will get "hooked" on those daily messages. In fact, they will be disappointed when the notes are not there.

Electronic Mail

Standard Insurance in Portland, Oregon, has found a number of creative uses for E-mail:

#91. Each of the customer service training classes of about 15 people at Standard selects an E-mail "alias" that anyone in the class may use to tell the rest of the class about listening skills or concepts that have worked for them, stories of good and bad customer service, etc. The company facilitators also use the "alias" to provide feedback from the participants' evaluations, to list participant responses to why they like working at Standard, and other "news" like parking lot issues (those that come up in a training but are not appropriate to spend time on in the class).

#92. Another creative use for E-mail at Standard Insurance is an electronic newsletter published by and for the Retirement Plans Division every two weeks. It is called the RP RAP and is sent out over their E-mail network. It contains news about what's going on (or upcoming) in the Division, staff changes, and always includes recognition for employees who have created PMCEs (Positive Memorable Customer Experiences) and other examples of good customer service, internal and external. It also lists the names of employees who have completed the customer service training. In addition, according to Doug Fritsch, Retirement Plans Trainer, there is an E-mail alias for people to submit news items, questions, or comments. He says, "We have been producing the RP RAP for over two years now, and it's become a part of the 'culture' for Retirement Plans—people look forward to reading it on alternate Friday afternoons. The RAP also goes to all the members of Standard's Management Committee and selected other interested people."

#93. All of our employees at Kaset International have a computer for internal communication. When the screen first comes up on the computers, it contains all the employee birthdays for that month. It is a wonderful reminder to celebrate your fellow workers.

#94. Mary Benfield of Iowa Electric Light and Power writes a "Morning Report" that flashes on the computer screens of the Customer Service Center employees and the Field Office reps. Each day it contains a motivational message such as "When we have done our best, we should await the results in peace" and "Learning is like rowing upstream. Not to advance is to drop back."

#95. Todd Gardener of Apple Computers told me of a global electronic mail system that every employee uses. When anyone anywhere needs help, he says, donations come rolling in. They had recently collected 5,000 empty boxes for the hurricane victims in Florida. The system is called "Apple Link" and includes a main window of about 20 different icons for information on such things as sales and marketing, employee purchase information, benefits, employee development opportunities, training, policies and procedures, all of which are virtually "up to the minute" in accuracy. Another icon is for an area called "Hot Links," which contains such things as Apple stock prices, 401K information, headquarter news, and community involvement, where individual and group needs become known almost immediately. In the last three major disasters in the United States, the two hurricanes and the earthquake in San

Francisco, 13,000 Apple employees all over the world could participate immediately in the relief effort because of "Hot Links."

#96. NEC America, Inc./ESD, Irving, Texas, has an "ESD Electronic Library," an innovative information service provided by NEC mainly for its distributors (associates) and customers. The opening screen of this PC based "Dial-up" service gives users 10 separate choices, including:

On-Line Subscription
News (NEC Corporation, NEC America, and ESD)
Product Information
Technical Documentation (including downloadable graphics)
Engineering Services
Training Information and Registration
"The Mailroom"

One of the most innovative is "The Mailroom," where associates and customers may leave questions and/or comments to the staff and management of NEC America's Engineering and Support Division. All inquiries receive an electronic response in a maximum of 20 working days (currently, the average response time is six working days). This unique medium allows subscribers the opportunity to contact the staff and management of ESD directly without the usual "filters" encountered in trying to reach any manufacturing organization.

The network also provides a distribution point for letters of appreciation regarding employees from satisfied customers. When a manager receives a letter from a satisfied customer, it's scanned into the E-mail system and sent to members of ESD's Customer Satisfaction Team, to the division's Vice President and General Manager, and to the corporation's Senior Vice President as well as to other members of the Customer Satisfaction Team in New York. Steve Winkle, the Manager of Technical Training says,

> If necessary, this medium can also be used to disseminate information on how we "stubbed our toes" if we ever fail to give total customer care and the emphasis it deserves. Not only does this remind all managers of whom we are really working for, it also recognizes superior customer-oriented performance with the individual's peers. Recognition and praise from one's customers, managers, and peers is an essential part of job satisfaction. Using resident electronic capabilities speeds up the recognition process as well as conserving natural resources.

#97. Cindy Powell, the Manager of Credit Collections, Centel Cellular, Raleigh, North Carolina, sends out an "FYI" message on E-mail every afternoon to her department members. This message tells about the people in the department who have done a good job with customers that day.

Computer Technology

#98. Gary Wheaton/First Chicago Bank has used its computer technology in a variety of ways to serve customers better. All of the new account information is completely automated. Video pictures of products appear on the screen with detailed images and multiple colors. The bank representative punches the product code for what the customer wants into the computer, and it does all the paperwork. This allows the employee to spend more Human level time with the customer rather than spending all the time filling out forms.

#99. AMP Inc., 150th on the *Fortune 500* industrial list, has a new internally developed computer system that

> has made front-line phone reps more responsive to customers. It enables reps to access information about inventory, pricing, future factory orders, and other data while fielding phone calls. "In the past, they would have had to put a customer on hold or promise to return a phone call while they retrieved the data from elsewhere," says Keith Drysdale, AMP's vice president for quality. "Order processing could take days. We had a bad case of internal constipation."
>
> The new system created new process flows that have improved AMP's on-time shipping record. If a customer needs an item sooner than might normally be possible, the rep can (while he or she is still talking to the customer) send priority electronic mail to the production control department. Production can then instantly indicate to the rep whether it is possible to deliver, so the rep can make the promise and complete the order. The company now ships orders on the promised day 93% of the time, up from 65% in 1986.[4]

COMMUNICATION CHALLENGE. Think of ways to "humanize" your E-mail system as well as creative ways to use the computer technology you possess to better satisfy both your internal and external customers. In particular, take a new look at what first appears when employees turn on their computer screens.

FAX MACHINES

Nearly every day we ask ourselves, "How did we ever get along without fax machines?" In my job it is the piece of equipment I use second only to my telephone and my computer. We have all made, up to this point, very utilitarian use of the fax machine; however, I believe that it possesses great potential for creative communication that is untapped at present.

#100. Buckner Corporation automatically faxes to customers an inventory of anything the company shipped to them that day. That way the customer knows when his merchandise will arrive and is able to immediately handle any corrections. In order to keep communication with international customers current, they fax them technical information, all new product information, and information about product availability on a weekly basis.

OH MY GOD, IT'S THE NEW GIRL WITH THE LONG HAIR IN OUR L.A. OFFICE!

Source: ©Kaset International.

#101. AMP Inc. has been using its technology in an extremely creative way they call AMP FAX.

Prior to June 1991, customers could call into AMP to request documents such as product specifications sheets, catalog pages, or drawings. The person receiving the request had to contact the appropriate department, photocopy the document, and fax it. However, with 70,000 support documents from many different departments, the process was slow and unreliable, and you still never knew if the document the customer received was the most up-to-date version available.

To address the problem, the company created AMP FAX, a fax database system available to all customers via an 800 number 24 hours a day, seven days a week. Those 70,000 documents were scanned and centralized in a single database. Now, customers needing a document can simply call the number and follow a series of instructions to enter the document number, fax number, and their company name, using a touch-tone telephone. The average call takes about three minutes. A maximum of 20 pages are then automatically faxed to the customer. If there's a busy signal, the system calls the customer back five times at 15-minute intervals. What used to take an average of five days now takes an average of about 12 minutes.

About 23,000 customers use the system each month and 93 percent give AMP FAX the highest approval rating possible on a survey the company sends out automatically with each fax request. Because 70 percent of callers have used the system more than once, AMP now offers the option to enter a seven-digit identification code that precludes customers having to tap out their names and fax numbers each time they request a document.[5]

#102. Yellow Freight System, an Overland Park, Kansas-based trucking firm, has a new Phone Resource system which allows any customer with a touch-tone phone to receive rate estimates, routing, information on shipment tracing, shipment status, and transit time, as well as a roster of Yellow Freight employees who are members of the "Answer Team," trained to handle problematic situations. The most notable improvement, however, says Carol Goergen, product development specialist, "is that any customer with a fax machine can now call the 800 line, punch in a number, and get instant written confirmation of cost estimates or routing data faxed back to them. Previously, such information was available only to customers with a computer and a modem." Bi-lingual service for Spanish-speaking customers will be initiated later in the year.[6]

COMMUNICATION CHALLENGE. Brainstorm with your colleagues creative ways to use your fax machine.

VIDEOCONFERENCING

Because the cost of this technology has become within reason for many large organizations, we are hearing of more and more uses of teleconferencing for communication. In an article entitled "You'll Get the Picture," Jim Meyer states, "The price of installing a system has dropped significantly. With current prices averaging around $40,000, it often takes a firm less than a year to recoup its initial investment." He says tabletop videoconferencing systems typically run about $15,000.[7] Videoconferencing is a particularly good tool for organizations that are spread out over large areas. The "humanness" of the interaction helps to create a spirit of company bonding even across long distances.

#103. United Services Automobile Association trained regional employees who could not leave their jobs for more than a day in Kaset International's customer service training using two teleconferencing sessions and one "real" get together. Participants were from Texas, Virginia, Colorado, and Washington, D.C.

#104. Hughes Aircraft in Long Beach, California, uses video conferencing to help employees in any of its 15 farflung locations work on projects together. According to user surveys of the equipment, the most important advantages of video conferencing are: involving more people in meetings, improving communication, and speeding up project completion.

#105. Davis, Wright, Tremaine, a legal firm, was created by the merger of two separate companies—one in Seattle and one in Portland. The new company decided to link the two locations with video conferencing equipment to make the merger go smoothly.

#106. Video conferencing can also help women on maternity leave stay in close touch with the office. Joan Nevins, vice-president of finance for PictureTel, one of the major US manufacturers of video conferencing equipment, had a system installed in her home to accommodate her during maternity leave. . . . This enabled her to take part in regularly scheduled meetings, and she found that screen-to-screen meetings made her more effective than a speaker phone setup. Nevins predicts that . . . [soon] video conferencing systems will be used to help executives keep in touch when they have to stay home for any reason—bad weather or a sick child, for example.[8]

Examples #104 to #106, all from an article in *Executive Female* magazine, show organizations communicating a commitment to employees to make their jobs easier, save them from the wear and tear of traveling, help them feel a part of things, and accommodate those who have families by using teleconferencing equipment.

#107. Tom Heslin, the Manager of Benchmarking and Comparative Analysis for AT&T in Morristown, New Jersey, uses video to benchmark other companies through teleconferencing rather than traveling all over the country to visit them. They have set up meetings with such highly respected companies as Hewlett Packard and Digital Equipment Corporation to have them share their best practices with AT&T. The information they have gathered through teleconferencing has been invaluable—helping them improve their practices and systems as well as being much less costly and tiring than travel, which is the usual way organizations benchmark others.

#108. Students at the University of Waterloo and the University of Guelph, both in Ontario, Canada, can now attend graduate level physics classes on either campus. "Our goal was to create an electronically transparent wall between two classrooms on two separate campuses some 15 miles apart," explains University of Guelph physicist Jim Hunt, project manager.[9] Not only have the universities communicated their commitment to the students by solving some problems on the Business level, but they have also saved them travel time and hassle on the Human level!

#109. John Holthaus, director of information services for the Chicago-based law firm of Winston & Strawn, views videoconferencing

as the most significant new communications technology since the advent of the fax machine. . . . We have offices in Washington, D.C., New York, and Chicago, and we regularly videoconference among them. Our executive committee holds monthly meetings via video, as does our associate evaluation committee. We've made visual presentations of new benefit programs, with staff in all three cities attending. I've interviewed potential employees by videoconferencing, and we occasionally use it to meet with clients.[10]

COMMUNICATION CHALLENGE. Are there any situations in your organization that could be solved, made possible, or enhanced by videoconferencing? I challenge you to *open up* your thinking to new possibilities.

VOICE MAIL

Voice Mail has become the great dichotomizer of American business of the 90s—you're either for it or against it! Joel Gruber of Information at Your Service in Brooklyn, New York, has been quoted as saying: "Used well, automated phone systems save time, money, and effort. Used poorly, they may make your customers absolutely crazy."[11] He shares three ideas to help avoid pitfalls:

- Bring in people from the customer service department to help design the messages and the menu.
- Make sure the escape option to a receptionist always exists, and tout that option early in the message.
- Voice mail messages should include at least some specific indicator of the meaning of the standard line, "I'll-get-back-to-you-as-soon-as-I-can." That way, customers will know if they need to seek another source for urgent help.[12]

YOU HAVE REACHED OUR 800 NUMBER... IF YOU ARE A PREFFERED ACCOUNT, DIAL "W-E-L-O-V-E-U" NOW... IF YOU ARE A REGULAR ACCOUNT, DIAL "S-O-W-H-A-T" NOW. IF YOU HAVE A COMPLAINT DIAL "D-O-R-K" NOW...

Source: ©Kaset International.

Ron Zemke says:

If the last couple of weeks are any sign, there is an enthusiastic, and, may I add, long overdue voice mail revolt under way. At the very least, some changes are in the offing for the way companies use technology as a low-fidelity substitute for human contact. Many companies that once saw auto-mated answering, information-providing, and call-routing systems as a boon to productivity and controlling customer service costs are rethinking their as-sumptions.

He suggests the following ways to minimize the potential damage when the voice mail bug strikes your company:

- Voice mail is a good place to "hide" from customers inside and out. Test response time. Leave messages on your internal and external systems and see how long it takes to get a response.
- Have your voice mail system shopped by clients and/or a professional shopping service that can recruit shoppers from your entire popula-tion base. Different age, economic, and racial groups have different reactions to voice mail systems.
- Do not let cost per call be the only driver of voice mail decisions. You also need to know how much market and image damage a voice mail system will do. Conducting focus groups before installation will give you an indicator of your customers' view of organizations that use voice mail.
- DO NOT give in to the temptation to install voice mail on your cus-tomer complaint and 800 service numbers. . . . Our research suggests that from a customer retention viewpoint, complaint calls are THE LAST thing you want to automate.
- Make voice mail an option. A company I regularly call has a human on the switchboard who gives me the option of leaving voice mail or a paper message. At another organization, salespeople have fax, voice mail, and switchboard numbers listed on their business cards.[13]

So, it is evident that in order to be effective, voice mail must be tailored to the needs of your customers and your organization. If used properly, it can enhance your communication in creative ways.

#110. NEODATA Product and Distribution Services in Des Moines, Iowa, uses a call processing mailbox to communicate infor-mation in their customer service centers. According to Valerie Wiese, Coordinator of Customer Service, "It's logical because CSRs are audi-tory people, so why not use voice mail, i.e. listening, for updates?" It works on their voice mail system. Each caller gets a greeting and then is asked to push 1 for the message for Monday, 2 for Tuesday, etc. The clients can even record messages for the CSRs, says Ms. Wiese.

#111. Dennis W. Melton of Northern Telecom, Inc., tells of their NewSource voice-mail news delivery program to provide up-to-date information to employees:

We conceived of NewSource as a way of allowing both internal as well as several thousand Installation and Field Service employees who work outside major office locations daily access to industry news and company information. The program uses the "menu" feature of Meridian Mail™ to provide different levels of information for different types of employees: for example, Dallas employees can get Dallas-area news under selection "3"; Field Installation people can choose selection "2," etc. The main selection, number 1, has a professionally produced 3-minute daily update on industry and company news of general interest. An important feature which we adapted from a built-in Meridian Mail™ capability allows callers to leave a message at any time by pressing a number on the menu. This allows for "two-way" messaging for follow-up.

Over 100 callers per day have used NewSource since its creation. The chief advantage is getting information daily to a large group of geographically dispersed employees and being able to tailor information via the "menu" to the needs of different groups.

COMMUNICATION CHALLENGE. Although you may not have a great deal of control over the *system* your organization uses, you certainly have control over the messages you leave. In a recent column in the *Chicago Tribune* titled "After Hours in the Electronic Office," Bob Greene tells how, by dialing a wrong number on a weekend, he got "lost" in a company's internal voice mail system. He says: "As impersonal as large corporations are supposed to be— as impersonal as electronic voice messaging is supposed to be—the voices told a different story. . . . These were like resumes, these were like studied presentations at an ostensibly casual corporate retreat. These were like fingerprints."[14] So, as you leave your message, consider what kind of "fingerprints" you are leaving—your message is a Moment of Truth for your customers, both internal and external! Become the internal champion to find some creative ways to use this vast technological system to its fullest capacity to enhance communication in your organization.

TELEPHONE

One of the questions I am often asked by our customers is, "How can we get representatives to be friendlier on the telephone?" As a result of this question, I have done a lot of thinking about telephone strategy skills. One of the keys, I believe, is to "whack" the reps' thinking—to constantly remember that each person on the other end of the line is a unique, living, breathing human being with a story.

Here are some strategies I have discovered that help me communicate a commitment to customers:

1. Draw a picture of what you think the person looks like as you talk to him or her. Even if you're as poor at drawing as I am, it will keep you focused on the customer as a person.

2. Write out the customer's name as you're talking to him or her. This again helps me to focus on the individual.

3. Visualize what the customer is wearing. Some trainers even suggest that if you visualize a particularly difficult customer in his or her underwear, it helps you to not get hooked into an unproductive transaction!

4. Keep a mirror on your desk to remind yourself that to keep a smile in your voice, there must be one on your face! I also use the mirror as a symbol that each voice I talk to is a person *just like me.*

5. I often tell a story that is a legend in the DisneyWorld training about a new employee who was stationed as a hostess in Cinderella's castle. By noon she had been asked 87 times where the restrooms were—and they were within ten feet from where she stood, certainly obvious to her! When she was asked for the 88th time where the restrooms were, she was ready to scream at the customer, "Right in front of your nose, you dummy!" However, she remembered her training just in time and answered the customer politely. The moral of the story is that even though you might have been asked the same question hundreds of times, it is the *first time* that customer has asked it. Some of our customers who have heard the story wear Mickey Mouse ears when they are on the telephone to remind them of this thought!

6. And finally, when it is the end of a long telephone day and I am beginning to forget the Human level, I think of robots. I ask myself, "What would a robot say now?" That, in a silly way, helps me to remember that I do not want to be perceived as a robot!

#112.   After customers said a typical loan application process was like going to the dentist, Seafirst Bank of Seattle, Washington, implemented a more user-friendly "Loan by Phone" program. Interestingly, it now handles half of the bank's loan applications.[15]

#113.   When I called the City of Scottsdale, Arizona, for information, I was *glad* I got put on hold! Instead of local radio station music, they had programmed information about their city. In just a few moments, I learned about a presentation at the library on "How to Grow Wild Flowers," the fall sanitation cleanup, and "Gardens for Arizona Living Show." On a more recent call I was wished a "Happy Holiday" and given the schedules of refuse pickup dates for the holidays as well as when city offices would be closed. Then there was an especially impressive message about commitment: "We encourage your input. To schedule an appearance at Scottsdale's City Council Meeting, please call _____."

#114.   A call to Donna Kovaleski at PSI Energy in Plainfield, Indiana, was answered with the greeting, "Customer Caring." That has become the standard telephone answer for their department.

#115. Gary Wheaton/First Chicago Bank has a telephone banking area that is open from 8:00 A.M. to 9:00 P.M. seven days a week. The purpose of this area is to answer questions about any products or services of the bank and to make it easy for the customers. The bank also has a Touchtone service that allows customers to obtain their balance 24 hours a day as well as to order extra bank statements for the month if they need them.

#116. Even telephone numbers can convey a commitment. Pierce Leahy Archives, a firm dedicated to the storage and retrieval of business documents, has this phone number: 1-800-INTEGRITY!

COMMUNICATION CHALLENGE. How might you use your telephone service more creatively to show your commitment to customers? What will be your *personal* strategy to remember that all callers are unique human beings?

ACTION PAGE

Chapter Five

Face to Face Communication
Creatively Communicating Your Organizational Commitment through Personal Interaction

F ace to face communication can be either one on one or as a part of a group. Although most of the examples included here are group examples, ultimately all communication comes down to the "one on one" relationship. In his book *Principle-Centered Leadership*, Stephen Covey says,

> The key to effective communication is the one-on-one relationship. The moment we enter into this special relationship with another person, we begin to change the very nature of our communication with them. We begin to build trust and confidence in each other. In this context consider the value of a private visit with each employee, a private lunch with a business associate, a private chat with a client or customer—a time when your attention is focused upon that person, upon his or her interests, concerns, needs, hopes, fears, and doubts.[1]

He suggests, "Let your customer have you for an hour." What he is talking about is the Human level—so important in all our communications, but particularly important in communicating beliefs and values.

How do you communicate your commitment creatively in a face to face situation, whether it is a group experience or one-on-one? I believe that both you and the organization first must be clear, authentic, and sincere in your beliefs, honest and human in your expression of them, and be a living model of what you are communicating. In one-on-one communication be fully aware of your eye contact, tone of voice, choice of words, and body language. You want to send a consistent and clear message. Keep your communications fresh and changing—always ask, "What can I do differently this time?"

HIRING AND INTERVIEWING

Selecting people who fit your culture and beliefs is one of the most important ways you can communicate your commitment as an organization. If you are striving to be a customer-focused organization, for example, hiring people who are extraordinary on the Business level but who are cold and distant on the Human level sends a contradictory message, no matter what their position is. Instead, when you look for people who are extraordinary on the Human level, even if they might not possess all the Business level skills you need, you send a definite message that you value "niceness." You can always give people skills training to get them up to speed.

CLARK KENT INTERVIEWING FOR A JOB.

Source: ©Kaset International.

In his book *Busting Bureaucracy*, Ken Johnston says: "Mission-driven organizations will seek to hire for such human attributes as 'attitude,' 'desire,' 'commitment,' and 'caring,' as well as the necessary business skills. The organization is concerned with the human needs of its customers and its employees. Both customers and employees will be affected by the human facets of new employees joining the organization."[2]

Not only is the hiring process an important time to send a message of commitment to new employees by making your organizational values *very* clear to the employee before he or she joins the organization, but it is also a time to reaffirm your values to your current employees in the hiring decisions you make. Let's look at some of the ways other organizations have handled this process creatively.

#117.   Southwest Airlines has started asking frequent fliers to interview groups of flight attendant candidates. These potential attendants must prove themselves with customers even before they get on a plane!

#118.   When a recent college graduate was hired by Richard D. Irwin Publishing Company, Homewood, Illinois, three senior level executives called him at home on the night he accepted the job to congratulate him and welcome him to their organization.

#119.   In a recent executive preview in San Francisco a participant told me that he had heard that the City of San Jose, California, leaves a basket of fruit in the room of prospective employees interviewing for executive positions after the interview. Even if the person is not offered the job, the city has still created a Positive Memorable Customer Experience.

#120.   David Armstrong, President of Armstrong International, uses stories in interviewing job candidates. He suggests using stories in the following ways:

1. To recruit candidates—often telling legendary stories about your organization can convince an attractive candidate to accept a position with your company.

2. During job interviews—Armstrong says,

> If your stories are sincere and show the direction you want your company to take, they can be a valuable interviewing tool. After a job applicant reads a story—or stories about your company—and tells you what he agrees or disagrees with, you'll know if he truly believes in your company's philosophy. Be sure to pick the right story for the right person. If you are interviewing an engineer, for example, who will be designing new products, pick a story about innovation. If a person is interviewing for a management position, choose a story about leadership. You may want the prospect to read several different stories to get an idea of how he or she would work with departments other than his or her own.

3. Have the interviewee tell a story about his or her own work experience—this can tell you a great deal about the person's values, personality (note how the story is told), creativity, and contributions and commitment to other jobs.[3]

#121.   On the bottom of the application for a position in the children's dental practice The Youthful Tooth, the applicant is asked to rate himself or herself on a scale of 1 (low) to 10 (high) in the following areas: Enthusiasm, Teamwork, and Happiness/Fun. Dr. Jeff Alexander says that because their vision is for children to learn about healing in a fun and friendly place, they won't even consider anyone, no matter how great the resume is, who rates themselves lower than a "9" in any of these areas.

#122. United Airlines has an internationally enhanced Employee Resume Information Form that gathers information about language proficiency, passport and visa possession, and special assignment interest. The language qualification section has been increased to a list of nearly 30 languages. A language proficiency rating scale from one to five distinguishes the employee who studied 2 years of Spanish from the one who is truly bilingual. "When United inaugurates service to a new country, we have opportunities that must be filled immediately (to serve our customers)," Senior VP of Human Resources Paul George says. "And the enhanced ERS Resume Information Forms will let us quickly identify employees through the ERS database who possess the needed skills and are willing to take on international assignments."

#123. Beth Munkres, the owner of The Paige Collection, an exclusive boutique in Grand Junction, Colorado, does several special things whenever she hires a new employee. As soon as the person has accepted the job, she sends a plant and a note, welcoming him or her and expressing her delight that the employee will soon be a part of the staff. She says she always sends it, if possible, to a visible place—his or her current place of work if that is appropriate—even a college dorm! Then, on the person's first day, she and her daughters make a bright, jazzy *big* poster to put in the front of the store as a welcome.

COMMUNICATION CHALLENGE. What are you doing in your hiring or interviewing process to communicate your organization's beliefs and values?

EMPLOYEE ORIENTATION PROGRAMS

As in the initial interview process, this becomes a critical time to communicate and reinforce the organization's beliefs and values in a creative way. Likewise, when people are coming together for the first time, it is important to emphasize the Human as well as the Business levels.

#124. Nationwide Insurance in Columbus, Ohio, begins its employee orientation with a video entitled "The 'On Your Side' Relationship." The video incorporates service legends and customer experiences to show that customer focus, both internal and external, is an integrated part of the culture. The video is introduced by CEO John Fisher, and its purpose is to gain new employee buy-in and enthusiasm for the values and culture of the company.

#125. The Medicare Operations Division of Nationwide Insurance recently completed a video entitled "Team Medicare," which is used for new employee orientation for that division. The host is Bill Ramsey, the Vice President of Medicare Operations. The entire video is scripted using a team metaphor, including actual game footage from Ohio State University used with their permission. Mr. Ramsey talks about "hiring winners"; the "coaching staff" of department managers is introduced like players, each wearing a Nationwide sweatshirt; he talks about the various means they use of selecting "MVP's," and he tells the new employees, "You've made the cut. Now you're part of the team!" Throughout the video, pictures of Medicare Operations employees are shown, and the video ends with testimonials from real employees and the final song, "We're Reaching for the Top." As another part of new employee orientation, a new management trainee condensed government Medicare information into a "Team Medicare Play Book." This is a resource for everyone, and includes a glossary of terms and "everything you ever wanted to know about Medicare."

#126. When a new employee joins the SaskPower team, they are included in a one day orientation program. Also invited are employees from key areas that may impact them (e.g., Compensation & Benefits, Labour Relations, Safety). An 83-point checklist system for both supervisor and employee is also included in the orientation program. In addition, new employees begin their first customer relations training program at SaskPower.

#127. A specially chosen group called "The Ambassadors" helps to welcome new students to Harlan High School in Harlan, Iowa, including students new to the community and foreign exchange students. They hold a bonfire with hot dogs and marshmallows donated by the local Hy-Vee grocery store at the beginning of the school year. Also, each representative is assigned a new student with the same lunch hour, and he or she meets with that new student during lunch their first week of school. This assures them a "friend" to whom they can ask questions and get advice. The Ambassador also introduces them to other students at the school and invites them to two other parties during the year—a Christmas party and a Goodbye celebration for the exchange students. This idea could work for new employees as well.

#128. New Associate Orientation at Rosenbluth Travel in Philadelphia is held each Monday and Tuesday, so everyone begins on those days. On the first day, people get to know the other new associates who have joined the company that week while learning about the company's philosophies and values. The second day is all about service. Rosenbluth describes the day like this:

Groups of 4 or 5 share the worst service experience they can think of. . . . The groups then decide which service experience is the worst and embellish it, making it as ugly as it can be. They get to vent their frustrations by acting out the episode they dreamed up. Next, they return to their groups and make their service story a positive one, improving on it in every way they can imagine. Then they perform the good-service experience in skits.

They expect that's all, but it's not. Even the very best of service can be improved upon. So back to their groups they go to create superior service—elegant service. But the point is that it shouldn't even stop there. Service can be taken from bad to good and from good to exceptional, but there are infinite ways it can go beyond exceptional—and that's the range we're interested in. . . .

The group then tours the facility, and the day ends with afternoon tea served by the top officers of the company. Rosenbluth says, "By serving our new associates, we're showing them that we're happy they're part of the team, they're important to us, and our people come first."[4]

#129. Ron Chapman shared Alberta Power's new orientation program:

We've developed a new employee corporate-level orientation program to supplement the operational-level orientation. The corporate-level involves bringing employees into a central location, the head office, during their third month of employment for a day-and-a-half session. Integral to this program is a video we produce to set the stage for each of the six segments in the overall orientation. The unique aspect is that we were able to obtain, as the on-camera host, the son of a 37-year company employee, now retired. The son is an actor, well known for his role as an RCMP constable on the long-running Canadian TV series, "The Beachcombers." He was able to personalize many of his remembrances, including bringing in his Dad's scrapbook, linking them to the company's focus on serving its customers.

As an adjunct, we edited a five-minute video that we show to each new employee on his/her first day on the job and then *give* the "Welcome to Alberta Power" video (the label is personalized to the individual) to the new employee. The emphasis in the welcoming video is on the importance of *everyone* being focused on serving the customer.

COMMUNICATION CHALLENGE. Are you including something creative and memorable in your employee orientation that communicates your beliefs and values as an organization?

SPECIAL EMPLOYEE BENEFITS

#130. At Apple Computer every employee from the janitor to the President is required to take a sabbatical of 10 paid weeks every five years. The company is so serious about this that they even cut off the person's electronic mail! Employees may combine their

4 weeks paid vacation with the 10 paid weeks if they so choose. They are encouraged to "do something they have always wanted to do." Another special benefit Apple Computer gives to its employees is a $500 cash gift when they have a new baby. This company certainly values its employees' families!

#131. A special benefit for all those who travel at Kaset International is a membership in your choice of airline club. The company feels that if one has long waits in an airport, the person should be as comfortable and as safe as possible.

#132. All employees at John Hancock Mutual Funds in Boston— even those who have never spoken to an external customer—have a good grasp of customers' needs and expectations. That's because every employee *is* a customer! The company gave each of its 250 employees $50 to invest in any John Hancock mutual fund, says Jerry Beauchamp, director of quality. The idea was to help them see the company from the outside looking in— the customer's point of view. "They learn what it's like to be an investor and shareholder, what goes into filling out an application, what happens if there's an error on their monthly statement," he says. The plan is the brainchild of Tom Baird, an in-house quality service consultant. Says Baird: "I was monitoring a call recently. A phone rep was talking to a shareholder who had some questions. The phone rep was able to say, 'I have shares in that fund as well.' It creates a bond with shareholders when our people own the same shares as they do. It also tells customers that employees feel strongly enough about the product to own it themselves."[5]

#133. Armstrong International does not offer its employees' children college scholarships; instead it *guarantees* them a summer job. David Armstrong says, "Not only does this help kids pay for school, but it also serves as a training program. During their four summers (plus winter and spring breaks, if they want) students get a chance to see how we do things. There's a benefit for us, too. We use the program as a way of spotting new talent."[6]

COMMUNICATION CHALLENGE. Get your creative juices flowing. Can you think of any special benefits you can give your employees to show how important they are to you?

SKILLS TRAINING

The single most important thing (in helping adults learn) is to create a climate of mutual *trust, openness, authenticity and helping—a HUMAN environment.*

Malcolm Knowles

Skills training in and of itself is definitely a way to communicate your commitment to your employees. Whatever training you are offering them indicates a value for the organization, and the more creative you are in advertising, presenting, and reinforcing the training, the greater the learning will be.

#134. To ensure a common language and encourage teamwork, Seafirst Bank established Seafirst College. Through the "college," an integrated approach offers extensive training in skills for interacting with the bank's internal and external customers.

#135. ServiceMaster, a Downers Grove, Illinois, based "handyman" company, has a strong commitment to training:

Employees receive intensive orientation training and retraining every six months. Managers conduct much of the training, and since they've taken the classes themselves, they know firsthand how to wax corridors and disinfect hospital rooms. The training doesn't end with technical skills—employees are also taught communication and customer service skills such as the following:

- "Life Skills" training offered through its Council Meeting Program. Employees can attend classes on company time in personal finance, stress management, etc.
- Advanced educational opportunities for front-line managers. An intensive, twice-yearly course conducted in the Downers Grove headquarters by professors from local universities offers those managers the equivalent of about 75% of a typical MBA program, says Dick Armstrong, Senior Vice President for People Services and Education Development. The program takes 4 years.
- ServiceMaster is also committed to training workers with limited literacy skills. The company offers both conventional and unconventional training tracks, the latter employing color-coded instructional materials and pictorial images to help workers master basic tasks and improve their productivity.

"Our root motivator for committing so much time, money, and effort (to train the whole person) is the company's second corporate objective: To use our business as a tool to help people grow and develop," says Armstrong.[7]

#136. QUIPS (Quality Improvement Plan for Service) was implemented by a team of service representatives from each Financial Services division of the City of Scottsdale, Arizona. The goal was to give frontline employees a chance to review the way they serve customers and to look for ways to improve. Customer questionnaires and an employee suggestion program were introduced throughout the department. Feedback from the internal and external customers served as the focus for division action plans and a training/orientation program. These sessions, which were attended by all Financial Services employees, included an introduction to the customer service values, new communication standards, and ways to handle difficult customers.

#137. Motorola's commitment to training is legendary. In 1990 the Training and Education Center became Motorola University with the intention of providing education and training for their own employees, their customers, and their suppliers. The company has spent between 2.5 percent and 3 percent of payroll on training every year for the last 8 to 10 years. Every employee must spend at least 5 days per year in training—a policy Susan Hooker, director of Planning, Retraining, and External Affairs, calls the "ground-floor requirement."[8]

#138. Northwest Airlines has initiated a unique three-day training program they call NorthBest U—Masters of Service. Northwest is currently using the Masters of Service program to train 15,000 customer-contact employees.

Recognizing the pin-point coordination required among ticket agents, gate, security, ground crew, maintenance, flight crew, controllers, and everyone else, Northwest has made a major departure from previous training efforts by combining in-flight and ground personnel in the same classes. The side benefit has been increased respect and cooperation among the diverse groups. Geographical and cultural diversity of the participants also enriches the classroom environment. For example, a recent class included participants from Singapore, Taipei, Hong Kong, and Seattle.[9]

#139. "Skyline University" is the new name for the Gary Wheaton/First Chicago training center. It got this name because all First Chicago products feature a Chicago skyline theme. Internal training classes from employee orientation and financial planning to customer service skills and computer training are offered to employees seven days a week until 9:00 in the evening. Just as the bank has "community-focused" hours for its external customers, they also have special hours for their internal customers, ensuring that everyone can have access to the training he or she desires. The center also provides a special training seminar once a month for managers. These seminars cover a variety of topics from product knowledge to ideas for coaching customer service and are often presented by outside speakers.

#140. Chrysler Corporation developed a multimillion dollar training program for dealerships that will not only train general managers, salesmen, and mechanics as in the past, but others like phone operators and the workers who clean and deliver customers' cars. The training will focus on things like how to handle telephone inquiries and follow up with customers. Tom Pappert, a Chrysler sales vice president, says, "The real story is that we are trying to deliver a cultural message to 5000 dealers that Chrysler has to shake the feeling among consumers that they'd rather have a root canal than buy a new car."[10]

#141. At USAA, a financial services company in San Antonio, Texas, there is a strong emphasis on training, both on the Business and on the Human levels. On the Human level, they offer training in cultural diversity, parenting classes, and Spanish lessons for all employees. They also have classes on how to deal with their senior members, teaching interesting things like the care needed in preparing brochures because older person's eyes may lose sensitivity to certain colors. On the Business level they have a program called "One Company." This consists of five one-hour presentations on each of the divisions in the company. Employees from one division are taught what the other four divisions do so that they are knowledgeable when customers ask about other services.

COMMUNICATION CHALLENGE. First, is training valued in your organization? Second, I challenge you to look at the *kinds* of training you do—how much of your training is on the Business level (technical, product knowledge) and how much is on the Human level (customer service, communication, personal and professional development)? What does this say about your organization's values? What are some creative ways you can advertise, support, or reinforce the training you are currently doing? What kinds of training do you need to do more of according to your organizational beliefs and values?

PRESENTATIONS AND PROMOTIONS

Sometimes an opportunity arises to communicate a belief or value through either a presentation or a special promotion. Both of these vehicles offer a wide latitude of creativity as well as "something different." You will notice that many creative ideas can go into a company-wide promotion!

I recently trained a group of facilitators at Nationwide Insurance in Columbus, Ohio, in two of our Customer Service training programs. In order to get upper level management support as well as to "spread the spirit" of this effort, a decision was made to have this group do a 45-minute presentation to the CEO and the top 300 senior level managers. Although some of them had never spoken before a large group before (and this was an especially challenging group with which to begin), they did an amazing job of communicating their enthusiasm, knowledge, and commitment. At times during the preparation, they had doubts about their ability to pull this off, and yet when the presentation ended and they saw the impact they had had on this important group, they all were ecstatic. In fact, the CEO, Mr. John Fisher, was so impressed that he asked to speak spontaneously at the end of their presentation in support of them and their effort and the impact it would have on the organization. I applaud Nationwide's decision to let the spirit come from *their own people* rather than an outside vendor. Not only did significant personal growth and stretching occur in the individuals involved, but also the obvious and immediate buy-in from senior level management gave an impetus to this effort that might have taken months and months to achieve.

The program was divided into several sections:

1. An introduction and explanation of the training process by the selected leader of the group.

2. A humorous "before" and "after" telephone skit.

3. An explanation by each of the group members of one of the models or concepts from the training and how it applied to their jobs.

4. Individual testimonials of what this training meant to them in their jobs and personal lives.

The program was a powerful blend of the Business and the Human levels.

#142.   Steve Carter, Assistant Vice President of Quality Service for Standard Insurance, told me that at an annual meeting attended by all Home Office employees, they empowered a volunteer group of employees to introduce the Quality Service Vision Statement in a theatrical way. This was a huge success, according to Steve. They interpreted the vision by depicting employees becoming empowered and wrote creative lyrics to a popular song. As a reward, they were made "President's Associates" (Standard's Reward and Recognition program), and all 16 were allowed to be an intact class group for the customer service training. The "performance" was videotaped for posterity.

#143.   The Department of Motor Vehicles of the Commonwealth of Virginia recently held an Employee Appreciation Week. The theme for 1992 was "The DMV team is blooming—look what we have accomplished." The idea of the week was to celebrate the many accomplishments of the agency made possible by the employees working as a team. In addition, it gave employees an opportunity to show appreciation for one another. The week was planned by The Customer Service Advisory Board, The DMV Employees Association, and the Wellness Action Board. Each of these three groups took responsibility for certain activities that would take place during the week. In addition, members of the Executive Staff were asked to plan an activity.

Below is a brief description of the variety of things that were offered:

- WELCOMING EMPLOYEES—The Commissioner's Staff greeted employees as they came to work on Monday morning and gave them a schedule of events for the week. In branches, they were greeted by managers as they came in.

Play Exec-U-Share

and win a member of the Commissioner's Staff for your work unit.

The executive you win will spend time in your work unit to lend a hand, listen and learn.

Send in your entry form for the big drawing during Employee Appreciation Week. Linda Mitchell, DMV's Employee of the Year, will spin the Wheel of Executives at 10:00 a.m. on September 16 in the cafeteria at headquarters.

Send in your entry form today--you can't win if you don't play.

Exec-U-Share

Name _____

Phone number _____

Office _____

If you work in the field, send this form through the interoffice mail to: **Customer Service Office, Headquarters, Room 730**

If you work at headquarters, deposit this form in the Exec-U-Share box at the security desk.

Return by September 13.

Source: Department of Motor Vehicles, Commonwealth of Virginia.

- EXEC-U-SHARE—All work units were eligible to win a member of the Commissioner's Staff who would spend a day in the work unit/branch to listen, learn, and lend a hand with the daily tasks.

  The Prize: A work unit won a member of the Commissioner's Staff for a day of fun and learning.

  Benefits: This allowed each working unit to show a member of management how much they are appreciated and the key role they play in the agency, to get to know a member of the Commissioner's Staff, and to share ideas and concerns. Commissioner's Staff members had the opportunity to show appreciation for the "DMV experts" in a work unit, to learn the details of how a particular work unit operates, and to improve the visibility of management.

- COLORS-OF-THE-DAY—Each day of the week was coordinated with a color which tied into the theme of the week. Employees were encouraged to wear clothes that were the color of the day to show their enthusiasm and support.

- CHILDREN'S ART CONTEST—Children of DMV employees were asked to draw a picture of what their Mom/Dad/Grandparent, etc., did at DMV. All entrants were awarded a prize and a certificate signed by the Commissioner.

- BRIGHTEN MY DAY CARDS—These cards were placed on bulletin boards. Employees could take them, sign their name, and hand them to co-workers to show appreciation.

- YOU ARE VERY DMV IF... —This contest gave employees an opportunity to creatively share situations or things that were typical of DMV.

- FUN ON THE RANGE—This was an outdoor activity that took place during the lunch hour at Headquarters. Employees were encouraged to bring a picnic lunch and participate in a

wide range of activities such as games, music, dancing, and
health checks.

- MEDIA SAFETY DAY—This activity was sponsored by the
  Transportation Safety Administration and the Public Information Office. Employees were encouraged to "buckle up" and
  drive safely.
- TIME CAPSULE—All DMV employees and work areas were
  asked to contribute ideas for a time capsule to be opened on
  DMV's 100th anniversary in the year 2027. A capsule containing documents and other items representative of DMV in 1992
  was buried on the last day of Employee Appreciation Week.

#144.   Guest Quarters Suites Hotel in Columbus, Ohio, had
an exciting promotion they called "007" because it involved "spying"
on other departments. On one selected day of the week every employee spent one hour in every department learning exactly what
people in that department do. One manager acted as a leader for
each employee "team" that went through this process. One hour
was spent in each of the following departments: Housekeeping,
Food and Beverage, Kitchen, Dining Room, Banquets, Front Desk,
Sales, and Maintenance. They learned such things as how to run
the washers in Housekeeping, how to use the PBX behind the Front
Desk, how to answer the phones, how to book a function, and even
how to repair some of the fixtures! All employees were issued "007"
certificates and T-shirts that said "Guest Quarters Suites Hotel" on
the front and "007 Team" on the back. A total of over 800 employee
hours was invested in this program; however, the rewards were a
new spirit of understanding and empathy for each other's jobs and
a new sense of teamwork. This program has now become a part of
the new employee's orientation.

#145.   Jean Scheffenacker told me about a promotion that is
currently underway at Provident Bank of Maryland. It is called "Q-
Tip," and is a reminder of their quality service focus. They are using
a variety of media, with a different "surprise" each week. Week one
was an E-mail message that said, "Q-Tip is coming. . . . " Week two
the surprise was a box of Q-tips. Week three was a special "Quality
card" to keep on desks or at their teller windows with reminders
about quality. Week four included an article on quality written in
their company newsletter, "Team." They also plan to have a "Quality
Quip and Quote" on the E-mail screen each week as an ongoing
reminder.

#146.   Moore Business Forms, Lake Forest, Illinois, has an
annual Quality Week celebration during National Quality Month. A
letter noting the 500th anniversary of the discovery of North America
kicked off the 1992 event by describing the enclosed "Navigator Kit,"

which it invited employees to use to "chart their course through Quality Week and beyond."

The kit contained the following bounty:

- Letter—"On Site Celebration of National Quality Month"
- Memo to All Employees
- Sample letter for Customers
- Journey Log and Menu—(Ideas for quality awareness and a calendar for charting them.)
- Menu items on Cleantac for easy positioning on Journey Log
- Five Navigator Newsletters—one for each week of Quality Month

MENU OF QUALITY ACTIVITIES
CHOOSE & USE IN YOUR LOCATION

WEEK 1	WEEK 2	WEEK 3	WEEK 4	WEEK 5
Q WEEK	CUST/SUPP WEEK INTERNAL	CUST/SUPP WEEK EXTERNAL	ED/TRAINING WEEK	MAINTAINING MOMENTUM WEEK
• Name Q Person/team of the week	• Most improved internal supplier award	• Visit another company to share Quality ideas	• Hold a seminar using material from Discovery sessions	• Halloween (Qualiween) contest/ cookout
• Letters to Customers re Q Week	• Contest between departments/awareness	• Discuss Quality with external customers	• Review QAT tools	• Show 1992 Quality Week video
• Show last year's SAM video	• Quality scavenger hunt	• Customer tours of local plants	• Poster contest	• Dress up as Mr./Ms. Quality
• Fewest errors contest	• Individual dept. Idea Fair displays	• Send in an extra order	• Open house - family (plants and sales offices)	• Create a Quality mascot
• Review/post Q activities for 92	• Best Quality slogan contest	• Make two additional sales calls week	• Cost benefit analysis comparing 1991 - 1992	• Identify falling tables day
• Create a Wall of Fame	• Managers/supervisors trade jobs with each other day	• Attend an outside Quality function ie training/semi- nar/ support session	• Plant tour (employees) training	• Future Quality projects contest
• Sign mission statement	• Manager take Q person of the month to lunch	• Invite a customer or supplier to a QAT/council meeting	• Cross functional training day	• Catch an Error (of the week/ month) award
• Thank Sam teams day - internal presentation of Sam entries	• Invite sales to plants and vice versa	• Thank your vendors day	• Reduce long distance calls day (Use the FAX)	• Build a thermometer to chart QAT progress
• Answer phone with a quality message - Change voice mail to include a quality message	• Post/display Idea fair items from Q week in Chicago	• Survey external customers to determine gaps (things that you can personally improve)	• Benchmark somebody day	• Post/display Idea fair items
• Recognition day for indivi- dual suggestions	• Say only positive things day	• Post/display Idea fair items	• Post/display Idea fair items for benchmarking purposes	• Goodies and refreshments
• Submit a clean order contest	• Survey your internal cus- tomers to discover gaps	• Goodies and refreshments	• Goodies and refreshments	
• Goodies and refreshments	• Goodies and refreshments			

MOORE   (QUALITY MONTH 1992)

Source: Moore Business Forms, Lake Forest, IL.

There were five major themes for the month:

- Quality Week 1992
- Internal Customer Week
- External Customer Week
- Education & Training Week
- Maintaining the Momentum

Each week of the Journey Log and its corresponding Navigator Newsletter was based on one of these themes. The Journey Log was prepared to assist employees in planning their Quality Month activities. They could choose items from the menu (or use their own quality ideas) and insert them in the appropriate spaces (days) in the log to have a whole month of activities that could be posted in their location.

#147. August is "Associate Appreciation Month" at Rosenbluth Travel. Something special happens every day of the month. Rosenbluth says, "We encourage our suppliers to each sponsor a day, hosting a breakfast or a lunch for our associates. Every office has its own celebration. Usually the events center around getting to know and appreciate each other better. For example, we'll have a contest to match people with their favorite story about themselves. We always end 'Associate Appreciation Month' with our leaders sending a personal note to each of our associates."[11]

#148. American Express in Fort Lauderdale, Florida, has a training department that makes use of accelerated learning techniques to make the learning fun and memorable for their adult customers. Whenever they do a training, they use a theme throughout the presentation. For collections classes, they decorate the room like a casino with green tablecloths and paper money. They use games like the $10,000 pyramid to review concepts, and they play money songs on breaks. When they were training their customer service reps about the Lodging industry, they created a live case study, concocting a "restaurant" and a "gift shop" as well as a front desk to teach them about all the transactions that go on in a hotel. The extra time and effort involved shows a commitment to their customers and to the best possible learning.

COMMUNICATION CHALLENGE. Can you think of a special presentation you might be able to do with a work group or class or team to communicate an organizational belief in a new and different way? Using the 12-month Action Plan at the end of the book, consider planning a creative promotion at the end of the 12-month period. Involve others in your organization and begin planning *soon!* These are the events that keep your commitment alive.

REGULAR LUNCH MEETINGS

#149. Many facilitators trained by Kaset meet once a month in their organizations for brown bag lunches to share ideas and enhancements. In Grand Rapids, Michigan, a group of facilitators organized sharing meetings across industries and organizations. They asked us for the names of all facilitators trained in their local region and contacted them to get together on a regular basis.

#150. Bob Ward from the Department of Professional Regulation, State of Florida, has created brown bag "Video Lunches" for employees. Every three weeks on Tuesday and Thursday, a training video is shown during lunch. Employees bring a bagged lunch to a large conference room and watch the video while eating lunch. Immediately following the viewing, they hold an interactive session to discuss and recap the main points of the video. Bob describes the purpose of the session: "To provide training to employees which is interesting, takes little time away from work, and is in a relaxed atmosphere to maximize learning. This type of training is especially beneficial for those employees who feel that they cannot afford time away from work. The video lunch concept actually works as a public relations campaign to pull in those employees who are unsure about the formal training classes offered. We hope to plant the seed, 'If training can be this fun, what am I missing?'" Several other enhancements for this idea are movie tickets used in place of class registration receipts, a movie marquee to advertise the "show of the week," and popcorn served to all!

#151. One of Kaset's general managers recently told me that she and whoever is available on her team meet once a week to discuss different professional development books. One person volunteers to be the "leader" each week, and he or she summarizes one to three chapters of the current book. This allows others to learn even though they might have had time to only skim the book. A discussion follows, applying the book to both their working and their home lives.

#152. The Centura Parents program, a series of lunch meetings for parents who work for Centura Bank in Rocky Mount, North Carolina, features discussions of parenting issues such as how to communicate with your child. "The 'Centura Parents' program is, truly, a trendsetter, a model for businesses that wish to promote student achievement," said Lela Chesson, Community Schools Director in Rocky Mount in a letter to Bob Maudlin, Centura's president. "Families are important to Centura because people are important at Centura," said Les Rutledge, senior vice president and director of Human Resources Administration. "We can't expect employees to function at top efficiency if they're worried about their families."

COMMUNICATION CHALLENGE. What kinds of discussion groups might you be able to encourage or organize during lunch times to reinforce what is important in your organization?

PEOPLE-TO-PEOPLE MEETINGS (INTERNAL)

Information is at the very core of what makes a group of people an organization. It is a source of power and effectiveness in organizational coordination and cooperation.

Edward E. Lawler III, *High Involvement Management*

These get-togethers across divisions and teams and functions not only show your commitment to employees as your most important resource, but they are also an invaluable way to gather employee input and help them feel significant and "in on things." They should not only be educational, but they should also have some fun, Human time built in.

#153. Recently the Accounting Department of Kaset International decided to hold open houses for its internal customer departments. They have had a different theme for each gathering, and their purpose is to get to know their internal customers better and to have some fun as well. They have been planning one open house a month, each for a different group of internal customers, and according to Beth Ann May, "We always have food!" In March they hosted one of the departments for a formal English tea. In April, the event was an Easter Egg hunt for several corporate groups like Human Resources. In May, Operations was their guest for a beach picnic out by the lake, where they played volleyball and had 3-legged races. In June, another department was entertained with a presentation entitled "Once Upon a Time" in which Accounting wrote a story that recognized an extremely significant recent accomplishment of the department. Another group was honored in July with a game called "Who am I?" The Accounting Department got special information about each member of the guest department, and 3 teams had to guess who the person was. Points were collected to determine the winning team. In August, the special guest event was an indoor baseball game with nerf balls and plastic bats in the recording studio at Kaset. All the internal customer groups have had a wonderful time, and the Accounting Department has provided all the food and planning for every event.

#154. Open houses were held at Standard Insurance in Portland, Oregon, hosted by members of the Service Quality task "Forces." Everyone was encouraged to come to get more information on the Quality effort and to volunteer if they so chose. About 300 employees attended.

#155. GE gathers employees for a three-day town meeting forum they call "Work-Out." The purpose is to solve problems and to take unnecessary work out of their jobs. Some of the changes that have resulted from the "Work-Out" sessions are the elimination of useless paperwork and the start of meetings to choose the best quality suppliers.[12]

#156. In November of 1992 the City of Gillette, Wyoming, had an "Excellence Luncheon." The city catered lunch to all employees. The buffet line was set up in City Hall with a number of round tables in the lobby area with different topics at each table. The employees were invited to sit at the table that interested them and participate in the discussion that was facilitated by a member of the Excellence Committee. Some of the topics that were proposed for the Excellence Luncheon were "Pay for Performance Program," "Employee of the Month Program," "Picnic and Awards Banquet," "People Who Do Good Work but Don't Get Recognized," and the "Luncheon Awards by John." These round tables encouraged an open discussion of the issue and solicitation of strategies or solutions to the problem, with a summary report going to the City Administrator for further action.

#157. The Culture Committee of Southwest Airlines is made up of 43 mostly nonmanagement employees from all around the system. Membership is rotated every year except for 5 members who stay on the committee another year to add some consistency. This committee hosts employee "town meetings" all over the country in every city (37, to be exact) and in every location, including reservation centers and marketing offices. These town meetings are for employees to share with committee members what is going on in the field, their concerns, and their questions. It is truly a grassroots communication effort!

#158. The Virginia Department of Motor Vehicles has created a Customer Service Advisory Board. The mission of this board is to promote and reinforce outstanding customer service beliefs, values, and practices. The board is comprised of representatives from all agency administrations and a cross section of position classifications. This dynamic group of individuals is the force behind many of their customer service activities.

#159. Approximately every two months, the President of Kaset International, Dave Erdman, holds an open and very frank meeting with all employees at which they discuss all the latest items floating around in the rumor mill. These meetings, called "Grapevine Sessions," are taped for off-site personnel so that they may also feel a part of the communication process. Answers to employee questions and concerns are handled by Dave or the most appropriate person. After the formal session, the group relaxes and shares a beer, glass of wine or a soft drink, and the discussion continues in a more relaxed setting. Dave says, "People tell me these sessions do a lot to address the nagging concerns that build up from day to day."

#160. On the first Wednesday of every month Edwin Quinones, the President of Coopertiva de Seguros Multiples de Puerto Rico, an insurance company located in Puerto Rico, meets with all the employees in the headquarters office. The Human Resources department distributes slips ahead of time so all employees can write down their concerns, questions, ideas, and criticisms, and Mr. Quinones addresses them all. He also discusses with them several Moments of Truth (interactions with customers) from the preceding month. With the difficult ones, they discuss what happened and how they could have made it better, and they celebrate the good ones. The whole session is videotaped and passed out to the branch offices.

#161. Clark Public Utilities in Vancouver, Washington, is launching a new effort to enhance employee communication they call "The Grapevine"—it's a monthly process for sharing information throughout the utility by face to face communication. "For a variety of reasons, we sometimes forget to tell people what's going on and why we're doing what we're doing," says General Manager Bruce Bosch. The Grapevine is centered around the Managers' Information Forum, which includes all managers and supervisors and one member of the Administrative Team (on a rotating basis). The group meets once a month to share information about work activity, programs, services, upcoming projects and events, and personnel changes.

Within three days following the Forum, an outline of the information that was shared will be posted on all bulletin boards. Within 10 days following the Forum, managers and supervisors will meet with their work unit teams and communicate in more detail from the Forum. In a two-week period each month, there will be a flow of information from the top to the bottom and between departments throughout the utility. "The Grapevine is a real opportunity for two-way communication on topics that are presented and discussed in team meetings," Bev Lynch, EIC representative, said.

The Committee's research also identified the effect of communication on the bottom line. "Our customer service efforts in recent years have emphasized empowering employees to satisfy customers," Chief Dispatcher Richard Hays said. "One way to empower employees is to keep them informed."

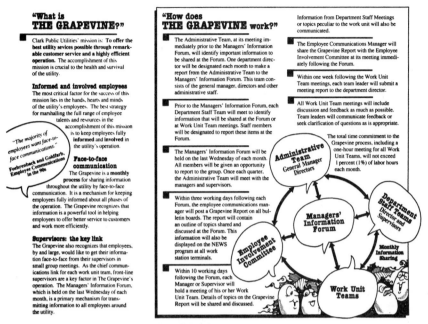

Source: Clark Public Utilities, Vancouver, WA.

#162. Provident Bank of Maryland has a program they call "In-Touch." This is a program designed to have Operations employees trade places with Branch employees for two to three days. As a part of this program, the Operations employees go through one day of teller training and even run a teller window for a day, all to experience "what it feels like on the other side." This has promoted a new understanding and feeling of teamwork in the organization.

#163. Wes Williams, Business Office Operations Director, Metropolitan Edison Company, Reading, Pennsylvania, cooks and serves breakfast to groups of employees as a special FACE TO FACE thank you for their outstanding work. A business office employee group, empowered by Wes, helped create an innovative program called TLC (for Teamwork, Learning, and Communications). The program recently won an award from the American Gas Association/Edison Electric Institute Customer Service Committee as one of the four best in the nation reflecting outstanding efforts to offer value-added service not normally associated with providing energy.

#164. Max De Pree, Chairman of the Board of Herman Miller, Inc., tells how he uses internal meetings:

> When I started working at Herman Miller, all 100 people there knew everybody else by first name. Now over 5000 people work for Herman Miller, and it's difficult to stay in touch. As CEO, I required each member of my work

team, six of us, to meet once a month with no agenda with twelve to fifteen volunteers for at least an hour over a meal. It's amazing what you can learn when you don't have an agenda. It's tough for some hard-driving vice presidents to go into meetings without an agenda, but it can be done. A lesson I learned from this experience is that organizations communicate whether a leader plans it or not. The best, sometimes the only, way to discover just exactly what is being communicated is to make it possible for followers to tell you.[13]

#165. Moore Business Forms has what they call SAM Teams. The name means "Success at Moore" and has even more significance because Samuel Moore was the company's founder. These Quality Action teams, some of which are cross-functional, get together at various times during the year to solve problems. If they come up with a project that has a significant impact on the company, they can apply for awards. They first write up their project and submit it. From those, "finalists" are selected who then do an oral presentation at the all-company Quality Week meeting. This year over 200 projects were submitted, representing some 1,500 people and *lots* of teamwork. The winners receive silver and gold certificates.

COMMUNICATION CHALLENGE. Does your organization provide any forum, formal or informal, to allow employees the chance to share their concerns and to get to know one another across divisions, job functions, and positions? If not, let these ideas stimulate your thinking and plan a vehicle that can combine sharing as well as some fun!

CUSTOMER MEETINGS

It is essential for organizations to listen to their customers if they are truly going to become a customer-focused or customer-driven organization. One of the best ways to do this is to provide ways for your employees to "meet" with your customers, either in person or by telephone. This allows you the chance to gain valuable customer input as well as to create a relationship on the Human level that will promote customer loyalty. And it becomes particularly helpful for those employees who rarely get to interact with customers or to see how the organization's products and services are used "out there." It gives them a greater sense of mission by seeing how their job fits into the "whole."

#166. The MassMutual Pension Division in Springfield, Massachusetts, has a "Keep in Touch" program. It encourages employees to "just call a customer" simply to say hello and to inquire about the quality of the service they've received. What a wonderful way to surprise their customers and to make them feel important!

#167. According to Jack Zenger, Chairman of Zenger-Miller of San Jose, California, an interesting communication strategy is to invite clients to come in to speak to your home office employee population. These people do not often see the way in which your products and services are utilized. Having a client come in and explain that from their perspective is highly energizing to the organization. As an example, Zenger-Miller has brought in two of its key clients, Solectron Corporation, a recent Malcolm Baldrige award winner, and Avis, a long time user of ZM products, to conduct such sessions. "These sessions were warmly received," said Zenger.

#168. Kenneth J. Peterson, Executive Vice President of Gainsco, an insurance company in Fort Worth, Texas, told me that they have a tremendous relationship with their agents, their primary customers, who are independent dealers of wholesale excess and surplus insurance lines throughout the United States. They invite their agents in periodically for product training sessions. They also bring them in for two-day, all-expenses-paid seminars, with outside speakers on such topics as marketing, financial analysis, technology, and customer service. Ken said, "The agents not only learn, but they have fun, and good relationships are developed with our organization."

#169. In the City of Grand Junction, Colorado, the second annual round of neighborhood meetings styled after old-time ice cream socials began again in May. The eight meetings are divided by neighborhoods and meet at places such as the new Fire Station, parks, Mesa College, and Orchard Mesa Middle School. "These meetings give citizens the opportunity to talk to Council members in an informal setting. It's more comfortable talking with folks in a park than it is in the auditorium," says Mayor Reford Theobold. ("I'm glad you came out," Madge Bowersox says to the Mayor. "I've got some questions I'd like answered.") Like many people who attend these meetings, Mrs. Bowersox got her questions answered that night. Usually Council and staff have been able to address the citizens' complex problems or concerns within one or two days. The Police Department uses information from these meetings to tackle specific neighborhood problems and gets good results. "The best thing about these meetings," says Police Chief Darold Sloan, "is that people who talk to us get to see results almost immediately. We're very fortunate to have a community that really cares about its neighborhoods and city employees who care about the citizens."

#170. With a desire to increase visibility in the community and to create a positive image of the company, Hawaiian Electric Company developed "HECO In Your Community." It was created with the idea of bringing together departments throughout the company to share their story/role in the company and to show how they serve the people of Hawaii, educating customers on energy-related issues while at the same time gathering feedback and creating a positive memorable customer experience. The plan was to take the fair to a site that was a "natural draw" for a crowd of people, so shopping malls were selected. Fun, informative, attractive and professional in appearance, the high-energy exhibits designed for the entire family were staffed by more than 100 employee volunteers, with some family involvement, and entertainment by volunteer employee groups added a festive atmosphere. This project had the full support and approval of officers of the company, union officials, and key shop stewards and was so successful that what began as a two-year trial presentation has developed into a major program and has been presented in malls, lobbies of businesses, and museums. The company's directors were so impressed with the contribution of time and effort by employees and the positive customer feedback and interaction that resulted that they issued a resolution commending these employees.

COMMUNICATION CHALLENGE.   Think of creative ways to get your employees interacting with customers in situations that transcend ordinary business.

COMPANY MEETINGS

Because most organizations have company meetings, the area to focus on here is *creativity*—how can you make these meetings different and inspiring and still communicate your organizational beliefs and values? I would suggest always having some Human level interaction in every company meeting. This might be a time devoted to telling company stories and legends, celebration of people, testimonials of what the company means to people, or contests. When I held a position as manager of training at Kaset International, I gave a challenge to all the trainers to create a metaphor for our company. The winners were read at the next all-company meeting, and they were both touching and hilarious! Another time I played short segments of popular show tunes and divided the company into teams who had to guess what song represented each of the six parts of behavior, a model used in Kaset training to describe the various parts of behavior from which all human beings choose to function. It was entertaining, relevant, and memorable.

#171.   William J. McGurk, President and CEO of The Savings Bank of Rockville, Connecticut, livens up staff meetings by interspersing role playing with business, using Jack Whittle's "motor mouth" contest. The person speaks on a bank-related product or service for up to two minutes, receiving $1 per second. The person is disqualified if he or she pauses, repeats himself or herself, says "uh," etc. They also place door prizes, such as lotto tickets, under selected chairs.

#172. Rockville Savings Bank also sponsors sessions of "A.M. Schoolhouse," wherein volunteers gather 45 minutes before the start of the work day to review a current management book. The bank provides breakfast, and participants can read the book from cover to cover or confine themselves to the one chapter assigned to them to present. Their effort is reduced, and they can enjoy listening to one another's remarks as well as the social ambiance that these sessions create.

#173. Comerica Bank in Detroit, Michigan, utilizes monthly Sales and Service meetings to reinforce skills in both areas. An actual "toolbox" labeled the "ECE Toolbox" (Exceeding Customer Expectations) was sent to each branch. Then, with each month's meeting, some type of fun, visual reminder is sent out that relates to the meeting. Each reminder is then placed in the toolbox, which is kept in the kitchen or other employee area within the branch. Kathy Carnacchi, Branch Administration, says, "We can tell we're accomplishing our objective because if you select any of these tool reminders and ask an employee what meeting it relates to, he or she can likely recall the exercise and what ECE skill(s) it reinforced." Here are two examples she shared:

One meeting dealt with being flexible to change and offering alternatives for our customers. The "tool" was a bright eraser which states "Erase Unproductive Tapes—Be Flexible to Change." Another meeting asked participants to evaluate themselves on their customer service skills. Included was a mirror that asked, "How Do I Look?" with a border of various customer service skills.

#174. The executive management committee of the National Exchange Carrier Association, Inc., conducts a quarterly review of current quality projects within the organization. These meetings celebrate the quality process and provide opportunities for the quality teams to talk about the process and how it is working. They also provide much-needed recognition for team participants. Jean Kahn, the Director of Corporate Planning, says,

> Our company president sets the tone for the quality concept in the organization. His support of the process was typified by his recent actions. Unable to attend a recent quarterly review, he made a point to visit with each team representative individually prior to the meeting. He expressed regrets for being unable to attend the meeting, then showed support for the process by encouraging each team to continue their efforts. This way, he demonstrated the quality concept by setting a personal example through his own leadership.

#175.   The owner of The Paige Collection in Grand Junction, Colorado, has monthly staff meetings where they discuss what they have done well during the month and where they need to improve, as well as sharing fun things that have happened in the store. As a part of this meeting, she always gives the employees silly, personal gifts. During a really stressful time for one of the employees, she bought her a gallon of bubbles to blow! When another one had put in hours and hours planning and presenting a huge style show, she presented her with a mug that said, "OH NO!" A new, rather overwhelmed employee received a T-shirt with a picture of a little girl in a forest. Below it was the caption, "I'm lost!" These meetings are a wonderful combination of both the Business and the Human levels.

COMMUNICATION CHALLENGE.   Many organizations devote the first five minutes of all company meetings to some aspect of Service Quality—feedback reports, success stories, creative presentations, reminders, etc. This practice communicates their commitment to service quality as a true priority in their organization. What can you add to your next company meeting to creatively support something important to the organization? Have fun, take the risk, and try something new!

CULTURAL DIVERSITY AWARENESS

Having an environment where everybody thinks alike, acts alike, and comes to the same conclusions is what got us into trouble in the first place!

Lawrence Perlman, *Control Data*

This is another area that is new to most organizations. The acceptance of the changing workplace as being more diverse with women and racial minorities will result in a healthier work environment and a more productive workplace. The reality is that if we shrink the world into 100 people, only 30 will be Caucasian; 70 people will be nonwhite peoples of Asian, African, Native American, Pacific Islander, and Hispanic origins, according to a 1990 study by Dr. Patrick Coggins. And by the end of the 1990s, 85 percent of new entrants into the workplace will be minorities, women, or immigrants. These trends indicate that managing diversity is no longer an option for business and the public sector; it is an imperative mandate that will strengthen our overall productivity and interpersonal relations.

I asked Dr. Coggins, Jesse Ball Dupont Chair Professor of Education and Multicultural Education at Stetson University, DeLand, Florida, to share some of the ways he believes we can increase organizational awareness of this crucial issue:

Cultural Diversity is not a program, rather it is a philosophy, a perspective that recognizes the positiveness, contributions, differences, and humanness of all human beings regardless of gender, exceptionalities, and racial, ethnic, socio-economic level, religious or other distinguishing variables. A commitment to the philosophy of Cultural Diversity is but the first step in developing a culturally sensitive work-place. The next steps are in the organization's policies and practices and the way we interact with each other.

Here are some proven strategies that can be used to enhance cultural awareness in a culturally diverse world and work-place:

1. Eye Contact—Different ethnic groups use different styles of eye contact. While most Americans emphasize looking straight into the eyes when speaking to another person, Asians tend to look down or away. African Americans and Hispanics tend to look at you when they are speaking but away when they are listening to you. The point here is that depending on the ethnic group, we need to adjust our communication strategies. Do not interpret the looking away as "rudeness" or "not paying attention to what is being said." These are simply cultural differences.

2. The Animated Communicator—People have claimed that individuals who use emotional expressions and lots of pointing and great movement with their hands can be intimidating, especially as they observe the emotions and loudness of voice. Instead of being intimidated, concentrate on listening to the message and separate the emotions and animation. If the person is too close, step back. Often the sender will react by slowing down and acknowledge that you are experiencing difficulty with the communication.

3. Language Used Is Not Always English—When a customer speaks a different language, instead of saying, "I don't understand," learn some simple greetings in his/her language. Be sure to learn basic language pieces related to your customers. If a customer brings in a translator, still use your verbal and nonverbal skills to keep the customer involved in the transaction by looking at the customer every time you speak.

4. Make the Environment Ethnically Sensitive—I have a picture of children from all of the primary racial groups in my office. I model the need to have an environment—an office, a classroom, a training room, a lobby, which reflects culturally diverse people, objects, and thoughts. My customers have often remarked that the pictures provide a warm feeling and help them think broadly about other people who are different.

   Another example is Sun Bank of DeLand, Florida, whose manager agreed to display the Stetson University's Dubey Collection of African Art for two weeks during the African History and Culture Month of 1992. It was announced on the marquis, and the

continued

display was near the coffee section by the main entrance. The customers and staff were delighted by the art collection and reported that they gained a better appreciation of African Culture. Next year the university will add the collection of art and history of women to the bank during the month of March to celebrate the contributions of women and to recognize female employees. By creating an environment that celebrates diversity, the university, in cooperation with Sun Bank, is actively demonstrating its commitment to this value.

5. Multilingual Communications—I believe that every major communication document in an organization must be multilingual. For example, if you have Hmong or Mexican or Russian employees, devote a section or do a special newsletter in their languages. Make sure the signs in the bathrooms are multilingual. YOUR MISSION STATEMENT SHOULD BE WRITTEN IN AT LEAST THREE LANGUAGES. If you are working with an overseas/international company, be sure to use bilingual communication since this helps send the message that you respect their language and culture.

6. Diversify Your Ceremonies—Have a multicultural menu of foods, games and decorations. Focus on including women, men, racial minorities at the head table of a banquet to showcase your staff's diversity. Make sure the music and the decorations reflect the diversity of American life. Reggae is a favorite music cross culturally.

7. Cross Cultural Annual Calendars—There are many cross cultural calendars which highlight the contributions of ethnic groups to the USA and to the world. Also if you print a calendar, ensure that the pictures which accompany the calendar represent a different ethnic group each month. You can communicate your vision of diversity through what you print on your calendars!

8. Communicating Commitment to Cultural Diversity Through Your Mission Statement—I have been struck by the many businesses that display well-written mission statements in their lobbies; however as I have become more aware of them, I am also struck that most often there are no references to diversity as part of the values of the organization.

9. Model Cultural Diversity—The philosophy that drives cultural diversity requires that each of us model the desired behaviors. Role models for the organization should especially come from middle and top management since they are the policy implementers who will monitor the progress of interpersonal contacts in the organization.

Finally, the commitment to Cultural Diversity must be lifelong. My personal dream is to ensure that all human beings be given equal opportunity to achieve their best and fullest potential. People will be judged not by the color of their skin, not by their social class nor race nor religion but rather judged by the content of their character and their relative contributions to society.[14]

#176. Richard D. McCormick, the President and CEO of US West, Inc., expresses his vision and his commitment to cultural diversity in this way:

STATEMENT FROM THE CHAIRMAN

When I think about what I want this company to be above all else, I want it to be a place in which everyone has the opportunity to grow, to contribute, and to serve. I want it to be a place where we actively seek to attract and involve a representative group of all people—all races, all ages, varying backgrounds and physical abilities, women and men. I want them to be the kind of people we know will care about and understand the customer because they care about and try to understand each other.

Richard D. McCormick
President and Chief Executive Officer

#177. UPS has a program that has been around since the 60s that helps managers at the giant shipping company to learn—up close and personal—what it means to "appreciate diversity." The Community Internship Program has been an important part of the corporate culture since 1968. These are the mechanics of the program:

Take upper and middle managers off the job for one month and put them through an experience that will sensitize them to people who live in very different circumstances—people like some of the manager's employees and customers. Instead of sitting managers in a classroom, UPS plunks them down in communities and situations that they would rarely or never encounter in the normal course of their lives. As community interns, managers might find themselves serving meals to the homeless, helping rid an urban ghetto of drug paraphernalia, helping migrant farm workers build temporary houses and schools, or helping teachers manage a classroom of kids in a Head Start program.

This is not a voluntary assignment; if you're drafted, you go. Since the program began, UPS has sent about 800 managers on these internships. Currently, they're being packed off at a rate of about 40 a year. The main message the UPS interns carry away is that poor and disadvantaged people aren't nearly as "different" as they thought. What tends to strike home most to these managers is how much they have in common with the people they help.[15]

#178. First Chicago Banks has a BankMobile that travels all over the Chicagoland area, attending ethnic festivals and visiting schools. This educational vehicle contains information on banking: written materials, films, videotapes, and slides, and all the materials are translated into Spanish. Some of the people who travel with the BankMobile are bilingual in Spanish as well. First Chicago also considers its diverse customers by providing advertisements in Spanish and Korean in area newspapers as well as making some ATM machines available in Spanish.

#179. While waiting to speak to a manager at Northwest Natural Gas in Portland, Oregon, I learned through a recorded message that in order to improve communication with all their customers, they now offer translation services for their non-English-speaking customers and telecommunications devices for the deaf for those customers who are hearing impaired. I was impressed with the importance they gave this message as well as the fact that they offer such services.

#180. Max De Pree says, "Leaders can be, when they choose, significant bearers of gifts to the spirit. There was at Herman Miller (a furniture business) a department supervisor to whom many disabled people seemed to gravitate. This supervisor seemed to have a way of providing a place for them. I once asked him why this was. He answered very simply, 'Max, it's just a matter of letting people know how much we need them.' That man (Howard) is a real gift to the spirit."[16]

COMMUNICATION CHALLENGE. What can you do to celebrate diversity in your organization? Seize the opportunity to learn from people of different ethnic backgrounds through things like a "foods of the world" dinner or "holiday customs" or "music/art/dance of the world." Appreciate these differences and then you will learn to better appreciate one another.

ACTION PAGE

Chapter Six

Day-to-Day Feedback
Creatively Communicating
Your Appreciation on a Daily Basis

Just as the accumulation of small improvements can make a dramatic, lasting change in the organization's products or services, the repeated, numerous small occasions of taking note of the contributions of individuals and teams of individuals can create a different company.

Patrick Townsend and Joan Gebhart
"The Quality Process: Little Things Mean a Lot"
Review of Business, Winter 1990/91

Source: ©Kaset International.

This chapter is all about ways to give positive day-to-day feedback to persons around us as a way to communicate commitment to our beliefs and values. Because of the importance of praise and affirmation to all of us, I decided to separate formal reward and recognition programs from simple, informal ways to show daily appreciation to customers, both internal and external. Although the following examples are certainly forms of reward and recognition, they are inexpensive, simple to implement, and are designed to be used often.

Also, unlike rewards and recognition that are internal affirmations, day-to-day feedback—Acknowledgment, Appreciation, Affirmation, and Assurance—can also be extended to external customers to thank them and to create Positive Memorable Customer Experiences.

THE FOUR A'S

Kaset uses the term the "Four A's" to refer to four ways to communicate in positive ways to customers—internal or external. The "Four A's" are: Acknowledge, Appreciate, Affirm, and Assure. The use of these four response skills helps customers know they are being heard and taken seriously; they feel cared about.

"Acknowledge" means to let the customer know you heard what he or she said. Within the context of the Human-Business model, acknowledging the customer's concern on the Business level or need on the Human level is the first way to defuse potential anger or upset. When upset customers know that you understand what they said, they do not have to escalate further to get your attention. In an everyday customer situation when the customer is not upset, it is important to acknowledge personal things the customer has mentioned so that customer feels important as a human being.

"Appreciate" is just what it says. You can appreciate: the customer's business, their specific situation, their efforts to get the situation resolved, their viewpoints. You can even appreciate the fact that you and the person have different points of view. And you can appreciate them as a person on the Human level.

"Affirm" has a "Business" and a "Human" use. On the Business side, you affirm the choices the customer makes during the interaction. On the Human side, you affirm the customer in order for the person to feel valued. You might do this by giving the person a sincere compliment or mentioning something about them that you like.

"Assure" is indicating to the customers you will take personal responsibility for researching or actually providing whatever the customer is asking for. The goal is to create comfort that the ball will not be dropped. You can assure them by giving them your name, your extension number, and if you need to call them back, give them a definite time.

So, when a customer knows you heard their need/concern, believes you will see to it that it's taken care of, and feels both valued and appreciated in the interaction, the individual will take away a positive memory—the foundation for extraordinary customer relations.[1]

Source: Shannon Johnston.

Remember the three-column chart described in Chapter 1? In every interaction you have the *choice* to create either a negative (−) experience by making the person feel less important than you or your organization, a neutral (0) experience by only taking care of the business at hand with no concern for the Human level, or a positive (+) experience by using one of the Four A's—by acknowledging, appreciating, affirming, or assuring the person. Each time you create a positive experience for someone, you have contributed to making the world a little better. Consider the following quotation, which can become a philosophy of life and work:

> Be kind and merciful. Let no one ever come to you without coming away better and happier.
>
> Mother Teresa

So, making the choice to create a positive experience for someone and having the skills to do that (the Four A's and sometimes other listening skills) is what day-to-day feedback is all about. Sometimes you will be positively recognized for creating those + experiences for customers, and other times you will be the one to recognize someone else who has done that.

It is important to determine a personal strategy to remember to use the Four A's with people in your life. Here are some of the ways you might want to do that:

- Keep a 3 × 5 card with three columns, a − column, a 0 column, and a + column, on your desk for a week. Every time you interact with anyone, put a check in the appropriate column. At the end of the week, if you have more checks in the + column than in the other two, you have contributed to making the world a little better.
- Keep a large "A" on your desk as a reminder.
- Keep a pad of "Thank you" Post-it notes in your desk and in your briefcase or purse. Leave a note for someone at least once a day, and be creative about where you put them. Try rearview mirrors, lunch bags, desk drawers, someone's telephone, the mirror in the organization's bathroom, someone's coffee mug, coat pockets, or a special place in their work area!
- Keep a copy of a report card to symbolize "You can't do better than all A's!"
- Designate one day of the week as your "A" day. Do not let the day end without creating a + experience for someone!

As you read the ideas listed in this chapter, you will find many delightful and creative ways to remind people to use the Four A's with both internal and external customers.

#181. Terry Huntsman of US West shares this strategy for remembering the Four A's: Draw playing cards (four aces) on a flipchart. Use them to represent and demonstrate acknowledging, appreciating, affirming, and assuring. Tell participants, "If you use one of them, you have one good card already, and if you use all four, you have a winning hand for establishing rapport!" He says that people in his organization put regular playing cards (four aces) on their terminals as a reminder.

#182. TheVirginia Department of Motor Vehicles gives its employees pads of "DMV Grateful Grams," which say "thank you" in several different languages. These can be shared internally or externally with customers. At Bonneville Power Administration in Portland, Oregon, personal recognition cards are available on every floor in the service centers. Anyone can give one whenever it is appropriate. One of them says, "BRAVO" and the other says, "THANK YOU."

DMV GRATEFUL-GRAM

No matter what language you speak...this is a message of thanks

Merci

Grazie

Dank U

Take Someke

Arigato

Mange Takke

Gracias

Dank

Source: Virginia Department of Motor Vehicles.

Bravo

To: _____   Date: _____

Thanks for your help in
( ) providing information
( ) getting quick action on _____
( ) _____

You made my job a lot easier and I want to let you know that I appreciate it! Way to go!

_____
_____
_____

From: _____   Phone: _____

Source: Bonneville Power Administration.

#183. PTI Communications in Tomah, Wisconsin, has recently started a program called "HOORAY FOR CUSTOMERS." Diane Winchell wrote: "This is our way of showing our appreciation for all the hard work and dedication to our valued employees of PTI. And, for the external customers, this is our way of showing our appreciation for their patronage. Periodically we serve cake, coffee, and punch and are available to discuss any issues or answer any questions. There is a drawing for a door prize, too!"

INTERNAL CUSTOMER EXAMPLES

#184. At the end of a refresher session on customer service, Jeanie Hagen-Greene of Sunrise Bank in Roseville, California, passes out four or five "customer report cards" that are printed on bright yellow 3" × 5" heavy paper to each participant. She asks them to send a report card to a co-worker as a thank you when the co-worker

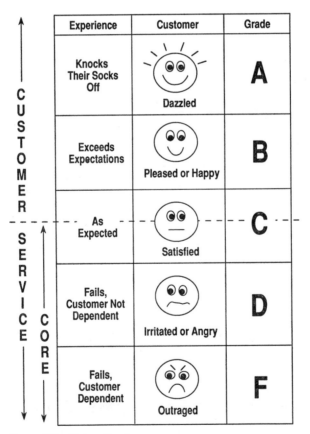

Source: ©Kaset International.

has created a Positive Memorable Customer Experience. The participant is to circle a grade, write a short note, sign the card, and send it to the PMCE creator to acknowledge a job well done. She also asks that a photocopy of the card be sent to her so that she may include success stories in the employee newsletter.

#185. At the conclusion of a very stressful presentation to the CEO and several hundred senior level managers at Nationwide Insurance by a group of newly certified facilitators in a customer service training program, one of their managers brought them each a red rose and a hug. Their extraordinary efforts had been immediately recognized and rewarded.

#186. At a recent training session at Nationwide Insurance, when we were discussing the four A's, one of the participants shared that when her husband got a special honor from the local police department, *her* department sent him a congratulations card. Both of them were very touched by this gesture, particularly because, as she said, "No one else in our lives sent a card to him." Anytime an organization acknowledges an important event in the personal lives of its employees or their family members, it makes those folks feel appreciated and special.

#187. Centel Cellular in Raleigh, North Carolina, encourages teamwork. Whenever someone in the department is having a hard time getting his or her work done because of things like a mistake, illness, a need to do extra research, or just too much to do, another co-worker can jump in to help. That co-worker becomes their "Star of the Day," and he or she is given a silver star to put in his or her work area. The co-worker who has offered to help has acknowledged the other employee's concern, has assured the person of his or her help, and he or she is then shown appreciation by the whole department for helping out.

Source: PEMCO Financial Center.

#188. PEMCO Financial Center, Seattle, Washington, promotes teamwork among all employees by the use of "Courtesy Cash." These $2\frac{3}{4}''$ × $6\frac{1}{2}''$ coupons have a value of 50 cents in the Center cafeteria. Employees request books of coupons from the Quality Coordinator. When they want to show courtesy and respect to a fellow employee who has helped them perform their job, they send a coupon. According to Christine Chalupa, Training Specialist, this has proven to be very effective, especially for crossing department lines and thanking someone the employee may not know too well.

#189. Mary Trowbridge of the Ohio Bureau of Employment Services designed a poster she called the "Small Wins Board." It said at the top: "CELEBRATE THE SMALL WINS (and the BIG ONES too, of course)." On the poster she drew a trophy, a certificate, a blue ribbon, a happy face button, and the words "BRAVO," "CONGRATULATIONS," "GOOD JOB!" Then she framed the poster and hung it in a place where all members must regularly go (mail box area), posted the explanation sheet next to the poster, and attached a pad of Post-it notes. The instructions were to write down things accomplished, both individually and as a team, honors received, good ideas, and appreciation of others—"Nothing that makes you feel good is unworthy of the Board." All messages were left up for a week and then recorded in a binder. Mary said, "Employees used the board in creative ways to communicate their feelings of pride and appreciation, and some heart-warming, encouraging personal notes went up there, too."

EXTERNAL CUSTOMER EXAMPLES

#190. After a recent purchase at the Saks Fifth Avenue store in Oak Brook, Illinois, I received a handwritten thank you note from the sales person stating, "I hope you will be happy with your new outfit." This is also a practice of H_2O Plus stores, whose employees send a thank you note to every new customer.

#191. The first time I tried Gateway Cleaners in Hinsdale, Illinois, the son of the owner offered to carry my cleaning out to my car. My husband was in the back seat with a full leg brace from a recent skiing accident, and the young man expressed his interest and concern as he put my clothes in the car. From that time on, each time I have returned to their establishment, he not only remembers and uses my name, but he also always asks about my husband. Their appreciation of us as customers and their acknowledgment of things in our personal lives have created some very loyal customers.

#192. When I had not returned to Hinsdale Hair Company in Hinsdale, Illinois, for several months, I received a note in the mail saying, "We miss you," and enclosed was a coupon for "$10 off your next haircut." That Human touch brought me back as a regular customer!

#193. United Airlines has a new program—"MANAGE-MENT EMPLOYEES ASKED TO DIAL UP A PREMIER, THANK THEM FOR THEIR BUSINESS." To let the airline's best customers know how much United Airlines values their business, President and CEO Jack Pope is asking all management employees to call a Premier Mileage Plus member and thank them for their business.

Each of United's 8,400 management employees will receive a computerized letter from Pope that contains the name and telephone number of an individual customer. It's part of the company's efforts to increase awareness of the contribution of Mileage Plus Premier Executive and Premier members. Together, those customers contribute approximately $2 billion a year to United.

"The Out-Call Program not only provides an opportunity for management employees to express their appreciation for our Premiers' business, but it also will offer one-on-one exposure to the customer—something many management employees don't experience daily," says Gayle Block, Director of Marketing Programs.

#194. Jeff Davis, a Training Consultant, gives his classes a picture of a large hand. It says, "POST THIS HAND ON A DOOR OR A WALL IN YOUR AREA. WHENEVER YOU DO A GOOD JOB, LEAN AGAINST IT FOR A FEW SECONDS AND GIVE YOURSELF A PAT ON THE BACK!"

#195. Jude Marchetti, a Realtor with Village Properties in Hinsdale, Illinois, believes her clients should be her friends and that theirs is a long-term relationship. She says her initial interview with clients takes about two hours. She asks them the following questions: What is your favorite color? What is your favorite vacation? What is your favorite hobby? She first finds out what their *needs* for a home are and then asks about their *desires*. She says she only shows them homes that match their needs and their finances. Other Realtors often try to "hook" clients with more expensive property than they can really afford; however, Jude feels this is deceitful and not considerate of the client's human needs. On the Business level she feels that her clients should have "one stop shopping," so she helps them arrange their financing, a lawyer, an inspector, and any other details they require. She always takes a picture of the couple in their new home, and for Christmas, she gives them something she has made especially for them, such as wreaths for their front doors and decoupaged baskets that match the colors of their homes. She sends them anniversary cards, birthday cards, and even learns the names of their cats and dogs! All of this creates a very special relationship, both on the Business and the Human levels, not to mention *lots* of referral business.

#196. Kansas City is the center of a special program called the "Kindness Campaign." It began when SueEllen Fried, founder of the Stop Violence Coalition, put together a very successful "Kindness" workshop for 4th grade children in the Kansas City schools. The following year Barbara Unell, the editor and publisher of *Twins* magazine, started a "Kindness" program in her children's school. One of the activities she created was to have two jars in the school foyer, a "PUT UP" jar and a "PUT DOWN" jar. Whenever the children saw anyone doing something nice, they put something in the "PUT UP" jar, and when they saw something hurtful, they put something in the "PUT DOWN" jar. As a result of this new awareness, they began doing lots of nice things for one another. Sometime later Channel 5 sent letters to all the Kansas City schools asking the children to nominate the "kindest Kansas Citians," and a special banquet was held honoring the winners as well as the children who had written the winning letters. The "Kindness Campaign" soon spread to 60 schools, and today there are over 200 schools in the greater Kansas City area involved. Barbara Unell has co-authored a book of "Kindness Activities" called *Kindness Is Contagious . . . Catch It!* to be used in the schools, and many, many folks have become involved in helping to bring more kindness and love to the lives of the residents of the greater Kansas City area and, as the circle of good deeds grows, spreading that kindness and love throughout the world. Rita Blitt has recently completed a sculpture for one of the city parks that she is dedicating to Kansas City, the "KINDNESS" city!

#197. Beth Munkres, the owner of The Paige Collection, gives special attention to her vendors. She often writes a personal note to the person she deals with in the shipping department and sends them a box of candy to recognize them when they have gone the extra mile for her, and sometimes just to thank them for always doing a good job. She says, "I like to recognize the 'little guys' who rarely, if ever, get any recognition. In fact, some of them tell me that I am the only customer they know! Then, when I really need something, they will pull merchandise from the great big companies for my little shop—just because I have taken time to care about them."

COMMUNICATION CHALLENGE.   Think of a unique, personal strategy to remind yourself to use the Four A's. What can you do in your organization to more fully and more frequently appreciate your employees? Your customers? Remember, we all need all the affirmation we can get!

ACTION PAGE

Chapter Seven

Enhancements and Reminders
Keeping Your Commitment Alive through Unusual and Innovative Extras

I STILL SAY WE JUST TICKET EM ¿ GET BACK ON THE ROAD.

Source: © Kaset International.

E nhancements and reminders are those delightful, creative ideas and events that "Keep the commitment alive!" A commitment usually involves a long-term experience, particularly when it concerns values and beliefs. Sometimes, though, the spirit ebbs to a flicker, and something is needed to fan the flames into brightness again. One of the best ways for this to happen is to encourage an atmosphere of fun in the workplace: "Playfulness, researchers are finding, can help people take a better, more creative approach to the way they work. The serious benefits of fun have been so well established that a number of firms have made it part of the corporate culture. . . . Don't let dogged determination kill your sense of fun. An element of playfulness will make you more creative, more satisfied, and, yes, more productive, too!"[1]

David J. Abramis writes, "Job satisfaction is certainly important. But fun is just as essential to productivity, and often harder to find." In answering the question, "How does fun affect people and organizations?" he found the following: "Compared to people who don't find fun in their work, employees who do, report they are: less anxious and depressed and more satisfied with their jobs and with their lives in general; more convinced that other people have fun at work; more motivated by their work; more creative at work; and better able to meet job demands and less likely to be absent or late to work."

Here are some ways to make work more playful:

1. Make a conscious effort to have fun. You might even include "having fun" as a goal when you set performance objectives.
2. Spread the word. Let people know that having fun at work is often appropriate.
3. Help supervisors and other managers have fun and suggest ways they can help their people do the same. Their influence is crucial, for good or bad. When we asked, "What would make your job more fun?" a number of people told us, "Get rid of my supervisor!"
4. Ask people what they think is fun.
5. Use rewards and recognition to let people know they are valued.
6. Create events.
7. Hire people who are interested in, and capable of, having fun.[2]

All of the following enhancements and reminders are ways of adding some creativity and fun to the workplace that will, in turn, help ensure that your organizational commitment is alive and well. So, lighten up and prepare to have your thinking stretched!

HUMAN LEVEL ENHANCEMENTS AND REMINDERS

These are the ideas and events that enhance the Human interactions in your organization.

CONTESTS

#198. The Limited Credit Services sponsors a "Kaset Olympics," a monthly meeting activity in teams to test and develop skills learned in Kaset training programs. Winners receive $25 certificates to the Limited store of their choice, an "Olympic" medal, and they are taken to dinner by the manager, assistant manager, and the Kaset facilitators.

#199. The Medicare Operations Division of Nationwide Insurance recently held an essay contest for employees on "Why I am proud to work at Nationwide." The winners were given "Ramsey Awards" (like Emmys), named after the Vice President of Operations, and were featured in a video for new employees entitled "Team Medicare." These employees articulated the values of Medicare Operations in their own words as testimonials for those just joining the team.

#200. The Virginia Department of Motor Vehicles is doing some fun things for its employees:

- As a celebration of National Customer Service Week, they are giving their employees an opportunity to send in their favorite customer service story. The categories are: Most humorous, Most unusual, and Most heart-rending. Winners will be selected, and all entries will be shared with all employees in a DMV booklet.
- Another fun contest that the Virginia DMV is sponsoring is a Halloween costume contest. In an effort to combine safety and service, they allow their employees to dress up on Halloween and to participate in a costume contest. They also provide their employees and their external customers with reflective stickers that they can put on their costumes to make them more visible on Halloween night.

#201. I recently read in the *InfoCanadian* about two contests that are occurring at Canadian Airlines International. One is a logo contest for the 1992 Charitable Donations Campaign, which is a fund-raising campaign of employees and retirees volunteering their time and energy to raise an expected $350,000 for a variety of causes. The winning artist receives two systemwide passes. The logo will be used for future campaign letterhead and posters. The theme of the campaign is "Canadians helping Canadians," and all logo entries should reflect the theme in some way. Submissions can be either hand drawn or created on a computer.

The second is an "It's a Kid's World" environment contest for children of employees aged 7 to 17. Young concerned citizens are asked to write an essay answering the question, "How could you make your home more environmentally-friendly?" First, employees are to encourage the children to look around their home to find ways the family can better reduce, recycle, or reuse. Then, they can help them put the idea or ideas into practice at home. Finally, the children can write a short essay on what their idea was and why reducing, recycling, and reusing is important to their family. "Children and young people are among the most active participants in the environmental movement today," says Malcolm Metcalfe, manager of Environmental Affairs. "This contest is their chance to tell us how they can help. We must teach our children that the combination of a lot of small things is as important as any one big solution to a problem."

#202. Odetics, a high-technology firm in Anaheim, California, has had a Fun Committee since 1982. It sponsors activities such as a 50s and 60s Day, featuring Hula-Hoop contests, bubble-gum blowing competitions, and telephone-booth stuffing.[3]

#203. Moore Business Communication Services recently had a contest offering its Logan, Utah, employees an opportunity to visit some of their internal and external customers. This was a drawing for a trip to Salt Lake City: "As part of 'Quality Month' and to provide a better understanding of Customer Supplier relationships, we would like to offer a trip to Salt Lake City to let you tour the Print Center, Sales Office and meet two external customers. Four people will be chosen. Lunch will be provided and the date to go will be decided among the people chosen."

#204. David Armstrong tells about the annual company bake-off at Warrick Controls in Royal Oak, Michigan. The contest is in the midst of winter, and almost everyone participates. The competition is fierce in the three categories: hot dishes, cold dishes, and desserts, and the entrants receive points on appearance, taste, and creativity. Armstrong says, "I remember one entree was a child's sand bucket filled with a dessert resembling dirt. (It was actually made of white pudding and ground-up Oreo cookies.) You were supposed to eat it with the shovel that was provided. It got my vote for the most creative!"[4]

#205. The corporate office of a large bank issued a "Laugh a Day Challenge" to all its employees. Employees were challenged to bring in a joke or cartoon every day for a month to share with their co-workers. Anyone who completed the challenge received a Corporate Challenge T-shirt and a book containing the best jokes and cartoons.

COMMUNICATION CHALLENGE.   Would a creative internal contest of some kind add a new spirit of commitment and fun for your employees? The most effective contests have something to do with the organization's commitment to beliefs and values; however, those that are simply for fun also create teamwork and camaraderie.

BUTTONS AND PINS

Here are some of the buttons I've seen that communicate a commitment:

#206. Puget Power in Washington state gives its customers and employees buttons that say "PUGET POWER CUSTOMER SERVICE—Ours is a partnership."

#207. In a large department store recently I saw a young man very proudly wearing a button that said, "I AM EMPOWERED." When I asked him what it meant, he stood up very tall and said, "It means that I can do things no one else except the manager can do, like authorizing refunds and checks, giving discounts for damaged merchandise, and scheduling breaks for employees." I replied, "Wow! That's just great! Did you get a raise too?" He answered immediately, "No, but that's O.K. I'm a lot more *important* around here!"

#208. A friend told me of a button she recently saw on a disabled person in a Target store in Minnesota. It said "Ask me, I like to help."

#209. When faced with a large, difficult project, Vision Financial Corporation decided to try a team approach. Comprised of members from all departments, the team analyzed the project, outlined the desired results, tested the system design, and celebrated the successful completion of the project. During the company recognition of the team's efforts during the celebration, each member was awarded a special button saying, "VISIONARIES MASTER THE IMPOSSIBLE!"

#210. On Mondays each employee of Sysco/Continental Produce in Portland, Oregon, wears a button with the slogan "Focus On The Flag." A flag flies outside company headquarters with the words "SERVICE EXCELLENCE." If a customer reports being dissatisfied with some part of the company's service, the flag comes down for the day.[5]

#211. The Stop Violence Coalition in Kansas City has created a button containing the words "Kindness is Contagious—Catch It!" These buttons were first given out at a banquet honoring the "kindest Kansas Citians," who were nominated by the school children of Kansas City. Each person who is given a button is told to "wear it into the world and to pass it on" whenever they meet a kind person. Legendary stories have evolved as these buttons have spread all over the world!

#212. Several organizations give their employees pins: Clark Public Utilities, Vancouver, Washington, gives each of its employees a high-quality black and gold lapel pin that says, "I can help" to wear whenever they are working. This reminds employees they have the authority to help, and it invites customers to ask for assistance.

REMINDS EMPLOYEES THEY HAVE

THE AUTHORITY TO HELP

INVITES CUSTOMERS TO ASK

FOR ASSISTANCE

Source: Clark Public Utilities.

#213. Every employee who goes through customer service training at PTI Communications in Tomah, Wisconsin, receives a "Hooray for Customers!" pin. When customers ask about the pins, it becomes a great opportunity for them to share their commitment to customer service.

COMMUNICATION CHALLENGE. How about a contest to come up with a button that communicates your organization's commitment?

SLOGANS, MOTTOS, LOGOS, SYMBOLS

#214. Most organizations have slogans that are short and concise, communicating their commitment in a few words:

- Standard Insurance uses the slogan, "You'll stay with Standard" to emphasize the commitment to building customer loyalty.
- Vision Financial shares its commitment to always go the extra mile for customers by its slogan, "Anything's possible with Vision."
- Seafirst Bank listens to its customers' needs, so it uses the slogan, "We make banking easy for you."

- Nationwide Insurance has a very reassuring slogan: "Nationwide is on your side."
- The City of Oklahoma City uses the slogan, "The City is ME!" They have stickers, posters, and small cards with the slogan as well as ballpoint pens with the three-dimensional letters "THANKS." They also give beautiful gold pins in the shape of a star with the seal of the city attached to employees who dazzle customers.
- NBD Bank has as its slogan, "QUALITY SERVICE IS NOT AN EVENT, IT'S A PROCESS . . . AND YOU ARE AN IMPORTANT PART OF THE PROCESS AT NBD!"
- At Peoples State Bank in St. Joseph, Michigan, they use the slogan, "People Come First" when referring to both their external and internal customers. This slogan supports their commitment to consistently provide service that will enable them to differentiate themselves from their competition.

#215. Jean Watson, a Senior Training Consultant, uses the following slogan puzzle as an icebreaker in her training classes to point out the impact that a slogan can have on an organization's image:

Q I J 1

W L To F and I S

Y D A B T

W Y C E To S The V B

L Y F D The W

R O and T S

H Y D A F L

G M I P

G To The L D

Y G The R O B

A Y G Y U D

Answers

Quality Is Job 1 (Ford Motor Company)

We Love to Fly and It Shows (Delta)

You Deserve a Break Today (McDonald's)

When You Care Enough to Send the Very Best (Hallmark)

Let Your Fingers Do the Walking (The Yellow Pages)

Reach Out and Touch Someone (AT&T)

Have You Driven a Ford Lately? (Ford Motor Company)

Get Met. It Pays. (Metropolitan Life Insurance)

Good to the Last Drop (Maxwell House Coffee)

You Got the Right One Baby (Pepsi)

Aren't You Glad You Used Dial? (Dial Soap)

#216. I recently spoke at the annual conference of the Georgia Division of Rehabilitation Services. One of the giveaways at the conference was from State Farm Insurance and was an extension of its motto. On each chair was a large plastic cup containing a pencil, a magnet, and two brochures, all containing the slogan: BE A GOOD NEIGHBOR. BE A DESIGNATED DRIVER.

#217. The Division of Rehabilitation Services of the state of Georgia initiated a competition to develop a motto for the division. More than 260 entries were submitted by both groups and individuals. They unveiled the winning motto at their statewide conference along with three other awards. The new motto is:

Dedicated
Responsible
Sensitive

#218. In the City of Scottsdale, Arizona, a Japanese character is popping up all over the organization. The symbol—or KAIZEN—didn't just appear; it was strategically placed in city offices to generate curiosity and enthusiasm for October as "Simply Better Service Month." KAIZEN symbolizes small, gradual improvements involving every member of a work force. The KAIZEN philosophy assumes that our way of life—be it our work life, social life, or home life—can always benefit from constant improvement. KAIZEN has been incorporated into the Japanese management style for years. Many believe it is the key to that country's competitive success. Dick Bowers, the City Manager, says: "Underlying the KAIZEN strategy is the assumption that all activities should eventually lead to increased customer satisfaction. This month, I hope we can be more aware of KAIZEN and begin to incorporate this philosophy into our organizational culture. In many ways we already are—but if we are truly applying KAIZEN, we realize that we can always strive for improvement. To quote a saying that is posted in all Japanese Honda plants, 'There will be no progress if you keep on doing things the same way all the time.'"

#219. Rosenbluth Travel prides itself on being different, blazing new trails, swimming against the tide. For that reason, they have selected the salmon as their corporate mascot. Hal Rosenbluth says, "Our people love having a mascot. It's a great morale booster and team builder." They have even designed and produced a salmon stuffed animal for their clients. An internal recognition program has been developed that is centered around the company mascot. The program recognizes employees who go the extra mile to help each other and their clients. Rosenbluth says, "We wanted the program to be alive on a day-to-day basis, so we created salmon materials our associates can use to recognize each other. For example, when we receive a letter complimenting an associate, the associate's leader sends him or her a copy with a salmon sticker on it. And associates send each other salmon note cards with messages of thanks or encouragement. The highest honor in our company is the salmon pin. We also have service pins to recognize length of service, but the salmon pin is reserved for associates who far exceed even a salmon's expectations!"[6]

COMMUNICATION CHALLENGE.   Do you have a slogan, a symbol, or a mascot? If you do, are they widely known and used by your employees? How do they communicate your commitment? These can be fun and creative enhancements for your organization.

BULLETIN BOARDS

Bulletin boards can be an extremely fun and creative way to communicate your organization's beliefs and values. Select different boards and locations for different purposes; however, use the most visible ones for your most important values. Use color, pictures, three-dimensional things—always remember the Human level! If your bulletin boards are drab, boring, and uncreative, that image will be projected to your entire organization. However, if they are vibrant, interesting, and fun, all customers, internal and external, will know that this is a committed organization and a fun place to work!

#220. The Limited Credit Services has an ongoing customer service bulletin board where they post articles on service, photos from training classes, reminders of concepts, service cartoons, quotes about service, and general information on the Service Quality initiative. It changes frequently and has become a "meeting place" for employees!

#221. Commercebank in Coral Gables, Florida, created a large board divided into two parts—"Forget Words to Avoid" and "Remember Words to Use." The words to avoid are written in black, whereas the words to use are all in fluorescent colors. In a Jeopardy-type game that the company occasionally holds, employees put Velcro-fastened words in the proper place.

COMMUNICATION CHALLENGE.   Consider adding a bulletin board in a visible place (like your lobby) and using it as an "advertisement" to your customers about what your organization believes.

COMMUNICATION OVERLOAD.

Source: © Kaset International.

POSTERS AND SIGNS

Most organizations already use posters and signs; however, many of them are pretty boring! You can enhance your use of these visuals by doing several things: Be creative in where you place signs and posters—the more unusual the place, the greater the impact on the viewer's thinking. Use as many bright colors as you can—make them noticeable. Make them three-dimensional if possible. Add borders, pictures, and illustrations to dull signs. Make them varying sizes, so they are not always the same. Change them often. For those you use frequently, check on the price of laminating. Many schools and universities have the technology to do laminating, and they are less expensive than commercial operations.

Notice the photographs of the posters on pages 116 and 117. These are flipcharts that my daughter Erin created for me to use in Kaset's programs. Very ordinary material, such as the list of the "It's O.K.'s," becomes extraordinary because she presented it in the shape of a rainbow and used bright colors. You will see a variety of ways to creatively and visually express ideas and quotations.

Every Customer Is A Unique Human Being

Source: © Kaset International.

The examples below illustrate how signs and posters creatively communicate what is important to the organizations they represent.

#222. Many organizations have created unique and colorful customer service posters, which they display prominently. Comerica Bank in Detroit, Michigan, uses two that have great impact: "If you think something is more important than a customer, then think again!" and "Quality is exceeding customer expectations of accuracy, timeliness, responsiveness, and professionalism in all that we do." The Bank of Montreal places reminder signs and posters about

Source: © Kaset International.

customer service all over the building—in the halls, the elevators, and even the restrooms!

#223. The Limited Credit Services in Columbus, Ohio, sponsors periodic poster contests organized around a theme or concept from the Kaset training, such as "the Four A's"—Acknowledge, Appreciate, Affirm and Assure, discussed in Chapter 6. Each department submits an entry, and the top four winners are displayed in a special place for a month. Many of these posters are *huge* three-dimensional, fantastic creations worked on by the entire department.

#224. Large black and yellow "YIELD" signs are hung from the ceiling over the phone reps' cubicles at the Limited Credit Services headquarters. The signs say, "QUIET ZONE: REPS LISTENING." Also around the perimeter of the ceiling are hung gigantic posters of the international symbol for "NO" with a fish hook in the center, indicating "No more getting 'hooked' by difficult customers."

#225. At Kaset's Florida headquarters, all the hallways are labeled with street signs to help visitors find their way around. The names are reminders of customer service: Dazzlement Drive, Ambassador Avenue, Friendly Freeway, Empowerment Lane, Extraordinary Way, and Reasoner Road. In the main entrance lobby there is a large area where everyone checks in and the phones are answered. It is the central meeting point for all. Whenever it is an employee's birthday, a large poster is created on the poster-making machine, hand colored, and hung where everyone can see it immediately upon entering the office. For example, it proclaims "Today is BARBARA GLANZ DAY." It is always special to see your name in print and to feel that others are celebrating you!

#226. At Aspen Valley Hospital, Aspen, Colorado, signs that read, "What have you taught your patient today?" were posted all over the facility.

#227. When SaskPower added "customer service" to its Mission Statement, it also wanted to make a copy available to each employee. In order to meet this objective in a timely and cost efficient manner, SaskPower printed the mission statement on a poster in the center of its monthly customer relations tabloid. The poster was easily unfolded and displayed.

#228. The Virginia Department of Motor Vehicles has gathered different sets of customer service posters that they display on all of the floors in their building. Every two weeks these motivational posters are rotated until they have completed a whole set.

#229.   Rita Blitt, a painter and sculptor from Kansas City, was asked by a friend of hers who was on the national board of Common Cause to create "something to send around the world to make the world a better place." Rita thought about this request for many months. A sudden flash of inspiration triggered these words in her mind—"Kindness is Contagious—Catch it!"—and she immediately added these words to a beautiful watercolor she had created in a special moment of joy. Sometime later Channel 5 sent letters to all the Kansas City schools asking the children to nominate the "kindest Kansas Citians." They were asked to write letters about why they had nominated that person, and a special banquet was held to celebrate the winners as well as the children who had nominated them. Rita was asked to present each of the children who wrote the winning letters with a print of her lovely watercolor. Instead of ordering a few prints to be made, however, Rita decided to order 2,500! She has made it a personal campaign to send them all over the world whenever and wherever she has heard of a kind person. They have been sent to nearly every state as well as 13 foreign countries.

#230.   Standard Insurance has a group of people who sponsored a "Poster Party" for frustrated volunteer artists. They created Quality concepts, quotations, and creative interpretations of models. They made 55 posters, with a plan to hang frames around the company and move the posters once a week. Over a year's time, each area of the company will have had each poster for a short period.

COMMUNICATION CHALLENGE.   First, become aware of dormant space around your workplace where posters could be effective. Second, you might purchase fun and motivational posters to use temporarily, but begin to plan to make some posters that illustrate your organization's beliefs and values. Perhaps someone could search out frustrated artists or use the poster party idea mentioned above. What it will add to the atmosphere of your workplace cannot be measured.

GIVEAWAYS

Giving reminders to your customers, both internal and external, is a good strategy for keeping your values and beliefs at a conscious level. Each time they see the reminder, it will reinforce what your organization stands for.

Internal Giveaways

#231.   Niagara Mohawk places clear stickers that say "Attitudes are contagious. Is yours worth catching?" on reps' telephones.

Other telephone companies give reps mirrors that say "You can hear a smile."

#232. Contel passes out purple fuzzy "weeples" with sticky feet to employees to put on their telephones or computers. One is wearing a hard hat, and the other is holding a telephone. They say "Thank a customer and make 2 people happy."

#233. Northwest Natural Gas Company, as a reminder to "FOCUS on Total Quality Customer Service," gives all field personnel a beautiful black Maglite flashlight with their motto "Customer Service with Personal Pride" near the head of the light and the employee's name in gold on the back. This tool keeps the motto in the forefront of their employees' attention each day, reminding them to go the extra step for their customers.

#234. The Georgia Division of Rehabilitation Services presented each attendee at their annual conference with a lovely brass bookmark that says, "We celebrate a belief that all people deserve the best we have to offer."

#235. The Department of Natural Resources in Minnesota has recently begun a campaign to "HIGHLIGHT Customer Service." The campaign has three objectives:

- To remind employees of the concepts they learned in the "Creating Satisfied Citizens and Customers" program.
- To stimulate discussion between supervisors and staff members about enhancing customer service within their work unit.
- To recognize the good work employees are doing in customer service throughout the DNR.

In a note to DNR Managers and Supervisors, Commissioner Rodney W. Sando said, "Customer service remains an important concept here at the DNR. You are receiving highlighter pens personally addressed to each member of your staff. The purpose of these highlighters is to create an opportunity for supervisors to reinforce the customer service concepts that are most vital to the successful operation of your work unit. The distribution of 3,500 highlighters creates the opportunity for 3,500 discussions in DNR this month about effective customer service." Special posters have also been designed for the campaign, showing pictures of citizens young and old with the caption "Customers are everyday people. They deserve your best, everyday. HIGHLIGHT Customer Service!"

#236. Centel Cellular in Chicago, Illinois, gives its employees "Keying in on Customers" calendars. This calendar was designed as a follow-up to the "Achieving Extraordinary Customer Relations" program. The calendar highlights one customer relations skill or group of skills each month until all the skills from the class have been reviewed. Persons who receive the calendars are encouraged to practice the "skill of the month" at least once a day in interactions with their internal and external customers and to keep the calendar posted in their cubicle where they can see it every day. As a part of the process, they also send out E-mail messages that review the skill(s) in detail and give suggestions on how the skill can best be used to provide extraordinary customer service.

External Giveaways

#237. My husband and I recently had dinner at a local restaurant. Although we had a lovely dinner and excellent service, what will make us return customers was the special touch at the end of the meal. When the waitress brought us our check, she also gave us two small complimentary glasses of dessert sherry because "they were glad we had chosen to dine with them!"

#238. Stouffer Concourse Hotels add a personal touch to their commitment to excellent service. They brought complimentary coffee and a newspaper to the room every morning, five minutes after a *personal* wake-up call. (After having wake-up call experiences with computers, recorded voices, and even dead silence after the ring, it was a pleasure to hear my name and speak to a real live person.) The coffee tray had the card shown on the following page with it. It presents the day's weather forecast in English, Spanish, Japanese, and even in pictures!

#239. The Savings Bank of Rockville, Connecticut, gives customers a foldover business card with the bank logo on the front. On the inside it says, "Who Says The Savings Bank of Rockville Doesn't Give Away Free Samples?" A dime is pasted to the card below!

#240. Chuck Harvey of American Speedy Printing Center in Grand Junction, Colorado, sends personalized note pads to all customers and prospects the day after his first contact with them. He finds this an effective tool to demonstrate his company's quality and turn-around ability as well as to show a personal concern for his customers.

#241. "Communications between an insurance company and its agents are usually weighted heavily on the Business side of the scale," said Liz Frenette of Vision Financial Corporation in Keene, New Hampshire. In an effort to also share good news and the Human level with its customers, the company purchased small

Source: © Stouffer Concourse Hotels.

jugs of New Hampshire Maple Syrup to mail in celebration of successes. Several little jugs were decorated with ribbons, and these were given as gifts during a Vision employee's recent visit to an agency in Tennessee.

#242. Rick Phillips, President of Phillips Sales and Staff Development in New Orleans, Louisiana, uses as his signature technique the giving of lovely parchment copies of his favorite poems to his customers with his company name, address, and logo at the bottom. He says, "Communications is our business, and we know that we must be in constant communication with our customers because we don't know when they will be making decisions about training or speaking. We like our clients to be constantly reminded of us and our message. We have found a way we can subtly stay in front of our clients all the time. . . . we hang around on their walls!" Rick goes on to say, "We began sending poems on walnut plaques to customers for Thanksgiving. People are accustomed to receiving gifts at Christmas, but we wanted our gift to stand out. We like our customers to know that THEY are what we have to be thankful for when we sit down to count our blessings at Thanksgiving. These plaques are now found, working for us, on the walls of hundreds of our clients." He also hands out copies of poems to his audiences whenever he speaks. "Over the years these poems have helped to carry our name and message to the four corners of the earth!"

#243. Daystar Productions of Lutz, Florida, a desktop publishing and promotion company, believes that "The Customer is the Star . . . in Daystar!" After an extended business relationship, Daystar sends out Star Lapel Pins to each customer with a special card that lets them know they are the star and their business is very much appreciated!

#244. AT&T decided to explore new ways to reach its customers. They started their research by asking a rather traditional question: "What can you do with a phone?" After a series of conventional answers, the group became inspired and began to think of things you *cannot* do with a phone, such as eat it, drink it, smoke it. This process led AT&T to send chocolate telephones to all preferred customers to stimulate business. The gift became a creative reminder of AT&T.[7]

#245. David A. DeFore, First Vice President of CB Commercial Real Estate Group in Sherman Oaks, California, sent a gift to both customers and prospects that was called a "crittle"—a movable magnetic metal sculpture designed to be a stress reducer. One of his purposes was to stimulate creativity and to create a more "human" level relationship with his customers and prospects. In fact, he was later told by the office manager of a law firm, one of the prospects to whom he sent a "crittle," that the only reason he saw David was because of the unique gift—he usually turns all brokers away!

#246. We have created a special calendar as a giveaway for our "Connections" workshops which were developed to help our customer facilitators "keep the skills alive." These calendars have a customer service slogan and cartoons for each month of the year. Each month begins with "BE KIND TO YOUR CUSTOMERS in . . . ":

- January! APPRECIATE what they've been through.
- February! GREET them with friendliness and warmth.
- March! ASSURE them that their needs will be met.
- April! EMPATHIZE with their concerns.
- May! AFFIRM that you know they are special.
- June! LISTEN to them and show that you care.
- July! Stay cool and SMILE often.
- August! HELP them through the "dog days" of summer.

- September! Create POSITIVE MEMORABLE CUSTOMER EXPERI-ENCES.
- October! Turn problems into OPPORTUNITIES for excellent service.
- November! THANK them for using your services.
- December! Give them EXTRAORDINARY SERVICE.

#247. The Metro Wellness Program, which provides well-ness services to 3,000 employees of the local school districts in Cedar Rapids, Iowa, delivered fresh fruit to *all* district buildings and de-partments in May. This gift of fruit was sent with the suggestion that a nutritious piece of fruit might get employees thinking about the things they could do to stay healthy. Thousands of pieces of fruit were delivered by Wellness staff. The fruit deliveries generated a very positive response from the school district staff members, who noted that they usually receive high-fat goodies from well-meaning parents and students. The fresh fruit was a nice change and was the Wellness Program's way of saying thank you to the employees for their health and fitness efforts.

Another "extra" they offered their customers was advertised on a brightly colored flyer: "RELAXATION BREAK: Take some time for YOU! A soothing, relaxing NECK & SHOULDER MASSAGE is a great way to relieve the stress of a busy day. Licensed massage therapist will be available to do free 10-minute neck and shoulder massages for ESC/Annex staff in the Wellness Office."

#248. Greenville Utilities Commission in Greenville, North Carolina, has an interesting and very useful giveaway. It is a plastic card with raised dots on it that tell the exact temperature according to the color they turn. It has adhesive strips on the back so it can be mounted on a wall. The card has Greenville's slogan, "See us first . . . for all your energy needs," as well as the company logo and can be used to confirm that your thermostat is accurate.

COMMUNICATION CHALLENGE. These giveaways be-come creative reminders of your organization and what is impor-tant to it. Why not have a brainstorming session for creative ideas of things that your organization could distribute to communicate its beliefs and values—perhaps one team for internal and another for external giveaways? Then work it into next year's budget.

SOCIAL EVENTS AND CELEBRATIONS

Celebrating provides a way to nourish the spirit of an organization.
                        Jim Clemmer, *Firing on All Cylinders*

If an organization values its employees as its most important re-source, it will encourage these employees to get to know one another as people, across divisions, positions, and functional work units. However, it takes creativity and a commitment to the employees for this to happen. It takes time and sometimes even money to sponsor these events, yet the team spirit and deeper understanding that result are not measurable in dollars and cents! Also significant are *customer* celebrations. Thanking customers in a fun and creative way will again reap countless rewards as well as communicate a commitment to them as the organization's only reason for existence. As I suggested earlier, many people today are writing about the importance of "fun" in the workplace. Employees are happier working in an environment where fun is acceptable, and customers like doing business with happy people!

Internal Events

#249.　At Kaset we observed National Employee Health and Fitness Day by hosting a healthy brown bag breakfast, a lunchtime 1.2 mile walk, and a tour of the Hidden River fitness center for all of our employees. Early that morning, smiling faces greeted those emerging from the elevators and offered them a free, nutritious, healthy breakfast of bananas, muffins, and juice, stuffed by a team of brown bag stuffing experts the day before. The bag had a specially designed sticker and a handout inside. Posters reminded everyone to burn extra calories on the stairs rather than use the elevators. The committee has decided to offer future events emphasizing the importance of health and fitness all year.

#250.　Every Thanksgiving week the Customer Service Center of Iowa Electric Light and Power has a huge Thanksgiving celebration, thanks to the special efforts of Christine Weaver, a Customer Service Consultant. She cooks all night to create the turkey, stuffing, potatoes, and gravy for 125 employees. Other employee volunteers bring desserts and pies, and the entire center eats heartily!

#251.　The Information Systems Services Department of Nationwide Insurance held a Teamwork Day '92 that was an unprecedented success. Held at the Ohio State Fairgrounds, the event brought ISS employees and their families together for four hours of nonstop quality-related games, fun, and entertainment. They had food, door prizes, entertainment by a jazz ensemble, Teamwork Day presentations, and a talk on the importance of teamwork. All employees signed the Quality Commitment Board that later was presented to Bob Saik, Vice President, ISS. They pinned the tail on the Q and got their faces painted. ISS remembered the kids, too, with exhibits, games, magic shows, clowns, and hands-on computer fun based on the theme of quality. There was even a babysitting concession for tired Moms and Dads! What a special way to recognize and reinforce Teamwork, both in the ISS Department (Business level) as well as in the family (Human level).

#252. Centura Bank of Rocky Mount, North Carolina, has sent a memo from its Service/Quality Team to all Regional Executives and Division Heads saying, "It's time to thank all of our employees for their hard work as well as celebrate the first year of our Service/Quality Initiative." They recommend that each region and division form an action team and charge them with coming up with a plan for their party. The general administrative budget is providing funding (the formula is number of employees × 2 × $15). The only other guidelines are:

1. Let your action team make the decisions.
2. Use the party to thank employees and build awareness about our S/Q initiative.
3. Make it FUN!

They also say that if invited, at least one member of the Executive Group will make every effort to attend.

#253. The Guest Quarters Suites Hotel in Columbus, Ohio, recently had a celebration they called "We Are Family." Each employee wore a black ribbon on his or her name tag with the words in gold, "We are family!" Not only did this celebration promote teamwork and a feeling of "family" within the hotel, but the company gave employees cameras to take pictures of their "real" families to share with others in the organization as well. Judy Myers told me that there has been no turnover in the management staff for $2\frac{1}{2}$ to 3 years. She said, "We really ARE a family!"

#254. We have many "spontaneous" social events at Kaset's Tampa office. Every few weeks, bells and sirens will go off, and an announcement is made over the intercom that everyone should meet downstairs in the atrium for a TGIF party. Another time the senior managers came around with a cart containing coffee, tea, and dozens and dozens of doughnut holes. They "served" each of us at our desks! One day, close to Valentine's Day, each of the senior managers "toured" the office in the middle of the day (wearing heart boxer shorts) and gave everyone a treat. Another day we heard an ice cream truck bell ringing. Lo and behold, it was the senior managers, dressed in white aprons, pushing a cart filled with ice cream treats for all! These events promote teamwork, are inexpensive, and create an atmosphere of celebration and spontaneity in the organization.

#255. Ben and Jerry of ice cream fame believe that *joy* is an important ingredient in their recipe for business. With growth and success, the spontaneity and camaraderie of the early days seemed to be missing, and the "fun" became more like work! As a result, they held a "Joy" meeting to get the company back on track. They first worked on "joyifying" the managers. According to Peter Lind, Ben and Jerry's research and development director, joy is "playful and responsive. It breaks patterns and makes people laugh." The company gives Joy Grants of $500 to work groups for long-term improvements in their work areas, and the Joy Gang plans events such as Elvis Day. They also have Tacky Dress-Up day, and earlier, during the busiest time of the summer, the company hired masseuses to ease the tension. Everyone was entitled to a half-hour massage. The best perk of all, though, is free ice cream. The company favorite is Gummy-Worm! The emphasis on joy in the workplace, they believe, directly impacts the productivity of the organization—the happier people are at work, the more productive they will be.[8]

#256.   I recently flew home next to a young man from the Chicago area. As we spoke about my book, he shared with me a delightful idea. He is from a very large family, and every other summer they hold a family reunion. Because this summer's reunion included 260 members of the family, the planners decided to have each branch of the family come in color-coded shirts with a logo or slogan. His Uncle John's branch had green shirts that said "JOHN'S GENES" with a family tree below. Uncle John, however, had a special shirt that said only, "I'M JOHN!" Another group was called "ELOY'S JOYS," and another was "CONERTY'S CLAN." He said what was really fun was that all the teams for games sort of evolved by color— "natural sides and family pride!" I thought this idea could be easily adapted for companies and organizations as well—most of us are not lucky enough to have such a large family!

External Events

#257.   Commercebank celebrated the completion of a corporate-wide training effort with a gala "Striving to Dazzle" day in every department and branch. Employees wore special dazzle buttons. Work areas and lobbies were decorated with balloons. Customers and employees enjoyed coffee, soft drinks, cake, and pastries, served with special "dazzle your customers" napkins. When customers asked about the celebration, employees told them about the training and said, "We're ready to dazzle you now." They also began to give service rating cards to customers in the branches.[9]

#258.   The City of Scottsdale, Arizona, celebrates October as "Simply Better Service Month." Held in conjunction with the National Consumer Information Month, this campaign seeks to reaffirm their commitment to providing quality service to Scottsdale citizens, create public awareness of Scottsdale's "Simply Better

Service" philosophy, gain inspiration and knowledge that will take their customer service skills to the next level of excellence, and have fun in the process. Some of the activities included are employees working side-by-side with Scottsdale's city manager, assistant city managers, general managers, and directors; brown bag seminars planned by Human Resources; fun activities such as "Simply Better Service Trivia," and a special "Kaizen Treasure Hunt." Employees can earn prizes for participating in these games and for being "caught in the act" of providing quality customer service. Some of the special events include Public Safety Day, Resident Orientation Day, an All Employee Forum, and a wrap-up featuring the "Not Ready for Private Sector Players."

#259. A Meeting Planner for a Medical Society suggests having a T-shirt exchange at the beginning of a conference to promote personal sharing. All attendees are asked to bring a new T-shirt from the area where they live. The shirts are put into individual bags and distributed during registration. This serves as a fun ice breaker when everyone tries to figure out who brought the T-shirt he or she received. It also allows each person to share something special about his or her home town. Later in the conference, a circle dance is held and people have an opportunity to exchange T-shirts as well as stories. This introductory exercise provides a networking opportunity that allows participants to enjoy one another on both the Human and the Business levels.

#260. The Service Quality Team of Centura Bank in Rocky Mount, North Carolina, recently sent employees the following memo regarding Casual Days:

> Our Casual Day was a big success based on all the comments we've heard from internal and external customers. We also understand that many of you have been having casual days in your department or branch from time to time with equal success. The purpose of this brief memo is to encourage occasional Casual Days and to declare 3 days each year as official **Centura Bank Casual Days.** Those days will be tournament Friday, the last work day before the 4th of July, and the Friday after Thanksgiving. We hope these Casual Days will be fun for you and that our customers will perceive Centura to be a more inviting, service oriented and enjoyable place to work.

COMMUNICATION CHALLENGE. What kind of social events do you sponsor for your employees? For your customers? Now, be creative in your thinking: even if your funds are limited, what can you do *next month* to celebrate your employees, and in *six months* to celebrate your customers? A caramel apple, a smiley face cookie, or an ice cream treat for each employee, renting a popcorn machine for an afternoon, or having a costume contest are not exorbitant in cost.

ADDED SERVICES

Some organizations have added new services to their customers on the Human level. These communicate their commitment to the belief that customers are unique human beings, especially children! Added services can dazzle your customers, both internal and external. One caution, however—added services soon become expectations, and their absence can cause a negative experience for your customers. For these to be most effective, your organization must periodically add new ones.

#261. To better serve children who travel, United Airlines has begun offering them McDonald's "Happy Meals" on flights. There is no additional charge; they simply have to be ordered ahead, and both children and parents are delighted!

#262. Besides providing childcare in the lobby for parents conducting bank business, Gary Wheaton/First Chicago Bank has a Junior Banker's Club for children 12 and under. "Breezie" the clown is president of the club and a goodwill ambassador to the community. He and his numerous counterparts (there are several "Breezies") perform in all the local parades and celebrations as well as appearing in the lobbies of all Gary Wheaton branches every other Saturday. They entertain the children with magic tricks and balloon animals while their parents bank. Another important part of the club is that for every $5 saved, the child gets a "Breezie" prize, such as a coloring book or a puzzle, to encourage saving at an early age.

#263. The Harlan National Bank in Harlan, Iowa, does an extra service for its customers. They have a printed folder that says, "You're in the news" on the outside, and on the inside, "And I thought you might like to have an extra copy." They then place clippings they have cut out from the local paper featuring the customer or his or her family and mail them to the customer's home.

#264. Charlie Roe tells of the added services he received at Herwaldt Oldsmobile/GMC in Fresno, California:

> I recently had my car tuned-up and had a really ENJOYABLE experience. First of all, the dealership had an older gentleman who was out in front of the service department at the crack of dawn with a coffee pot and cups for everyone who was lining up for service (first come, first serve). He was really good at providing alternatives for those who were unable to wait for the service doors to open at 7:30 A.M. He kept checking back to make sure everyone had coffee and even went the extra mile to get tea for my wife! The dealership, as an added service, provided a shuttle service to get customers back and forth to their offices or homes. I was really pushed for time that

afternoon and let the service department know that I had to have the car back by 4 P.M. It was about 3:45 and my phone rang—it was the shuttle driver "Poppa Bear" (they have a cellular phone so he can contact customers and make special arrangements). He said, "I know you need to get back to pick up your car in 15 minutes." I acknowledged that and asked how soon he would be there to pick me up. He responded "If you look out your window, I'm just pulling into your driveway." Now THAT'S EXCEPTIONAL SERVICE!

#265. If the success of the Automated Teller Machines (ATMs) is any indication, United Airline's "Tickets Plus" machines should prove very popular with customers. Their new machines will allow United's customers to take ticketing into their own hands. Beginning October 1, 1992, United will conduct a six-month test of nine self-service ticketing machines in Los Angeles and San Francisco. All of the machines will allow customers to create and ticket new reservations, ticket existing reservations, select seat assignments, and print boarding passes. "We recognize the need to simplify the ticketing process, especially for frequent fliers who enjoy the ability to select flights and ticket themselves in a fast, easy, convenient manner," says Susan Hinderaker, senior staff analyst, market research and development. "With people so familiar with ATMs now, we think customers will be very receptive to Tickets Plus."

#266. Suburban Hospital in Hinsdale, Illinois, has a Senior Citizen "Breakfast Club" that meets once a month at the hospital. Each month features an educational lecture presented at 7:30 and again at 9:00 as well as a brunch. Topics such as "Your Yearly Physical," "Taking Care of Your Heart," and "Eating Your Way to a Healthier Life Style" are included.

#267. When you are hospitalized or having surgery at Suburban Hospital and you don't have anyone to watch your children, they will reimburse you for their care at the day-care center of your choice upon presentation of a receipt for such child care. Reimbursement for child care is limited to three children for up to $60 per day per child and is limited to eight hours per day per child for each day you are hospitalized or having surgery. All you have to do is contact the Admitting Department for approval before your surgery or hospital stay.

COMMUNICATION CHALLENGE. Do you have customers who are children? Who have children? What extra service might you offer both to begin creating loyalty for "future" customers and to dazzle existing customers by offering something special for their children?

BUSINESS LEVEL ENHANCEMENTS

Some enhancements fulfill customers' Business needs as well as their Human needs. Although these special services "appear" to be Business or technical enhancements, don't they really still appeal to our Human needs for convenience and attention?

TOLL-FREE NUMBERS AND EXTENDED HOURS

#268. Buckner Corporation has a 24-hour toll-free hotline, staffed by an answering service specially trained to handle customer questions. They are also provided with a rotating list of employees to handle any customer emergencies.

#269. Gary Wheaton/First Chicago Bank prides itself on having "community focused" business hours. Their lobby facilities are now open from 8:30 A.M. to 9:00 P.M. Monday through Friday, 8:30 A.M. to 5:00 P.M. on Saturday, and from 10:00 A.M. to 4:00 P.M. on Sunday. The drive-ups are open from 6:45 A.M. to 9:00 P.M. Monday through Saturday and from 10:00 A.M. to 4:00 P.M. on Sunday. When Gary Wheaton was purchased by First Chicago Bank, located in the city of Chicago, the huge city bank learned a great deal about retail from this smaller, community-oriented bank. First Chicago now has extended hours as well—100 Chicago-area branches recently increased average hours of operation from 36 per week to 80 hours per week!

#270. Says Alvin T. Booker, publisher of *Service Dealers Newsletter,* "The shops that are doing well are those that offer flexible hours." Joe Thomas, service director of R-K Chevrolet-Peugeot in Virginia Beach, Virginia, says he first opened his service and parts departments on Saturday mornings in May 1989, and a year after that experiment extended his weekday service hours to midnight. He made the change based on a customer survey that revealed the main reason customers chose alternatives to dealerships was for convenience, with price a close second. He says the increased business has more than made up for the expense of the labor. In the first 4 months of the experiment, 80% of revenues came from first-time customers. He also created a separate and permanent 5 P.M. to midnight work shift. His promise to customers: if they bring in a repair on the night shift and it can't be finished by the end of the shift, it won't be completed by a technician on the next day shift. The work will be completed the next night by the same technician.[10]

#271. Borders Book Shop in Oak Brook, Illinois, has recently extended its hours to accommodate customers: Monday–Thursday 9 A.M.–9 P.M.; Friday–Saturday 9 A.M.–10 P.M.; and Sunday 10 A.M.–8 P.M. The book shop also offers speakers, programs on current issues, holiday celebrations, and children's story hours. All of these are highlighted in its newsletter "Cover to Cover."

#272. Vancouver, Washington-based Clark Public Utilities Electric Center customer service office is now open on Saturdays. The office is open on Saturdays from 9 A.M. to 5 P.M. for changes in service, dealing with credit matters, and for accepting payments. "To our knowledge, we are the first utility in the Northwest to offer Saturday office hours," said Utility Commission President Jane Van Dyke. "We are trying to make it as easy as possible for customers to do business with Clark Public Utilities." Because this is new for the utility and the customers, they place a sandwich board outside on Saturdays that says, "OPEN for Customer Service" with the Clark logo below.

#273. Pediatric dentist Dr. Jeff Alexander believes that the physical environment is an important part of communicating an organization's vision. Therefore, because his customers are children, he says he got down on his knees and asked himself the question, "What do children see in my office?" He noticed that all the pictures were far too high for children to see, so he moved them down. He also added a bulletin board at their level that has pictures of all the dentists as children themselves. He and his associates then created a "yellow brick road" so that they could easily let the children know where to go. The bright colors are aligned with the vision that this should be a happy place. There are different "theme" rooms for exams, X-rays, and dental work, such as a "jungle room" and an "undersea world." Instead of having to look at lights and the ceiling tiles while they are in the dentist's chair, the children see stuffed animals hanging from the ceiling. Also, all the dental chairs are in the same room so that children won't feel afraid and isolated. Dr. Jeff has used the Business level of the physical environment to share his vision of "learning about healing in a fun and happy place!"

COMMUNICATION CHALLENGE.   Are there extra services you can add that might benefit your customers, like extended hours or a toll-free number? In many cases the costs involved are quickly absorbed by the added business of loyal customers.

ACTION PAGE

Chapter Eight

Measurements
Creative Ways to Gather Information to Make Your Organization's Commitment Actionable and Effective

Source: © Kaset International.

M easurement can be thought of as a communication tool to show both employees and customers what is important to you as an organization—for employees, through feedback of what customers say; for customers, by the questions you ask. What you measure (or do not measure) is one of the primary indicators of what your organization values. If it is *truly* important to your organization to provide extraordinary customer service, for example, then you will measure things like how well you are meeting your customers' needs. If, on the other hand, you are only committed to the bottom line, then all your measurements will probably support that value.

Sometimes there are conflicting values expressed in an organization. If you say you value good customer service, yet you measure only such things as the *number* of phone calls handled in a time period rather than the *satisfaction* of the customer, you are sending a conflicting message to your employees. First, be very clear on what your values are, and then make sure that what you measure supports those values and beliefs. Finally, communicate the results of the measurements you take in creative, actionable ways to all employees. I believe that many organizations fall into the trap of doing measurement for measurement's sake. Always keep the big picture in mind—make sure you measure what you really value and then use those results in actionable ways to get better at what you value.

Chip Bell and Ron Zemke list "10 Ways to Get Information for Improving Your Delivery System":

1. Customer Surveys
2. Focus Groups
3. Employee Visit Teams
4. Customer Visit Teams
5. Customer Advisory Panels
6. User Groups
7. Employee Surveys
8. Mystery Shopping
9. Toll-free Hotlines
10. Benchmarking[1]

Although these are presented as ways to get internal and external customer feedback in order to improve a service delivery system, most of them are techniques that can be used to measure how actionable the organization's commitment is to other beliefs and values as well. Remember Tom Peter's statement, "What gets measured is what gets done!"

CUSTOMER SURVEYS

Customer surveys are one of the most commonly used measurement tools. Just the exercise of administering a survey that is focused on how well you are communicating your commitment through your actions as an organization sends a positive message to both employees and customers. However, many organizations use customer surveys and then do nothing with the results. This becomes a source of frustration and cynicism for employees and customers alike. If you are going to use surveys, design them so that you will have some actionable data, communicate the results, and *take action!*

Here are some key points to consider when using surveys:

- General questions yield "nice to know" information. Specific, action-able questions help set service standards and create momentum for change.

- Send out a few short, specific surveys measuring one aspect of service performance rather than one shotgun approach that tries to do it all.

- Tie survey data to market damage probabilities like customers lost or gained, percent who will recommend your product or service to others, and feature that data prominently—and plainly—in executive reports.

- Give satisfaction surveys new importance by tying them in to employee incentives.[2]

Dear Customer:

At SouthTrust, we consider the customer our most valuable asset. That's why we hope you'll take a moment to tell us **what's on your mind.**

We'd like your opinion of SouthTrust. We hope that you are pleased with our service. But if you're not, we'd like to know why, so that we may improve. Our goal is to provide top quality service to our customers at all times.

So please help us evaluate our performance by completing the attached questionnaire. You may leave the form with us or you may drop it in the mail at your convenience. No postage is necessary.

Thank you for your time and comments. Your input **will** make a difference!!

Sincerely,

Robert L. Henderson
Senior Vice President

SouthTrust Bank

MEMBER FDIC

(Optional)
Name: _____
Address: _____
Today's Date _____ Time of Day in Branch _____
Branch Location _____

		YES	NO
1.	Did we greet and help you in a friendly manner?	☐	☐
2.	Did we efficiently handle your transaction?	☐	☐
3.	Did we thank you for your business?	☐	☐
4.	Was our office clean and neat?	☐	☐
5.	Would you refer SouthTrust to your friends, relatives and/or associates?	☐	☐
6.	How long did we wait for service? _____ (minutes)		
7.	Do we have knowledgeable, well-trained employees?	☐	☐
8.	Do we promptly answer questions regarding account information or problems?	☐	☐
9.	Did we greet you by name?	☐	☐
10.	Do our services fit your needs?	☐	☐

11. What is your final grade on overall service?
(A is superior,   A B C D E F
F is inferior)   ☐ ☐ ☐ ☐ ☐ ☐

COMMENTS: _____
_____
_____
_____
_____

Source: SouthTrust Corporation.

#274. One way SouthTrust Corporation obtains customer feedback is through "What's on Your Mind?" survey cards displayed in branch lobbies. To focus on customer retention, they also conduct a quarterly survey of customers who closed a checking account to determine the reasons. By coordinating this information with account balances, they can project the bottom line cost of accounts closed due to poor service as well as learn from the experiences of unhappy customers.

#275. Daystar Productions in Lutz, Florida, measures customer satisfaction by sending a "Tell Us!" Gram to inquire about the level of satisfaction the customer experienced with his last design project. This enables Daystar to pinpoint opportunities for improvement. In appreciation for filling out Daystar's "Tell Us!" Gram, the customer receives a Certificate of Savings for a future job.

#276. Virginia Power recently conducted a Net Impression Survey, a specialized assessment created by a consulting group. The survey covered residential, assigned business (the company's largest customers that have an individual marketing representative), and unassigned business customers. The residential survey began with five customer focus groups, one in each division, from which the items of most concern were gathered. A seven-page survey was then mailed to 3,000 customers, 600 in each division. The Net Impression Surveys were designed to help the company identify areas where improvements in customer service would have the greatest impact on the customers' feelings toward the company. The survey also provided a snapshot of the customers' current impression of service and attitude toward the utility.

Virginia Power also does a quality of service survey once a month through telephone interviews with 10 customers in each district who have had reason to contact the company in the previous 30 days to gather current information about their customer service.

#277. Clark Public Utilities in Vancouver, Washington, uses two types of survey tools to poll the utility's customers throughout the year: The CUSTOMER SATISFACTION MONITOR surveys 200 customers every two months regarding a specific service they have received. Some of the areas covered are:

- Experienced inconvenience in reaching representative (1986—6%; 1992—1%)
- Satisfied request/problem received proper attention (1986—94%; 1992—99%)
- Satisfied with call/visit (1986—94%; 1992—99%)
- Contact handled professionally (1986—96%; 1992—100%)
- Representative courteous (1986—96%; 1992—100%)

- Reported something outstanding about representative (1986—34%; 1992—27%)
- Expressed dissatisfaction with service/policies (1986—5%; 1992—0%)

Conducted since 1986, the bi-monthly survey polls customers who have had contact with the Customer Services Department by telephone or in person. Market Trends receives computer printouts of these customer contacts, then randomly selects a few and calls them. The average interview takes about five minutes. "The monitor gives immediate feedback on specific customer transactions," says Public Relations Manager Rick Shutt. The information goes directly to the employee involved in the transaction. "It is a helpful tool for people in Customer Services to gauge their performance."

Customer Satisfaction Monitor

	1986	1987	1988	1989	1990	1991	1992
YEARLY TOTAL	1001	802	1200	1200	1200	1200	800
% Experiencing Inconvenience Reaching Representative	6%	4%	5%	4%	3%	3%	1%
Representative Being Courteous	96%	97%	98%	98%	98%	99%	100%
Contact Handled Professionally	96%	98%	98%	99%	99%	100%	100%
% Satisfied Request/Problem Received Proper Attention	94%	95%	96%	98%	97%	99%	99%
% Reporting Something "Outstanding" About the Representative	34%	31%	34%	38%	48%	53%	27%
% Satisfied with Call or Visit	94%	95%	96%	98%	98%	97%	99%
% Expressing Dissatisfaction with PUD Service/Policies	5%	5%	4%	1%	2%	0%	0%

Source: Clark Public Utilities.

The PUBLIC OPINION SURVEY is conducted three times a year. It polls 400 customers each time to determine their attitudes toward the utility and their perspectives on key services. Conducted since 1982, the survey sample is drawn from all utility customers. The research firm contacts them by random-digit dialing with a representative sample of 50 percent male and 50 percent female customers. Rick Shutt has worked closely with Market Trends to develop a questionnaire that pinpoints customers' attitudes on a variety of topics, as well as their service needs. Each interview takes 10–15 minutes. Some of the results are:

- Positive assessment of job the utility is doing (1985—94%; 1991—97%).
- Key phrases to describe the utility:
  - Friendly (1985—85%; 1991—96%)
  - Efficient (1985—83%; 1991—92%)
  - Believable (1985—63%; 1991—87%)
  - Hard working (1985—73%; 1991—87%)
  - Professional (1985—78%; 1991—95%)
  - Responsive to customer needs (1985—54%; 1991—70%)

Data is electronically compiled and has a confidence level of 95 percent. Shutt says that the opinion survey is very valuable in measuring Clark Public Utilities' performance—both strengths and weaknesses. "This research is also very helpful in identifying customer needs so we can respond with enhancements to our services," Shutt says. They share all the results with their employees in "Spectrum," their monthly customer service newsletter.

#278.   Another organization that believes in communicating the results of company measurements to its employees is AMP Inc. John Kegel, vice president of corporate logistics, says numbers such as the call abandonment rate, time customers wait on hold, and error rates are communicated to employees *daily*. "Even if you're satisfied with results," he says, "you have to continue to measure. Problems are less likely to get out of hand if you constantly analyze data." This data is used to drive process and systems improvements as well as employee training.[3]

#279.   The *Minneapolis Star Tribune* writes about the importance of customer feedback to the bus service in Maple Grove, Minnesota. In Maple Grove, when the new bus service began, routes and schedules were determined from a citywide survey asking what time people wanted to get picked up and where they wanted to board the bus. If riders regularly say that a route time is inconvenient, the city does a further survey to determine if the schedule should be changed. Most importantly, the riders themselves run the system—seven of them make up the city's transit commission. Because they ride the bus each day, they know how the system is working. To encourage riders on Christmas Eve, when most people take their cars so they can leave early, Maple Grove took a rider survey to find out what time to schedule an early bus home. They also gave riders pen-sized flashlights so that the drivers could see them on dark corners when they were waiting before dawn or after dark. Jim Koniar, the chairman of the Maple Grove Transit Commission and a regular rider, says, "Ridership is running almost 85% occupancy, which is almost unheard of in public transit." Listening to their customers and then taking action has paid off.[4]

#280. Deck House, an Acton, Massachusetts, based company that designs and manufactures post-and-beam houses, uses phone surveys to gather information from customers. Their success, however,

> hinges in part on the way that information is reported BACK to customers. Eric Stacey, assistant sales manager, tracks and inputs into a database some of the calls coming in to Deck's 800 "owner assistance hotline." After addressing the caller's concern, Stacey asks a few research-related questions, and then works hard to funnel that information back to Deck House customers. Stacey sends all customers a quarterly newsletter that reports back on what he's been hearing over the telephone. When more pressing problems are widely reported on the hotline, Deck House issues a technical bulletin informing customers of the potential problem and details solutions or preventive action. The line gets about 200 calls a month, according to Stacey.[5]

#281. Provident Bank of Maryland uses a customer survey with prepaid postage that is given to each customer after they do business with the bank. The questionnaire asks about things like wait time, how the branch looked, and how they were treated by the bank. These surveys are compiled and sent to the individual branches for action. Each branch then keeps a response log as they respond back to each customer. The branch results are communicated to the branch managers, highlighting both strengths and areas to improve. The results are then communicated to branch employees through individual branch meetings and to the whole company in "Team," the employee newsletter.

#282. The Defense Information Systems Agency (DISA) has incorporated a long-range strategic plan to bring customer focus into a government agency. Their challenge is to focus on both core service and customer service and to have more cross-agency participation. DISA's first step, according to Brigadier General Dennis C. Beasley, USAF, was benchmarking. Looking at AT&T, Federal Express, Marriott, and others, the Agency explored ways to measure service attributes. They discovered the value of periodically surveying customers to determine what's working and not working and then getting help from experts in the customer service field. For each key area, DISA established "shadow" organizations, headed by a senior leader with members from across the Agency. Their goal was to close the gap between where DISA is today and where their customers want them to be, placing as much value on internal customers as on external customers.[6]

#283. Dr. Jeff Alexander, the children's dentist in Oakland, California, uses a "Rapport Sheet" to measure his customers' satisfaction. His organization, The Youthful Tooth, gives these to both the patients and their families. They ask questions about how the office looked to them, how they were greeted, how they were talked to, etc. The scores are from 1 (poor) to 3 (excellent). The office staff has an agreement that if they average good or below at the end of a month, that month's bonus for the office is given to charity. This practice makes customer satisfaction really matter!

#284. When Hal Rosenbluth wanted feedback from clients and associates, he took the advice on the back of a 64-pack of Crayola crayons: "Crayons help people express thoughts they can't always put into words." He sent 100 of his clients construction paper and a box of crayons and asked them to illustrate what Rosenbluth Travel meant to them. He created a tradition that has never ceased to produce new insights into the business.[7]

COMMUNICATION CHALLENGE. If you are using surveys, are they designed to give you actionable information? Are you taking that action and letting your employees know what you are doing?

CUSTOMER FOLLOW-UP CALLS

These should be short telephone calls to customers as immediately after their encounter with the organization as possible. They are particularly valuable as a measurement tool because they are simple, short, and nearly always provide a Positive Memorable Customer Experience. If the customer was dazzled, they appreciate the chance to tell about their experience. If the customer was just satisfied, they are usually dazzled or at least pleased to receive the call and to know that the organization really cares what its customers think. And if the customer had a bad experience, the empowered caller has a chance to apologize and recover with that customer by fixing the problem and to create, in the end, a loyal client.

#285. Kaset has a Customer Feedback Team that calls customers, gathers evaluation sheets, tabulates surveys, and conducts focus groups and interviews. The members record customer comments in specially designed data bases, print reports, analyze the results, and recommend specific actions. The team, which reports directly to our president, finds the Service Quality Call particularly valuable in gathering information. Our Service Quality Call is a friendly two-minute transaction-based call to learn customers' perceptions of their experience with us. Input from Service Quality Calls provides valuable feedback about our people, processes, and products, and helps them improve the way they serve customers. The team is responsible for finding out what customers think about our service and products and translating those perceptions into continuous improvement actions. Because the calls are transaction based, specific actionable information is obtained. Some of the benefits team members have discovered are:

- An opportunity to be responsive at the individual level— initiating recovery or action alerts.
- A tool for personal development and growth at the individual service provider level.
- Specific data for making customer-driven product/service improvements on the aggregate level.
- A reality check for strategic planning.
- Direction for internal process improvements.

These Service Quality Calls are made at the request of one of the service providers, they are conducted as soon as possible after the customer interaction, and the results go directly to the service provider.[8]

#286. Hydro-Electric, Perth, Scotland, has made "Quality of Service Calls" a permanent feature of its customer satisfaction measurement system. This process was developed as an integral part of the Customer Focus program and involves calling samples of customers who interact with many different parts of the company within 48 hours of that interaction. For example, customers who buy a major appliance receive a "Quality of Service Call" within 48 hours of making the purchase and are asked about the standard of service. Around 15,000 telephone calls to the company's customers across the North of Scotland are aimed for in total annually, split across fifteen different types of customer transactions. The organization has dedicated three full-time staff members to the endeavor.

#287. At SaskPower in Regina, Saskatchewan, Canada, customers are randomly contacted 24 hours after they complete a specific transaction. Customers are asked to rate their service experience with the customer service representative. Customers are called back within 24 hours of the original contact by senior management when either a concern or problem has occurred or been expressed. This quick response, according to Wayne M. Bosch, Director of Quality Improvement, is achieved by the use of a comprehensive computer database.

#288. One of the individual goals of the "Goal Rush" incentive program of Clark Public Utilities in Vancouver, Washington, is "To have all employees make follow-up contact with at least six customers regarding their recent service from the utility." These calls have several purposes: to get everyone actively involved in the organization's customer service goal, to provide a nice extra touch of service for the customers, and to get some feedback about what their customers are looking for and how the individual employee's job helps deliver it to them even if they don't work directly with external customers. The data is collected on a form that is turned in every three months for analysis, resulting in recommendations for systems improvements, better communication, and additional training.

Customer Follow-up Record

Date _____ Account Number _____

Customer Name _____

Customer Address _____

Service or Situation _____

Customer Comments _____
_____
_____
_____

☐ Customer Satisfied   ☐ Additional action needed

Description of additional action needed _____
_____
_____

Action Taken _____
_____

Date of Action _____

Employee Signature _____   *I can help*

Source: Clark Public Utilities.

#289. Diane Winchell of PTI Communications in Tomah, Wisconsin, reported:

We have a customer contact program that allows the customers to speak up and be heard. The managers are involved in this based on a list of names that each one is given from an activity report. A series of questions are asked, and the results are compiled and shared with all employees. (The results are used to improve the organization's service delivery.) It's great to not only have the managers involved, but to hear the compliments as well as have the opportunity to make ourselves even better. We welcome complaints as another chance to deliver extraordinary service.

COMMUNICATION CHALLENGE. If you are not currently using service quality calls, decide if this measurement tool might be useful to gather immediate, actionable information from your customers, both internal and external, about specific transactions they have had with your organization. If so, then get some help, either an outside measurement consultant or an internal task force, and design a series of questions that will provide whatever information your organization needs from customers to better communicate its commitment.

QUALITY AND SERVICE STANDARDS, PERFORMANCE REVIEWS, AND BONUSES

If an organization wants to communicate to its employees what is most important to the organization, it will set specific service standards and measure employee actions according to its commitment. And the most significant way to do this is to make the expression of those beliefs and values through service standards a vital part of the employees' performance reviews—make it matter to employees whether or not they support the organization's commitment with their individual actions. A service standard is defined as "a set of instructions designed and communicated to promote consistency in delivering the service the customer expects."[9]

#290. A financial organization in the South publishes a booklet of standards that includes the specific guidelines they expect for core service and customer service. These booklets are given to all employees so they know exactly how their performance will be measured.

#291. Seafirst Bank of Seattle, Washington, ties the incentives of those employees dealing with new accounts to retention figures. The program is based on account openings and closings. Currently, closure goals and incentives are figured by looking at an individual's rate of closure from the previous year and asking for a 1 percent decrease. In the past, the policy read: reps would receive $5 for every new account opened, but would pay $10 out of a potential bonus for each closed. The plan was discontinued because at the time Seafirst was unable to sort controllable reasons for defections from uncontrollable (for example, a customer moves away).[10]

#292. When AT&T launched its new Universal credit card, the president believed that the best way to create a service orientation was by linking pay at all levels to quality performance. "Whether it's the president or an entry-level customer contact person, some portion of everyone's compensation is tied to our quality indicators," says Pam Vosmik, Vice President of Human Resources. AT&T developed 150 quality indicators that are measured daily. To promote teamwork, all employees must meet the indicators for their jobs 96 percent of the time or that day's allotment doesn't get into the bonus pool. Nonexempt employees can earn up to 12 percent of their base pay, paid quarterly on a prorated basis. Managers can earn up to 20 percent of their pay and receive bonuses annually. Quality results are tallied daily and displayed on color monitors throughout the company."[11]

#293.   Larry Harmon, president of De Mar, a small plumbing, heating, and air conditioning firm in Clovis, California, ties employees' pay to customer satisfaction with a unique point system. The 16 plumbers (called "service advisors") are awarded points each month based on positive comments from customers via phone and letter, and on survey results compiled from phone interviews with each customer upon completion of a job. The top three service advisors for each month receive A 50 PERCENT PAY RAISE over the next month. A customer call that praises a service advisor is worth 250 points, a complimentary letter is worth 500 points, a service request that asks for a specific service advisor is worth 1,000 points, and a service advisor who works extra holidays earns 3,000 points. Sales efforts are also rewarded and the system takes points away for negative feedback.[12]

COMMUNICATION CHALLENGE.   Take a close look at your performance reviews. Do they measure what is really important to the organization?

GATHERING FEEDBACK THROUGH CUSTOMER MEETINGS—INTERNAL AND EXTERNAL

We at Kaset International describe a customer as "a person whose evaluation of your service impacts your ability to continue to deliver that service." Here are some of the characteristics of today's customers to consider:

- Customers have needs and expectations; these needs and expectations tend to be self-serving.
- The customer's needs constantly change over time.
- Customer have less tolerance for poor service than they used to.
- Customers, both external AND internal, have an increasing number of options.
- Customers make judgments from perceptions—not facts—from their emotional heart, not their rational head. As Tom Peters said in a speech, "Customers perceive service in their own unique, idiosyncratic, emotional, erratic, irrational, end-of-the-day, and totally human terms. Perception is all there is."[13]

So, in order to understand customers' perceptions of your service and to continuously improve your service delivery, you must constantly ask them about their needs and expectations and how you are doing in serving them. Meetings with customers, both external and internal, become one powerful way to do this.

#294.   Hal Rosenbluth created "The Happiness Barometer," a systematic approach to measuring staff morale. Twice a year Rosenbluth spends a day with 18 associates, chosen randomly. He uses a written survey in these meetings, and its findings are later distributed to the whole company. One result of these get-togethers was the introduction of the company's 401(k) investment plan.[14]

#295. Provident Bank of Maryland conducts focus groups of both internal and external customers several times a year. According to Jean Scheffenacker, the external customer focus groups are always held whenever they introduce a new product. They hold internal focus groups to look at internal systems and processes. They ask employees, "What systems and processes are getting in the way of providing good service?" and "What are your ideas to fix these processes?" The information is then used to improve those systems and processes.

#296. Seafirst Bank of Seattle began a new accounts customer retention program to develop a relationship with customers so that they wouldn't be afraid to talk to them if there was a problem rather than just walking away without the bank ever knowing what went wrong. The day the account is opened, a customer is sent a personalized thank-you letter by the representative who opened the account. The same rep also calls the customer no more than 14 days later to see whether the checks and an electronic bank card have arrived. Marie Gunn, Executive Vice President in charge of quality service, then issues a survey 30 days after the account is opened, asking the customer to rate the bank on its process of introducing new customers to the bank and the handling of the account to date.

Another letter is sent out after six months with a special offer of a financial product to generate new business and, Gunn says, "to keep the bank in front of them and let them know if they have a problem they can call us." After one, two, and five years of loyalty, customers will be sent an anniversary letter, and the line "A valued customer since . . . " will begin appearing on checks and ATM cards. The first box of checks, deposit slips, and withdrawal slips of new customers are printed with a special star, making them easily recognizable to bank personnel.

As tellers recognize these new customers, they are expected to solicit feedback from them. Seafirst has made some important changes because of that feedback. When new customers told the bank that check orders weren't being filled on a timely basis, Seafirst found a new vendor. They have extended their hours and offered a service guarantee of $5 for customers who have to wait in line more than five minutes. They have also opened small branches in grocery stores as a result of customer feedback. Gunn says, "We're trying to open the lines of communication and make customers comfortable about bringing problems to us so we have a chance to fix them. There aren't too many problems we can't fix, but we need to know about them to take action."[15]

#297. Shelby Insurance Group in Shelby, Ohio, has an Agents' Council group (agents are their primary customers) that serves as an advisory board to them. They are responsible for gathering opinions from other agents and offering helpful feedback.

#298. As a result of research that showed only 21 percent of Apple Computer's customers were satisfied with how the company and its authorized resellers handled their problems, senior management agreed to implement a dedicated 800 number and a well-trained, centralized customer service unit called the Apple Assistance Center. This center consolidated customer relations and technical support under one roof. The center's staff consists of 45 customer service reps, 30 technical phone reps, 22 trouble-shooting engineers, plus a staff of 30 "escalation engineers" who work directly with Apple's design engineers to resolve quality and design issues. Each phone rep spends a minimum of six weeks in training before taking a phone call. "The goal is preemptive problem resolution," says Jackie Whiting, Apple USA's Director of Customer Response, "gathering real-time customer feedback and driving that back to design engineers, salespeople, and marketers to constantly improve products and services." The center sends monthly reports to major divisions summarizing what customers are saying about products, programs, or services.[16]

#299. Ron Zemke writes about GTE telephone company's "Quality Advocate Program." He says,

> Employees from any area of the company can volunteer to be customer "advocates" and once trained, are assigned a list of customers. The advocate is responsible for making periodic contacts with assigned customers, discussing service satisfaction, and ensuring that corrective actions are taken if unresolved problems exist. Initial contacts are made in person and repeated twice a year. Customers are encouraged to contact their advocates whenever a problem arises and they are unsure of normal channels for information or assistance or when a problem situation hasn't been resolved to their satisfaction.[17]

COMMUNICATION CHALLENGE. Have you used meetings with customer groups to gather their feedback—internal or external? I would suggest two cautions for those of you who decide to do more of this in your organization: Be sure you are sincere, open, and nondefensive when you ask for feedback. And let customers know that their feedback has made a difference by communicating to them actions you have taken as a result of it. Why not combine this kind of customer feedback meeting with a social time as well?

MYSTERY SHOPPING

Some organizations use mystery shopping as a measurement tool. They either hire and train persons to be shoppers or they use their own employees from a different locale. The term "mystery" refers to the fact that the employees do not know which customers are "for real" and which customers may be the mystery shoppers. For this tool to be effective, the shoppers must appear and act just like ordinary customers, with the same problems and concerns. After the interaction, they rate the organization and the employee on previously agreed upon criteria. That data, if accurate, can be used to drive service improvements in the organization.

Ron Zemke makes these suggestions about using mystery shopping as a measuring tool:

> Take a close look at your mystery shopping program. Are you shopping beyond the basics? Most mystery shopping looks only at standard operating procedures. Mystery shoppers should present tricky problems to be solved, so you can evaluate (tellers') behavior when they're faced with a difficult situation. If your mystery shoppers are telling you that your (tellers) are terrific people, but overall customer satisfaction scores are mediocre, take it as a strong signal that you may need to change your systems, policies, or procedures. Ask your tellers what gets in their way, what barriers exist to their providing high-quality service. . . . One more thing: make sure your mystery shopping reports are giving you real data. CIA operatives might learn a thing or two by going underground to watch seasoned front-liners pick out members of the "smile police" at 50 paces![18]

#300. To ensure excellent customer service, SouthTrust Corporation conducts 5,000 mystery shops a year. Shoppers, both external customers and internal employees, are hired and trained to observe the expected performance level. They are then sent out to all 400 branches to conduct transactions. Each branch employee with whom they interact is rated on a 10-point scale. Achieving a "9" rating is considered good. Anything under an "8" calls for a reshop one month later so that the manager has time to coach the employee. Managers receive feedback sheets for each employee with specific actions/recommendations to coach. The results of the "shops" impact the employees' performance appraisals and raises as well as the branch as a whole.

#301. Gary Cino, CEO of 98 Cent Clearance Centers, West Sacramento, California, uses an interesting version of mystery shopping.

> When he finds someone who is a first-time visitor to one of his retail stores—where every item costs 98 cents—he hands the prospect an envelope. Inside is $5, another envelope stamped and addressed to Cino, and a single sheet questionnaire with a dozen questions such as, "Did the cashier greet you at the time of checkout?" The first-timers are also asked to rate the store's appearance and products. Customers are asked to attach a copy of their cash register receipt when they return the questionnaire. He and his executives pass out some 500 packets a year, amounting to just $2500 cash expense.

About 85% of shoppers return the survey within 90 days. Responses are posted in each store.[19]

COMMUNICATION CHALLENGE. Are you using mystery shopping to its full advantage in gaining actionable information?

MEASURING CUSTOMER COMPLAINTS

Many organizations think of a customer complaint as a "negative." I encourage you to reframe a customer complaint as an opportunity—an opportunity to recover with the customer and "fix" the complaint as well as an opportunity to find out what upsets your customers. Current research shows that only a small percentage of upset customers even bother to complain—most just leave. So, those that tell you what concerns they have are, in essence, doing you a favor. What has upset them has probably upset many other customers—the others just didn't stay to tell you! Whatever time and effort you put into gathering customer complaints and then taking action on what you find will not only communicate your commitment but will also ultimately keep your customers returning.

#302. The Florida Department of Health and Rehabilitative Services customer complaint department has recently been doing some extremely innovative and powerful measurement. They have been measuring the number of complaints that occur because of the Business level of the transaction (unfriendly or confusing policies, bureaucratic or inefficient systems, poor product quality, etc.) and the number that revolve around the Human level of the transaction (employees being unfriendly or rude, not listening to customer needs, refusing to jiggle the system or go out of the way for the customer, etc.). This measurement will help them to know where to concentrate training and support efforts.

#303. Provident Bank of Maryland believes in the importance of surveying people who have closed their accounts to find out why customers were unhappy with the bank. They measure both the processes and the service, and they have found that most often it is the service that causes the customers to leave. Their hope is that by doing these surveys, they may be able to recover with the customer and the customer will return to the bank, as well as learn how they can provide better customer service to all their customers.

COMMUNICATION CHALLENGE Do you measure the way employees are communicating the values and beliefs of your organization by measuring customer complaints about service? Do you measure both internal and external actions? Do you measure on a regular basis? Do you communicate the results of those measurements in a creative, actionable way?

ACTION PAGE

Chapter Nine

Rewards and Recognition
Creative Ways to Make Confirming the Commitment Matter to Your Employees

AND THE WINNER IS...

Source: © Kaset International.

The most neglected form of compensation is the six-letter word "thanks."

Patrick Townshend, *Commit to Quality*

T he *National Underwriter* reports that recognition for a job well done is the top motivator of employee performance. It was rated 4.9 on a scale of 1–6, according to the results of an interactive telephone survey of more than 200 employee communications managers conducted for the Council of Communication Management by William M. Mercer, Inc. Recognition surpassed money (4.8 on the scale) and challenge (4.3) among the top three employee motivators. Fear—including concern over possible job loss—ranked fourth (3.4) and was the only negative consideration. Ownership and freedom ranked 3.3 each and free time 2.7.[1]

Jeffrey M. Horn, Mercer managing director, said, "All too often, large, complex organizations overlook something as basic as recognition, and that can be a big mistake. By recognizing employee contributions in non-financial as well as financial ways, companies can take a giant step toward building morale and becoming more productive."[2]

Recognition can be defined as "treating someone as a worthwhile human being." Fran Solomon, Ritch Davidson, and Jeff Randall of Playfair in Berkeley, California, list the following principles of recognition:

1. Make sure the program rewards and is consistent with a highly held value in the organization.
2. Reward and recognition work best when EVERYONE has an opportunity to win.
3. The broader the scope of recognition, the greater the potential benefits. Don't restrict recognition to one or two big events. Recognition must be ongoing and every day.
4. Use it, don't abuse it! Overdone or insincere, rewarding loses its impact.[3]

They also suggest some characteristics of effective reward and recognition:

1. BE SPECIFIC. Don't be vague in giving feedback, such as, "Thanks for your help." Rather say something like, "Thanks for assuming the extra responsibility for getting that report done at the last minute and on time for our customer meeting."
2. BE INDIVIDUAL. When rewarding a team for a job well done, it's important to recognize individual efforts that allowed the team to succeed. Also, be sure to recognize individuals who consistently recognize and appreciate others.
3. BE PERSONAL. Each of us appreciates praise in a different way. Remember the "Way It Is model"? Do your homework. Ask people how they would like to be acknowledged. Information can be gathered from the employees themselves, as well as from family and former managers in your organization regarding their likes, hobbies, personal interests, etc., for extra clues as to how to appreciate them in tangible ways. Then use your creativity to make it special.
4. BE TIMELY. Don't wait until the end of the year to sing your people's praises. Too often someone complains, "When I do something wrong, it only takes 5 minutes for me to be called on the carpet. Yet our awards ceremony happens only once a year."
5. BE PROPORTIONAL. Make the size of the acknowledgment commensurate with the project or deed being recognized.

6. BE SINCERE. Sincerity is established, in part, by following the other characteristics. That is, when we are timely, specific, and proportional in our praise of an individual, there's a much greater chance it will be perceived as honest and well-meant recognition. Walking around and randomly stopping employees you don't know, patting their backs, and saying, "Good work. You're doing a great job!" is unlikely to be experienced as sincere and may have a backlash effect of stirring resentment. Don't mix praise with a request for something else. It dilutes the power of the praise and puts the recipient in an awkward position for giving an honest "yes" or "no" to the request itself.

7. HAVE FUN. As in all the work you do, enjoy the process. Whether you are creating a major reward and recognition program for your organization or simply thinking of ways to informally acknowledge people for what they do, the process should be as much fun for you in the planning and giving as it is for your people in the receiving![4]

One of the most significant things I have learned about rewards and recognition, mentioned in number three above, is to *Ask your employees what they would like.* It is human nature to give someone else something *you'd* like; however, that gift might not be meaningful to them at all. Because the importance of rewards and recognition is to honor the employee in some way, managers must communicate with them to determine what *is*, in fact, a reward for each individual.

When I was working with a large state government several years ago, one of the major concerns we dealt with was how to reward the employees and still stay within financial limitations. The management assumption was that the state workers would only feel rewarded with things that cost money. I asked them if they would be willing to poll state workers to determine what *they* would like as rewards and recognition. The managers agreed, and when the results came in, there were two requests that overwhelmingly occurred:

1. That they could spend one hour in their commissioner's office, just watching what he or she did—to give them a feeling of "being in on things."
2. To change jobs with someone in the state for a half-day.

The amazing thing was that neither of these requests cost any out-of-pocket money, and they were relatively easy to implement. In fact, within two weeks various departments of the state had begun to implement these requests as rewards for extraordinary service to citizens.

Let your creative juices flow and get out of your mental locks as you begin to think in a different way about rewards and recognition. Here is a creative list of rewards and recognition that a recent management class I facilitated put together. Notice how their ideas got more and more creative the longer they brainstormed:

"Ways to Reward and Recognize Your Employees"

Give affirming feedback.

Give Chocolate.

Write a thank you note.

Put something positive/affirming in the employee's file.

Give a promotion.

Increase their responsibilities.

Recognize special accomplishments publicly, in meetings or celebrations.

Give comp time.

Have a party.

Invite them to lunch or dinner.

Have a "beer bust" after work.

Give special tokens or mementos.

Hand out Lifesavers.

Send them flowers.

Send a bunch of balloons.

Give them tickets to a movie/play/cultural event/sporting event.

Give them opportunities for special training or seminars.

Let them choose a cross-functional assignment.

Suggest a salary increase.

Give them opportunities for overtime.

Give them casual dress days.

Allow them to exchange positions with someone else in the company for a half-day.

"Sit in" with an upper level person for part of a day.

Recognize them privately.

Write a letter to their spouse, family, or significant other.

Allow the employee to choose a special project.

Allow flexible work time so the employee can participate in outside professional activities.

Sponsor a membership in a professional group.

Give a subscription to a professional periodical.

Purchase a professional book of interest to the employee and his or her development.

Give special bookmarks.

Sponsor a catered lunch.

Buy pizza for everyone.

Send a fruit basket.

Give them a surprise for their work station—a desk organizer, a picture or poster, a new pen, etc.

Give them a coupon for an extra 30 minutes for lunch on the day of their choice.

Send a T-shirt or something from the company or community to the employee's children.

Choose a company executive to give a one-hour question and answer speech to an organization of the employee's choice.

Let them attend meetings in your place.

Name some place in the building after them.

Take out an advertisement in a local paper and include their names and pictures.

Make a donation to their favorite charity in their name.

Give them a coupon for a massage as a stress reliever.

Give them coupons for some of your time.

Give them potato chips!

Write a fun story about them.

Do all their copying for one week.

Serve them coffee each morning for a week.

Name an item in the company cafeteria after them.

Finally, and most importantly, think about what you are rewarding—are you rewarding behaviors that exemplify the beliefs and values you are committed to as an organization? If not, your reward and recognition programs need some revising!

Now let's see what creative things organizations are doing to reward and recognize employees who are supporting the organization's commitment. Recognition has been defined as costing little or no money and rewards as involving a more significant cost.

LOW COST IDEAS FOR RECOGNITION

Simple observation suggests that most of us are trinket freaks—if they represent a genuine thanks for a genuine assist.

Tom Peter, *Thriving on Chaos*

#304. Centel Cellular in Raleigh, North Carolina, rewards its "credit consultants" for going out of their way to help customers and doing such things as providing special resources. The department has a "Dollar Tree," an artificial Christmas tree decorated with many different things that cost a dollar, such as Post-it notes, candy bars, Pac-Man note cards, and other items. Whenever a rep has gone above and beyond for a customer, he or she gets to choose a reward from the Dollar Tree.

#305. The Medicare Department of Nationwide Insurance in Columbus, Ohio, has a recognition program called GEMS: "GIVING EXCELLENT MEDICARE SERVICE," which recognizes positive performance. Each division creates its own requirements to receive the Quality/Production Awards and the Outstanding Achievement

Awards. The Outstanding Achievement Awards are reviewed by the GEMS Committee each month. All supervisory Medicare employees are eligible, and magnets with the appropriate "gem" are awarded to them as they meet the requirements for each. A recognition celebration is held at the end of the fiscal year for the TREASURE CHEST recipients. These are the qualifications for each of the GEMS:

Attendance—Ruby
Quality/Production—Diamond
Outstanding Achievement—Emerald
Gold—Treasure Chest

AND WE WANT 200 OF THESE AWARDS BY 3:00 PM.

Source: © Kaset International.

#306.   At a large Eastern bank, they use the form on the following page to recognize internal customers. It is based on their "Five Cornerstones to Quality Service: COURTESY, RELIABILITY, RESPONSIVENESS, KNOWLEDGE, AND ENVIRONMENT" and includes a place to describe the service performed and the date it took place.

#307.   The Virginia Department of Motor Vehicles has an Employee Recognition program they call GEM, for Go the Extra Mile. Lois Lavery, the Customer Service Director, says that when the

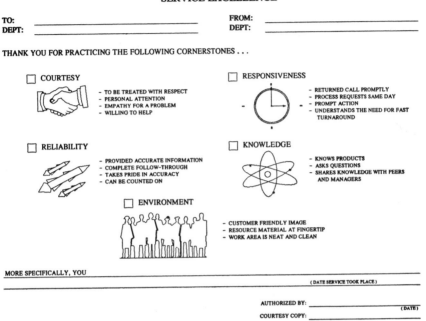

department determined that a program was needed, several things were done to research different options. These included talking with other companies who had successful recognition programs as well as surveying employees to find out what was important to them. She states, "The GEM program has now been in existence for 14 months. Employees have definitely appreciated the opportunity to recognize others and to be recognized for going the extra mile for internal and external customers. At this time, over 3800 GEM's have been awarded. This is 3800 times we have been able to recognize and reinforce the type of service behavior we are looking for." These awards give employees a quick and easy way to recognize one another as often as they like and they don't need approval by a committee.

Two interesting details of the program are:

The first time an employee is recognized they are given a card with their name on it and a GEM sticker. Each subsequent time they are recognized they receive another sticker. Employees display this "tent card" on their desk or counter so they are publicly recognized.

The GEM tent card and/or sticker, the nomination form stating why the employee was recognized and by whom, and the congratulations card from the Customer Service Office are sent to the employee's manager, who presents them with the GEM. This was done in response to employees' requests to inform their managers that they had received a GEM. It also provides managers with an opportunity to recognize their employees. The award comes with a card that says, "GREAT NEWS FROM THE CUSTOMER SERVICE OFFICE— You have an employee who has been recognized as a GEM. To make this recognition even more meaningful for _____, we are requesting that you personally present the attached GEM award to him/her. Thanks for your help and support of customer service."

GEM (Go the Extra Mile)
Information Sheet

What is GEM?

GEM is DMV's new employee recognition program. This program lets you formally praise any DMV employee for going the extra mile to provide customers or fellow employees with outstanding service. In turn, the Customer Service Office will recognize the employee you commend. Feel free to recognize a co-worker, your supervisor, employees who report to you, a work unit or a branch office. **GEM** is not limited to employees who work with the public. This program is for all employees.

When does GEM start and how can I recognize someone?

GEM starts March 15. To recognize someone, fill out the attached recognition form. Recognition forms will be available on all DMV bulletin boards. You may also recognize employees by calling the Customer Service Office at (804) 367-9230.

Why is this program at DMV?

Employees are DMV's most important asset and deserve to be recognized for all they do. **GEM** is a tool you can use to acknowledge other employees who go the extra mile to give extraordinary service. When you recognize people for doing jobs well, you take the essential step in helping them feel proud about what they do.

Here are some **examples** of why someone should be recognized:

● For going the extra mile to help a customer or fellow worker.

● For doing a great job ahead of schedule and under budget.

● For changing an angry customer into a satisfied one.

● For solving an unusual problem.

These are only suggestions. Feel free to recognize a fellow worker for other reasons. The goal of this program is to recognize and reward DMV's spectrum of employees whose skills and personalities bring this agency closer to being a model agency for customer service.

Go ahead, recognize the GEMs you know!

Source: Viginia Department of Motor Vehicles.

#308. Colleen Dykes, the Communications Manager for Iowa Electric Light and Power, shared with me an employee recognition program that she started several years ago called "Customer Service Second to None." She said the company used to have an employee recognition program that recognized only a small number of employees with a cash reward. It was well received by the few employees who won, of course; however, it caused morale problems for the other 1,800 employees who weren't recognized! So, Colleen decided to start a program that was simple, cheap, easy to administer, and able to provide lots of recognition.

She began by making pins that said "Second to None" with a #1 on them. They were sent to all employees with a letter from the President of the company introducing the program and explaining that they all had customers, whether they were internal or external. The program consists of the employees nominating anyone, their peers, subordinates, or even their bosses, for giving extraordinary customer service. EVERYONE who is nominated is recognized without anyone making judgments or comparisons. Each person nominated receives a gold metal #1 pin and a personalized letter from the Chairman of the Board. Colleen stated, "I thought the program would last a year, but everyone loves it. It is a program that refuses to die!"

#309. Heather Moreton and Lynne Foster of Canadian Airlines have created a Recognition Handbook for all employees that was developed in support of and in conjunction with the company's Recognition Excellence Program. It begins with a section on "Who is responsible for recognition?" It says:

> Personal recognition and praise are essential in maintaining a motivated workforce. Unfortunately, the "no news is good news" approach to recognition is the more common practice. Reversing this cycle to build a culture of recognition and thanks begins with each one of us. A single stone thrown in a pond creates a ripple; multiple stones can fill the pond with ripples. In the same way, recognition can fill Canadian with motivation. You are the stone to create the ripple. There are no restrictions to giving or receiving recognition. Find ways to recognize all employees, therefore stimulating motivation for all. It is everyone's responsibility.

Another section deals with "What can you do?" This section contains an action plan with the following questions:

- What activities can you undertake to increase recognition here at Canadian Airlines?
- When are you going to begin?
- Who hasn't been recognized lately?
- How often will you give recognition?
- How are you going to sustain the process?
  This week?
  This month?
  This year?

RECOGNITIONGRAM

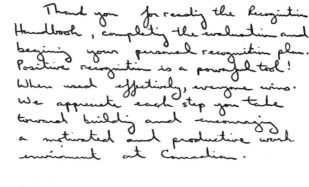

Thanks for Your Contribution!
Sincerely,

Source: Canadian Airlines International.

The booklet ends with a RECOGNITIONGRAM from the President of the airline.

#310. Centel Cellular in Raleigh, North Carolina, sets goals for each individual employee, and these goals are to exceed the corporate goals. After their goals have been decided, the company lets the representatives assign the values to their goals. In other words, they determine when they should be rewarded, *and* they determine their own rewards, depending on whatever is important to them.

Some of them choose concrete reminders of their achievement, such as plaques and certificates, but others choose more practical things like flextime.

#311. Commercebank in Coral Gables, Florida, has a special recognition program called the Dazzle program. The bookkeeping department, for example, chooses a person to be "motivator of the week." This person wears a hat for easy identification and is responsible for "pumping people up" when they begin to run out of steam. One division votes for a "Dazzler of the Week" every Friday and posts the results on Monday. This person is the one who has "dazzled" the most customers, both internal and external.

#312. Shelby Insurance Group, Shelby, Ohio, has an Associate of the Month. The people selected for this are often chosen because of their ability to provide quality customer service. Associates of the Month receive a certificate to have their car washed and waxed, a prime parking spot for the month, and lunch with Dan Carmichael, the president of the company. At the lunch, Dan asks them about ideas they may have to further improve customer service.

TIME TO ACT

Employees who have gotten into the "ACT" by submitting their revenue generating and cost-cutting ideas to Award Creative Thinking have added $73.7 million to United's bottom line since the program began in 1989. More than 35 percent of all the suggestions that have passed through the ACT evaluation process have been approved.

"Now is a great time for employees who have ideas to submit them to the ACT program." says ACT Manager Beverly Hawkins. "Employees have proven that they are the experts in their fields by the creativity of the more than 10,000 ideas generated in just over three years."

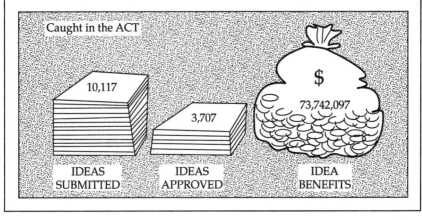

Source: United Airlines.

#313. This example is a creative way to gather employee ideas. United Airlines has a program called ACT—Award Creative Thinking. It encourages employees to submit their revenue-generating and cost-cutting ideas. These employees who have gotten into the "ACT" have added $73.7 million to United's bottom line since the program began in 1989. More than 35 percent of all the suggestions that have passed through the ACT evaluation process have been approved. Says ACT Manager Beverly Hawkins, "Employees have proven that they are the experts in their fields by the creativity of the more than 10,000 ideas generated in just over three years." Pictures of the employees and a brief description of their ideas are published in the monthly newsletter.

#314. In line with broad strategic objectives of the company, Hawaiian Electric introduced its Team Incentive Plan (TIP). The primary objective of the plan was to replace the focus from a previous incentive program that recognized outstanding individual performance with a program that recognized the successes of team performance. One of the four TIP performance goals is based on Hawaiian Electric's customer satisfaction rating. The remaining three goals indirectly relate to their overall objective of meeting customer needs through reliable, efficient, and quality service. A company publication reads, "In its own way, the existence of the incentive program is a highly effective and potentially rewarding form of communication. Ongoing communication of our commitment to customer service to the public is an important, strategic objective of the company, carried out by the Corporate Communication Division. Yet communicating the customer service commitment internally, to the employees, is deemed just as important as external public communications."

#315. Max De Pree, the Chairman of the Board of Herman Miller, Inc., a furniture manufacturer, tells about a special kind of recognition he created for his company:

> In the life of an American Indian tribe, the watercarrier held one of the most important and respected positions. Water, like food and air, is essential for survival. . . . To be a watercarrier suggests continuity, longevity, commitment, dependability, and resourcefulness. Watercarriers transfer the essence of the institution to new people who arrive to help us and, eventually, to replace us. . . .
>
> Before I stepped down as CEO, I searched around for a way to honor the watercarriers I had known and the ones who would come after me. I discovered a wonderful sculpture in Arizona by Allan Houser. An American Indian, he knew all about watercarriers. His own culture honors them. The result of his talent is a wonderful and evocative sculpture titled *Watercarrier*. Around it on a low granite plinth at the company headquarters are the names of people who have served Herman Miller for 20 years or more, an investment of their lives that has contributed to the continuity of our company. Every year, of course, we add new names. . . .

A small version of Houser's sculpture sits outside the CEO's office to make sure that Herman Miller's leaders don't forget the importance of continuity and history in the rush of everyday business. Inscribed next to both sculptures is: "The tribal watercarrier in this corporation is a symbol of the essential nature of all jobs, our interdependence, the identity of ownership and participation, the servanthood of leadership, the authenticity of each individual."[5]

COMMUNICATION CHALLENGE. What can you do to begin a formal recognition program if you don't already have one? Remember recognition costs little or no money. Have fun and remember to ask for employee input!

REWARDS THAT REQUIRE MORE MONEY

People will do exceptional work for a company that expresses its gratitude for their efforts–even if the most expensive symbol of that gratitude is a fifty dollar item.

Patrick Townshend, *Commit to Quality*

AND THE BAD NEWS, FARBUSH, IS YOU'RE FIRED.

Source: © Kaset International.

Consider the following fable about the importance of reward:

A weekend fisherman looked over the side of his boat and saw a snake with a frog in its mouth. Feeling sorry for the frog, he reached down, gently removed the frog from the snake's mouth and let the frog go free. But now he felt sorry for the hungry snake. Having no food, he took out a flask of bourbon and poured a few drops into the snake's mouth. The snake swam away happy, the frog was happy and the man was happy for having performed such good deeds. He thought all was well until a few minutes passed and he heard something knock against the side of his boat and looked down. With stunned disbelief, the fisherman saw the snake was back—with two frogs![6]

Michael LeBoeuf says that the fable contains two important lessons:

1. You get more of the behavior you reward. You DON'T get what you hope for, ask for, wish for, or beg for. YOU GET WHAT YOU REWARD. . . .
2. In trying to do the right things it's oh, so easy to fall into the trap of rewarding the wrong activities and ignoring or punishing the right ones.[7]

What is the "greatest management principle in the world?" REWARD, of course!

#316. David Armstrong tells about a time when Armstrong International's employees were given a retroactive raise and how it was done in a dramatic, memorable way:

THE $125,000 THANK-YOU

All companies go through tough times, and Armstrong, unfortunately, is no exception. In 1987, for the first time since the Depression, we put a wage freeze into effect to help us get through what looked like it would be a very difficult year.

Our employees were amazing. They accepted the freeze with very few complaints. "The company has always been fair with me" seemed to be the prevailing attitude. "Now it's my turn to be fair to the company."

A few months into the new year, it looked like 1987 was going to be much better than projected. We decided that not only could we give everybody raises, but we could afford to make them retroactive. The back pay came to about $400 per employee.

We didn't give our employees that $400 by check. Instead, we called everybody into the recreation building where my father, company president, was standing behind a large table covered with a white sheet. He explained that since Armstrong was doing better than anticipated, the company wanted to share its good fortune.

With that, he lifted the sheet, and everyone saw that the table was covered with $10 bills—some 12,500 of them—stacked two feet high.

Continued

One by one, each employee came up, shook my dad's hand and those of the company's managers, and was told, "Thank you for your understanding." They walked away with forty crisp, new $10 bills.

If there's a point to be made, either good or bad, do it dramatically. People will remember.

THE MORAL OF THE STORY

- Integrity is a two-way street. Both sides showed integrity here. The employees took the wage freeze with few complaints. They wanted to help their company. But the company demonstrated integrity, too. It didn't have to make the raises retroactive. It could have kept the $125,000, and nobody would have been the wiser.
- Thank-you's must be sincere. We wanted to let our employees know we really appreciated their actions. Sure, we could have given everybody a check, but it wouldn't have had the same effect.
- Messages with a smile. There is nothing wrong with a little fun. Seeing $125,000 up close is dramatic, entertaining—and when part of that pile of bills is yours—definitely fun![8]

#317. Beth Munkres, the owner of The Paige Collection, gives thoughtful rewards to her employees who have gone the extra mile or to the person who has achieved the highest percentage beyond her individual percentage of the store goal for the month. She tries to give them rewards that include their families, and she also writes notes to the family to thank them for "sharing" their mother, sister, or wife. This month, for example, the winner received tickets to the play "A Christmas Carol" in Denver and a certificate for a hotel room to go along with it.

#318. Nationwide Insurance has a company-wide reward and recognition program called SOAR (Service Over & Above Requirements). The Human Resources SOAR Committee states, "SOAR is the program designed to:

- Stimulate creative ways to serve our customers.
- Expand our vision of service opportunity.
- Recognize those who exhibit exemplary service.

SOAR allows us to applaud and learn from each other's successes."

Each region decides its own SOAR nomination criteria, selection process, awards, and methods of presentation for spontaneous, monthly, quarterly, and annual SOAR recipients. Some regions have very rigid selection processes, giving out only monthly and annual awards. Others honor all spontaneous nominations submitted but are selective in choosing quarterly and annual honorees. Nearly all regions involve management level in presenting the SOAR awards. (It is interesting to note that two regions recognize SOAR nominators.) Each operation decides its own rewards, which vary from stuffed animals, items with the corporate logo, and calculators to savings bonds, dinner tickets, and gift certificates.

#319. Max De Pree talks about rewards in his company:

> To win a Frost award at Herman Miller you have to be named an outstanding employee by your peers. Then the senior management team must select you as one of two or three outstanding contributors in the entire company. It is a real honor and now carries with it a five-thousand-dollar stipend for continuing education. One can go to school for a period in London or Lausanne or Sao Paulo. Many have. Manuel had won a Frost award and came to ask me if he could use the money in a different way. He was still commuting every weekend from Mexico to our Irvine, California, plant and was enduring the separation every work week from his wife and four children. His goal was to immigrate to the United States. He told me that before the family immigrated, he wanted each of his children to be fluent in English. He wanted to use the stipend for language lessons for his children. Naturally we agreed. I was reminded in a touching way that rewards and recognition are not the same for all of us.[9]

#320. The City of Gillette, Wyoming, has special awards that reinforce their customer service orientation. When an employee gives extraordinary customer service, a letter is sent to the employee's spouse or significant other (at their home) that contains a coupon for the two of them to go out to dinner at a local restaurant to celebrate. This Immediate Recognition Award is in its fourth year of use, and all nominees also receive a Letter of Commendation in their personnel file.

#321. "Goal Rush" is the name of an incentive program used by Clark Public Utilities in Vancouver, Washington, to provide financial rewards to employees for outstanding individual and company performance. The reward for exceptional performance can be as much as 60 hours of annual leave for each employee. But the challenge to earn that reward is a tough one.

There are six major goal areas. Each one has a specific target for achievement. Three of the six goals—System Watch, Customer Follow-up, and Community Involvement—will be measured on an individual basis. The bonuses for these goals will go only to those employees that participate in them. In addition, each employee must complete at least two of these individual goals in order to receive Goal Rush incentives. A minimum of four of the six goals must be met to trigger the incentives for each employee. Goal Rush bonuses

Goal Rush '92
Quarterly Report Form

Name _____ Department _____
This is a report of my activity in quarter number 1   2   3   4   (Circle one)

System Watch

I have submitted the following operating orders this quarter:

Operating Order #	Date	Operating Order #	Date
_____	_____	_____	_____
_____	_____	_____	_____
_____	_____	_____	_____

Customer Follow-up

I have made follow-up contact with the following customers this quarter regarding their service with the utility:

Customer Name	Date	Customer Name	Date
_____	_____	_____	_____
_____	_____	_____	_____
_____	_____	_____	_____

Community Involvement

I have participated in the following authorized outreach activities this quarter:

Activity	Date	Hours
_____	_____	____
_____	_____	____
_____	_____	____

Signature _____ Date _____

Please record only the activitiy in the quarter indicated above. Return to: Communications Department, 3rd floor, Electric Center, the first week of April, July, October and January.

Source: Clark Public Utilities.

will be awarded as annual leave that may be exchanged for cash within the limits of utility policy. The rewards increase with the achievement of each additional goal:

4 goals × 8 hrs. annual leave = 32 hrs.
5 goals × 9 hrs. annual leave = 45 hrs.
6 goals × 10 hrs. annual leave = 60 hrs.

The amount of the bonus depends on how many of the six goals an employee and the utility reach by the end of the year.

Individual Goals

System Watch—To have all employees identify and report at least six needs for electric or water system maintenance.

Customer Follow-up—To have all employees make follow-up contact with at least six customers regarding their recent service from the utility.

Community Involvement—To have all employees participate for six hours in one or more authorized outreach activities outside of normal work hours.

Utility Goals

Customer Satisfaction—To achieve a positive rating from 95 percent of customers regarding the overall operation of the utility.

Employee Communications—To achieve a 90 percent participation of work unit teams in The Grapevine; to achieve a 50 percent participation of employees in the incompleted "Over the Top" orientation training activities.

Labor Efficiency—To increase labor efficiency by 2 percent over 1991.

#322. Whereas the "Goal Rush" program rewards mostly team performance, Clark Public Utilities has another program called "Hats Off" that gives special recognition for individual achievement. What kind of actions by an employee may result in a Hats Off award?

1. An individual act of exceptional customer, community, or emergency service which exceeds the normal expectations of the job.

2. Extraordinary performance of one's job resulting in an outstanding accomplishment or significant contribution to the organization or the utility industry.

3. A suggestion which results in an improvement to the operation of the PUD.

4. A suggestion resulting in a positive financial impact to the utility, either by saving money or producing new revenue. Recommendations for a Hats Off award may be made by any utility employee. Employees may recommend themselves for an award.

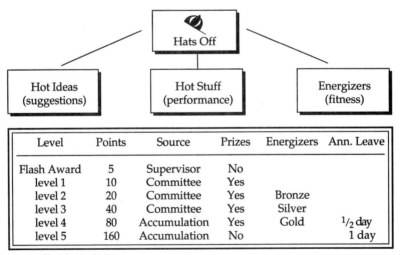

Level	Points	Source	Prizes	Energizers	Ann. Leave
Flash Award	5	Supervisor	No		
level 1	10	Committee	Yes		
level 2	20	Committee	Yes	Bronze	
level 3	40	Committee	Yes	Silver	
level 4	80	Accumulation	Yes	Gold	$1/2$ day
level 5	160	Accumulation	No		1 day

Source: Clark Public Utilities.

The Hats Off awards are set up on three levels. Level-one and Level-two awards are merchandise, such as ball caps, T-shirts, and jackets. Level-two awards are of higher value, commensurate with a greater accomplishment or contribution. The Level-three award is three days of annual leave and is reserved for clearly superior or outstanding accomplishments. The awards are all in the form of a certificate with points attached to it. Employees will be able to cash the certificate for a prize or save it to accumulate points toward higher-level awards.

Hats Off awards are rewards for both big and small suggestions and accomplishments by employees. The review committee evaluates approved Hot Ideas and performance nominations with an eye to creativity, initiative, effort, impact on customers or the organization, and any potential cost savings or efficiency improvements. Hats Off awards can result from HOT IDEAS (implemented suggestions), HOT STUFF (exceptional job performance), or from ENERGIZERS (fitness achievements).

To improve the timeliness of recognition, Hats Off now includes a *Flash Award*. It can be given by supervisors directly to employees at any time for going beyond the normal requirements of the job. Previously, all Hats Off awards were made by a review committee in response to written nominations. "The Flash Award gives supervisors a tool to provide instant recognition without waiting for someone to approve it," said Richard Cyr.

Source: Clark Public Utilities.

#323. Lori Orton, JC Penney Credit Services, shared one of the most positive ways they continue to recognize the importance of customer service with their frontline staff:

All Thank You letters received are shared during monthly department stand-up meetings. They are then forwarded to our Personnel Department and again shared on a quarterly basis in an office-wide meeting. Each associate's name is placed in a drawing (1 for each letter) and the name drawn usually wins a $100 gift certificate. Yearly, we choose one associate whose customer relations skills have far exceeded our expectations. This is done in each of our 12 credit offices. These 12 associates will usually receive a weekend trip for two at a resort hotel. At our Fall Credit Manager's Meeting, when all 12 offices are represented, one associate is picked from among the 12 as Outstanding Customer Relations Associate of the Year. This person is awarded a trip for two to Hawaii or other destination of pleasure. This is a tradition that has been upheld since our program started in 1988, and all associates nationwide look forward to and appreciate this program.

#324. The Washington Water Power Company in Spokane, Washington, has a Quality Assurance recognition program to recognize outstanding customer service. Excellence is observed and measured through monitoring a sample of the Customer Service Representative's telephone calls and evaluating their performance. Expectations or criteria for completing a quality call were identified and communicated. A qualifying rep receives a one ounce silver bullion coin, a note of appreciation, and is honored in quality communications:

The silver bullion is pure and symbolizes the same high standard we are striving for in quality assurance. The message inscribed on the coin reads, "Quality is an investment in our future." In the center are the company's logo and shaking hands that symbolize:

- Our congratulations.
- Extending a helping hand to our customers.
- A commitment toward quality service.
- Teamwork for the benefit of the customer.
- A promise of mutual trust.
- Striving to exceed the customer's expectations.
- Personalizing our service.

#325. At Wisconsin Power and Light, every employee is given $200 in $20 certificates at the beginning of the year. These certificates are for employees to recognize one another for excellent customer service.

#326. The Awards for Creative Efforts Program (ACE for short) is the new name for Hawaiian Electric Company's employee reward program, through which you can submit suggestions for improvements in quality, productivity, safety, and health, or nominate fellow employees for recognition of their exceptional achievement or voluntary community involvement. Designed by a team of bargaining unit and merit employees, the ACE Program encourages creative new ideas, ensures that those ideas are heard, and implements them. A full-time administrator is employed to stay on top of suggestions and a team of in-house professionals is available to help evaluate and assist with suggestion efforts.

An awards committee reviews suggestions and nominations and determines awards. All suggestors earn ACE credits for their suggestions, whether or not they are implemented. Suggestions that contribute to the quality, productivity, and savings at HECO are awarded based on the calculated net benefit to HECO (hard dollar savings). Suggestions calculated to yield a net benefit of more than $1,000 are awarded 10 percent of the total net benefit up to a maximum of $30,000! Suggestions that improve the safety conditions of the work environment earn gift certificates valued from $25 to $100. Nominated employees who give generously of their time and talent via Community Service or Involvement can be assured of recognition and may be eligible to receive as much as $100 in gift certificates for their efforts. Suggestion evaluators can be recognized as the Evaluator of the Month/Year, and supervisors/managers can be recognized as Leader of the Month/Year for supporting their employees and urging constant peer encouragement and growth.

COMMUNICATION CHALLENGE.   Do you have a reward program in place for your employees? If so, is it creative and does it exemplify the beliefs and values of your organization? What kind of input have your employees had in creating the program and the rewards? If they have not been actively involved, perhaps it's time to create a task force and begin a new program. If you believe what Michael LeBoeuf and many other experts say, you can't manage effectively without one!

ACTION PAGE

Chapter Ten

Recoveries
Using Creative Recovery to Communicate Commitment

NICE RECOVERY, GEORGE.

Source: © Kaset International.

The art of simple apology is rare in business. And the art of skillful recovery and restitution to capture future customer loyalty is even more rare.

Karl Albrecht, *Service Within*

The word "recovery" means "to return to a normal state; to make whole again." In Kaset International's training, recovery is described like this:

> When a person has "fully recovered," it is a signal to us to expect that person to be or act the same as he or she was before something went wrong. The goal of *service* recovery is much the same—to at least return the customer to the state the customer was in before the service delivery "went wrong," and hopefully carry it beyond, so that the customer is dazzled.... One of the interesting things about recovery is that it creates a positive memory for the

173

customer. A customer who was terribly upset about service can be turned into a loyal customer who will tell others how good you are. The service failure, in effect, turns out to be an opportunity to create a positive memory for a customer.[1]

There are four steps in the recovery process:

• Apology with empathy.
• Urgent reinstatement (fix it).
• Symbolic atonement (do something extra).
• Follow up.

I consider Chip Bell, along with his colleague Ron Zemke of Performance Research Associates, Inc., to be the "gurus" of recovery. I asked Chip if he would share some of his thoughts on recovery as it relates to creative communication and commitment. He did this in "The Art of Strategic Apology."

THE ART OF STRATEGIC APOLOGY

Customers do NOT expect organizations to provide perfect service!

Now, before you lower your service standards, know that frequent foul ups WILL foster a fast exit for customers. However, if service failures are strategically managed, the customers' tolerance of a disappointing oops will not only be likely, it can be transformed into a delightful opportunity. In fact, research shows that customers who have had their service problem elegantly solved wind up more loyal than customers who have NEVER even had a problem! The secret to success lies in partnership communication.

Think back over the service encounters which left you positively stunned—the ones that gave you goose bumps at the time and became the "you're-not-gonna-believe-this" substance of a service love story later. No, really do, stop...and recall. I'll wait. Bet you the story was about how the service provider "kissed and made up" after leaving you in a state of illogical lividness! What did they do to turn your emotional decibel level from growl to glee?

Service, unlike product, is about partnership. The objects you purchase are not the result of your participation in their creation. While you are a partner in the buying process, you are an end-user in the making process. You do not show up at the factory to help the manufacturer make the objects you buy. Service, on the other hand, requires the active involvement of the customer. Whether getting a haircut, driver's license, or checking out of the supermarket, the customer and service provider join in a "partnership" to produce an outcome and hopefully meet a need of both.

Continued

Successful partnerships of all types require extraordinary communications. Ask ten friends who are or have been divorced for the number one cause of their breakup. Eight will tell you communications, or else an answer which is really communications stated in a different way. Customer partnerships are no different. Especially when amiable turns to anger.

The key to converting customer lividness into customer loyalty lies not in "buying" back devotion ("How about I give you... your money back? A coupon worth? A new mink coat?"). Sure, symbolic atonement can help. However, the key to recovery is the way you use communication in a healing manner.

Healing begins with Humility... an expression of authenticity. The negative reaction Exxon received over the *Valdez* tragedy when compared with the positive reaction Johnson and Johnson received over the Tylenol tragedy lay less with culpability and more with authenticity of the communication. As Exxon opted for delayed vagueness, Johnson and Johnson chose assertive realness. Look at before and after market shares and see who won the consumer.

Healing includes expression of Empathy... words and actions which let the partner know you can appreciate their pain, plight, and predicament. It does NOT mean frontline servers have to wallow in the mire of bad feelings. Empathy communicates understanding and identification, not "tail between the legs" shame. Just as customers expect caring, they also prefer confidence.

Healing communication includes Agility... words and actions which tell the customer they are dealing with someone with the where-with-all to correct their problem. They want can-do competence, attentive urgency, and take-charge "I'll turn this around" attitudes. It sometimes takes finding ways to enfold customers in a joint search for a solution. Practicing the "people will care if they share" philosophy can increase the customer's commitment to the outcome and bolster the very best of partnering.

And, healing communication includes Longevity... the after-the-fact experiences of the customer which say, "we will not abandon you now that we have hopefully regained your business." It is the opposite of "taking for granted." It is about continuous care and frequent follow-up. It is telegraphing that loyalty is always a two-way street in any effective partnership. The best service providers view recovery as healing a broken relationship—through humility, empathy, agility, and longevity.

We are approaching an era in which "exceeding customer expectations" is the ticket, not just to success, but to survival; where extraordinary is being pursued as the norm. The challenge in all relationships is that dazzlement as a goal is much more realistic than dazzlement as a standard, or most of us would not have stayed married past our honeymoon! And, the glue that cements relationships between moments of dazzlement is the security of the partnership. True partners remain loyal through good times and bad, through sickness and health, and through price increases and mistakes. Such closeness starts with and continues with effective communication.[2]

So, recovery becomes yet another way to communicate our commitment to our customers in a creative way.

#327. I recently stayed in the Portland Hilton, Portland, Oregon, and was very disappointed with the condition of the room. I wrote a comment card and indicated my feelings about staying in a room I considered "tacky"—wallpaper peeling at the top of the room, stained carpeting and spreads, and tile missing from the bathroom floor. Several weeks later I received a letter of apology from the manager. It included a photocopy of a newspaper story telling of the thousands of dollars they were going to spend this summer on renovation. He also asked me to make my next reservation directly through him so he could ensure that my next stay would be more acceptable. I especially appreciated the newspaper story, for it added credibility to his comments and assured me that they *were* doing something about the problems in their rooms.

#328. Buckner Corporation of Fresno, California, has an interesting customer complaint program. It directs the executive in an area receiving a complaint to call the customer, apologize, and let the customer know what steps are being taken to resolve the problem. Often the executive also writes a letter of apology and sends the customer a small gift, such as a paper weight made in their foundry or a Buckner coffee mug.

#329. David Armstrong tells how important it is for leaders to recover when they make a mistake in "Leaders Make Mistakes, Too."

LEADERS MAKE MISTAKES, TOO

Armstrong-Hunt in Milton, Florida, had received an order for copper coils that we knew would be tricky to produce. The work required intricate welding, and after we were finished it was clear the job was not up to our standards. We were certain that it was just a matter of time before the welds would crack.

Chuck Rockwell, the general foreman, knew there were two possible solutions. We could scrap the coils and start over. That would cost us about $2,000 in material alone, and you'd have to add our labor costs on top of that. Our second option was to grind away the bad welds and try to salvage the job. Because Chuck had to pick me up at the airport, he left the decision up to his foreman.

By the time Chuck and I got to the plant, the foreman and his welders had decided to scrap the product and start over.

"It's my fault we had this problem," Chuck told me in front of his staff. "I knew from past experience that welding copper is extremely difficult,

Continued

but I didn't spend enough time with either our foreman or our welders to show them what needed to be done."

Chuck estimated that we could recover about $300 if the coils were sold for scrap. He decided to take the $300 and throw a party to celebrate his mistake because he was certain people would learn from it. From this day forward, he knew, we wouldn't undertake a new job until EVERY-ONE understood what needed to be done. They would also learn that EVERYONE makes mistakes, even the boss.

I am very proud of what Chuck did—for two reasons. In front of his co-workers and his boss (me), he took the responsibility for making a mistake. And he decided to celebrate it. Here's an outstanding example of a leader who led by example. He said PUBLICLY it's okay to fail.

You have to be brave enough to fail as a leader.
—Olle Bovan, Hewlett-Packard

THE MORAL OF THE STORY

- Celebrate your mistakes—publicly. Seeing is believing. People will come up with more ideas when their leaders demonstrate *by their actions* that they will support failure, especially when something is learned from it. If the boss can admit failure, then the troops feel more comfortable trying new ventures. How can the boss get upset if a good idea fails? After all, he/she's failed, too!
- Supporting failure does not mean supporting (or even tolerating) sloppiness. The only time failure is good is when (a) something is learned from it, and (b) the idea is quickly modified.
- To fail is not enough. You must fail big. Tom Peters said that, and he's right. Significant gains come from significant risks.[3]

#330. At Castle Medical Center in Kailua, Hawaii, if patients aren't happy with some aspect of the hospital's service, any employee has the power to make up to a $50 adjustment on their hospital bill, says Linda Wysong, director of quality management. Patients are given a choice of compensation for shoddy service—if they don't want the bill adjustment, they can receive a hospital mug or a rose. "In the two years we've run the program, we've had more patients ask for a mug or a rose than the $50," Wysong says. The hospital has given out 250 mugs or roses—at an estimated cost of $900—and only four $50 credits.[4]

#331. We have a number of "Recovery cards" that are available to our customers:

- One has a picture of a homing pigeon and says: "SO sorry. We evidently sent your materials the long way."
- One has a burglar sitting at a computer. It says: "Sorry we held you up."

- Another pictures a man cracking an egg on his head. It reads: "Boy, have I got egg on my face!"
- One shows a cat sticking his paw in a light socket, looking rather wild. Inside it says: "We didn't mean to overcharge you."

Our customers have loved these—both to receive when we have "goofed" and to use for their own mistakes with customers.

#332. Vision Financial Corporation in Keene, New Hampshire, has found its native maple syrup a valuable recovery tool! A little jug of maple syrup was included with an apology letter to an agent who was put in a difficult position through an oversight on the company's part. The note attached to the syrup read "Sorry for putting you in a *sticky* situation!" The apology was well received and the agent enjoyed the treat!

#333. A midwestern bank has a planned recovery program they call "Boo-boo Banking." The bank has worked with a florist to create "Boo-boo Bouquets," which come in a mug that includes the words "We're sorry" with the bank's logo. Every employee is empowered to send these bouquets when the bank makes a mistake. When they first began the program, the officers of the bank were afraid that employees would "go wild" and give away more bouquets than they had budgeted for. In fact, after the first six months, they had not even come close to using up the actual budget for the program. The customers loved these bouquets and often good-humoredly asked the employees to "please make a mistake" so that they could have one!

#334. At MCI International, a small customer with a sudden case of chronic breakdown and disappointment is referred to as a Customer At Risk (CAR). Those customers immediately become candidates for "CAR Pooling," or extra special handling and attention by service personnel. The CAR Pool process begins when a customer with a history of "troubles" is nominated as a CAR Pool candidate by a front-line service person or supervisor. Quality assurance and customer service managers review the nomination and assign a CAR Pool "driver" to the customer.

Every one of the 60-plus employees of the QA/CS staff is eligible for a CAR Pool driver assignment. The driver's key role is expedition: to "drive the rest of the organization" to find a permanent fix to a customer's recurring problem. The driver is expected to look for root causes, create a plan for a permanent resolution, and stay on top of the situation. In addition, the driver immediately opens a dialogue with the customer, establishes him/herself as the key contact and assures the customer that a special investigation of the problem is underway. According to Kim Charlesworth, senior manager for Quality Assurance at MCI, the CAR Pool concept, which emerged from a front-line employee problem-solving group, is a hit with customers and employees alike. The program is being expanded to include sales staff, so the CAR Pool net can be cast even wider.[5]

COMMUNICATION CHALLENGE. There are certain recoveries you can plan for—those "mis-takes" that seem to happen over and over in your organization. While you are working on improving systems and processes and giving training to make them better, you can immediately begin to recover with the customers who are negatively impacted by having a Recovery Plan. Always keep in mind the four steps of recovery. Pick several of these mistakes and decide what you can do for the customer to truly recover in a dazzling way—do it *soon* (set a time to aim for, such as within 36 or 48 hours), and do *something extra* (plan *exactly* what employees are empowered to do in each case, such as send a personal card or note, a letter written by the President of the company, a small bouquet of flowers, a certificate for something free from the organization, a book or mug the organization stocks, etc.). The important thing is to have a plan and then to *communicate* it to everyone in the organization. This attention to recovery becomes another important way for the organization to communicate its commitment.

ACTION PAGE

Chapter Eleven

Personal Executive Actions
Creative Ways for Senior Management to Communicate Commitment

Source: © Kaset International.

Amidst the massive outpouring of data, computer printouts, and television's tasteless wasteland, people are starving for authentic, caring human communication for the workforce. [Research shows that] the "image at the top" has a more profound impact on job attitudes than any other single factor in the work setting. . . . A whole new way to communicate can be developed using the "image at the top" as the medium through which caring and truthful interaction can be created.

Richard S. Ruch and Ronald Goodman,
Image at the Top—Crisis and Renaissance in Corporate Leadership

Alan Zaremba states the following:

If you want to assess your organization's communication quality, you'll need to examine the quality of the humans who communicate in your organization. Moreover, you'll need to assess your managers' willingness (and ability) to meet the human needs of their subordinates—particularly when communications regarding these needs require perspicacity and diplomacy. These communications are every bit as important to the overall communication quality of the organization as video tapes, house organs, and E-mail capabilities. In fact, they may be more significant. Interpersonal interaction that is gratuitously brusque, condescending, or otherwise insensitive can affect the entire climate of an organization—indirectly, if not directly, undermining organizational communication and overall quality.[1]

So we see the critical importance of executive actions in communicating the organization's commitment. Their visibility, their humanness, their authenticity, their personal commitment, their actions— all determine to a great extent how it goes in the organization. If all of these are *consistent* with the professed beliefs and values of the company, then their commitment has been put into action, and others will believe. However, if there is inconsistency between the professed beliefs and the day-to-day actions of the leaders of the organization, then employees will only see the hypocrisy and most will shun any depth of personal commitment themselves. As the leaders go (especially the leader at the top), so goes the organization!

COMMUNICATE THE VISION

Intellectual strategies alone will not motivate people. You must have people's hearts to inspire the hard work required to realize a vision.

> John Naisbitt and Patricia Aburdene, *Reinventing the Corporation*

One of the most important things the senior leader can do in his or her organization is to communicate that organization's vision in a clear, memorable, and inspiring way. James Mapes says, "A vision is like a lighthouse which illuminates rather than limits, gives direction rather than destination.... It is creating an ideal, preferred future with a grand purpose of greatness."[2] He goes on to say that there are several characteristics of a "grand vision":

- It's idealistic.
- It's from the heart.
- It's authentic.
- It's extraordinary.

Thus, as a leader communicates the organization's vision, he or she is, in fact, living out what employees want and need from their leaders. Mapes says, "A vision of greatness is an expression of the spiritual and idealistic sides of our nature. After all, the business world as well as our day-to-day existence is mostly about practical matters. When we touch the spiritual nature of people, they are much more likely to be moved to action than if we try to appeal to their logic."[3] As a result of the senior leader's communication of and commitment to a grand vision that is idealistic, from the heart, authentic, and extraordinary, employees will be able to develop their own personal sense of mission or vision.

Charles Garfield has spent years studying what he calls "peak performers"—those people who are the very best they can be at whatever their job is. He has found that one of the primary differentiators of peak performers from ordinary workers is their sense of mission or vision. Wherever I speak, I tell this story from his book about how one group of workers found their sense of mission:

> In every organization that does unusually well, I see people all the way up and down the line operating with a strong sense of mission. . . . A senior vice-president of an aerospace company in Southern California piqued my curiosity one afternoon as we talked about a series of workshops I had just conducted for his managers and technical people. Developing a sense of mission makes sense at the middle and higher levels of a company, he said. But he suggested that there must be levels at which peak performance is just impossible because people have so little control of their circumstances.
>
> "For instance," he said, "there's a group here that puzzles me. They maintain the pipes in our thermodynamics plant, checking temperatures and pressures. The situation makes me nervous. On the one hand, the enormous cost of the parts we test and the delicacy of the equipment means the pipes have to work within strict tolerances or there will be expensive damage. On the other hand, the work is mechanical and repetitive; essentially it's plumbing, and it seems impossible to me that anyone would find it even interesting, much less an occasion for peak performance. But here is the surprise: This group's attendance record is terrific; they have the lowest turnover in the entire company; their motivation is obviously high; their productivity and performance are excellent. How come?"
>
> I went to visit the department. Sam Harrison, the foreman, gave me a tour. At one point I asked why all his people wear green surgical smocks. "Oh, you noticed," Harrison said, "I got them from my son. He's a cardiovascular surgeon, and he got them so I could give them to the gang." "Ah," I said, "you wear them for comfort."
>
> "No, no!" Harrison said. "It's because we are surgeons. Just like my son. He takes care of the pipes in the body—you're worried about a heart attack, my son works on your arteries. We take care of the pipes in this plant. It isn't going to have any breakdowns as long as we're working on its arteries. We take care of these pipes the way a doctor takes care of your heart."
>
> Sure enough, the stencils on their locker doors said **Dr.,** and Sam used the title—with a grin—as he introduced his colleagues. Their statement of their mission—"take care of these pipes the way a doctor takes care of your heart"—matched its importance. The way they spoke to one another, the

mixed humor and pride with which they used surgery as their metaphor, helped them to share the special value that their work had for them.[4]

#335.   Ms. Yvonne Johnson, the Director of the Division of Rehabilitation Services of the state of Georgia, developed her vision for the division, had it videotaped, and distributed it across the state for all staff to view. The video contains nine ideas she has for the division, including that it be run with a "mixture of head and heart," that the employees be responsive and enthusiastic, that it be community based, that the staff adopt an attitude of "lifelong learning," that they develop resources for a wide variety of needs, that they be collaborators, enablers, supportive of clients and their families, and proponents of "quality service." She ends the video with the following statement: "After all, Georgians with disabilities are the reason and the ONLY reason we are here!"

#336.   Dick Bowers, City Manager of Scottsdale, Arizona, expresses his personal values and goals for the organization. He says, "We, as a team, must:
Learn from the past . . . and honor it!
Examine the present . . . and improve it!
Envision the future . . . and achieve it!
Keeping this mind, I am confident that we will build a strong 'rock' on which to launch an exciting future."

#337.   The President of Republic Mortgage Insurance Company in Winston-Salem, North Carolina, has created a vision he calls STEP (Service, Teamwork, Efficiency, Performance). He periodically gives his "STEP" talk to all departments. He discusses with them what STEP means to him and what he hopes it will mean to them as employees. He also personally introduces all service training programs and was a participant in the very first class.

#338.   Tim Peterson, a Professor in the Department of Marketing and Management at the University of Tulsa, told me an interesting way he asks senior managers to focus on their vision. He calls this exercise "The shield of excellence." He gives each of them two blank sturdy paper shields and a box of crayons. He reminds them of the medieval knights who each carried a shield that was symbolic of what they stood for and believed in. He then asks them to draw their vision of excellence, first for themselves personally and then for their organization. After discussing their creations, he then asks them to take their organizational vision of excellence shield back to their place of business. He suggests that they ask their direct reports as well as some other employees to draw their idea of a vision of excellence for their organization and then to compare them with that of the senior leader. The amount of similarity in the drawings will indicate how well that senior manager has been communicating the vision!

COMMUNICATION CHALLENGE. Is your organization's vision of greatness from the heart? Do your senior leaders communicate it from the heart? Do your employees, no matter what their jobs, have a sense of mission of the importance of what they do?

MANAGE BY WALKING AROUND

All managers have heard, it seems, of the much-touted practice of Managing By Walking (or Wandering) Around. However, what I have found in working a great deal with middle managers is that many of them know what it means intellectually, but they don't know *how* to do it, and they especially don't know how to do it on both the Business *and* the Human levels! In our management training at Kaset International we say: "Management By Walking Around (MBWA) is based on a very simple idea: If you don't know what's going on, you can't manage it. . . . Today's managers know they need to keep in touch with their employees, and they do it by getting out of their offices and into the areas where the work is going on. They're walking around, they're observing, they're talking, and above all, they're listening to what their employees (and their customers) are saying."[5]

When you walk around, you, as a leader, are communicating your commitment to your employees just by the fact that you're "out there." However, you can affect employees' belief in your commitment by *how* you walk around and *what* you say. Do employees see an interested, friendly person who is willing to help, if necessary, and wants to learn more about their jobs, or do they see a policeman, ready to criticize and punish? Do you ask questions like *"What are you doing?"* (Big brother is watching!) Or do you ask questions like *"How are you doing?"* (I am here to help you.) Open-ended questions will always elicit more information and will allow them a chance to really talk with you.

Several other things to consider as you're walking around are:

- Do it frequently and consistently.
- Make sure you get to all areas of the organization or department.
- Ask questions that indicate your commitment, both to the organizational mission and to your employees.
- Be human and even have some fun.

This is a list of questions a training class at Nationwide Insurance suggested that managers who view themselves as coaches or developers of people might ask their employees as they walk around:

How are you doing?
Are there things I can do to make your job easier?

What do you need . . . from me? from others?
What ideas do you have to make things better?
How is your workload?
How is your day going?
What are the questions our customers most frequently ask?
Ask them for help in learning some of what they do.
Look around—acknowledge personal things in their office.
Ask about their families.

Two of the questions I like to ask are: "That project really looks interesting. Can you tell me a little about it?" and "What have you learned today?" The last question has become a special way to end each day for me as well. It helps me to keep things in perspective and also to feel that even on the worst day, I have still accomplished something! (I often share that thought with those I ask.)

#339. Joseph Shaute shares the following idea for Managing By Walking Around:

> A great trick is for the president of a company to stop by the finance department Monday morning and pick up two $50 bills. As they walk around during the week, they find someone doing something right and hand the employee the two bills, congratulate the person and say the company would like to take the employee and a guest to dinner because of whatever it was they were doing. Imagine how many employees want to be discovered doing something right.[6]

Another executive I know keeps a number of $5 bills in his pocket and passes them out as he sees employees doing great things. He feels $5 is an amount big enough to pay for the employee's lunch but not significant enough to cause resentment from other employees.

#340. Jeff Sullivan, Director of Corporate Development and Training for Southwest Airlines, headquartered in Dallas, Texas, told me that the company has a mandate for all managers to be out of the office for 33 percent of the time to see "what's going on." They sell tickets, throw baggage, and work in many different capacities to truly understand what it's like for their employees.

COMMUNICATION CHALLENGE. Brainstorm with other leaders in your organization some nonthreatening questions to ask your employees as you walk around. Then determine a personal strategy to remind yourself to do it frequently and consistently. David Armstrong asks another challenging question: "When was the last time you spent any time with the people who work the second or third shift? Did you meet them when it was the middle of the day *for them?*"

SPEND TIME WITH SUPERVISORS, MANAGERS, AND EMPLOYEES

When a CEO makes champions of his or her staff, the staff in turn makes champions of the customer and this is a surefire way to make winners of us all.
Michael H. Mescon and Timothy S. Mescon,
Showing up for Work and Other Keys to Business Success

Remember the Human-Business model? If your employees only know you on the Business level, it can affect both the quality of their work as well as their commitment to the organizational values. If they do not see their leaders modeling internal caring, how can they be expected to care for their customers? Taking time from your busy schedule to spend time with individual or small groups of employees *really* communicates your commitment!

#341. Mr. John Fisher, CEO of Nationwide Insurance, tells the following story regarding his contacting a Nationwide employee in another state. He called an adjustor in Mesa, Arizona, and said, "Hello, this is John Fisher, President of Nationwide Insurance. How are you this afternoon?" The adjustor immediately responded, "WHAT THE HELL KIND OF PRACTICAL JOKE IS THIS?" So, if you are a senior level executive and have not made it a practice to contact employees frequently, be prepared for some humorous responses!

#342. Several organizations use breakfasts or lunches as special times for senior management to get to know employees better. "Lunch with Management" is a popular program at Iowa Electric Light and Power. People from meter readers to clerks to managers are invited to have lunch or breakfast with officers of the company. Each company officer commits to doing at least two lunches in each nine-month period of time. A schedule is sent out of who will be where, and employees can sign up to share that time with senior management. Some of these events are held in the general office, some in operations locations, and others in the power plants. Colleen Dykes, Communications Manager, says, "It is a wonderful opportunity for the senior managers to get 'out in the field'—each location decides what kind of lunch they will have, and sometimes these are box lunches on the backs of the trucks! Both managers and employees love these occasions."

#343. Greenville Utility Commission has an "Eat 'N Chat" program in which employees can have an informal breakfast or lunch with GUC general management. By filling out a coupon, randomly selected employees get to know Mr. Green and Mr. Ferren and have an opportunity to get together with co-workers they don't ordinarily see.

"THE BOSS SAYS THESE 'GETTING TO KNOW YOU' LUNCHES ARE WORTH THE EXTRA BUCK."

Source: © Kaset International.

#344. Hal Rosenbluth tells about his program to reach people:

> A couple of years ago I initiated a program in which anyone in the company could spend a day with me. Whatever my day includes, their day includes. They read what I read. They are a part of every phone call, client visit, meeting, or whatever else makes up my day. The only exception is any confidential human resource issue that might betray another associate's privacy. We call this our "Associate of the Day" program, and at first it took place every Tuesday. But it was so well received that I began to host an Associate of the Day each Tuesday, Wednesday, and Thursday, and sometimes two associates per day. The tradition still continues each week, but now we've expanded it to all leadership positions. Associates can also spend a day with the vice president or director of their choice.[7]

#345. To reinforce the importance of their safety efforts, President Fred Hafer and other Metropolitan Edison Company executives in Reading, Pennsylvania, have stood on chilly mornings in the parking lot to meet employees on their way to work, providing cafeteria gift certificates to celebrate their attainment of safe work hour goals and giving ice scrapers and thank you's to employees who were wearing seatbelts.

#346. President Joseph Viviano has begun an extremely creative and bold management program at Hershey Chocolate, U.S.A. He has committed Hershey to rotating senior-level employees between line and staff positions. In a novel experiment, a vice president for human resources was rotated with a plant manager. Over a six-month period and through many sleepless nights, both gained unique insights into the other's role and a newfound respect for line/staff relations. The experiment has been so successful that dozens of executives are on a waiting list for placement outside of their units. Viviano is dedicated to building multifunctional champions.[8]

#347. Stephen Wolf, Chairman and Chief Executive Officer of United Airlines, personally holds annual Chairman's Conferences all around the world. All employees are invited to attend one of the sessions. The final round was held in the cities of Los Angeles, Seattle, London, and Newark. Throughout his presentation and the question-and-answer session, Wolf mentions employees' outstanding efforts.

#348. Some senior leaders with whom I've worked have gotten involved with charitable endeavors sponsored by the organization, working alongside their employees at all levels to cook pancakes, load food on trucks, and collect and distribute used clothing in the inner city. When I spoke recently at the annual conference of the Georgia Division of Rehabilitation Services, I was privileged to stay for part of the evening. One of the activities at the end of the day was a dunk tank to collect money for the hurricane victims in Florida. One of the first very willing "victims" was Yvonne Johnson, the Director. When I was leaving, she hurried up to tell me goodbye, sopping wet and enjoying the laughter of her employees!

COMMUNICATION CHALLENGE. Do your senior leaders spend time with employees at all levels, and especially in an informal setting? Not only will the leaders learn "what is going on out there," but there will also be a new spirit in the organization as more and more employees experience upper management as human beings!

SUPPORT SERVICE QUALITY TRAINING EFFORTS

In an article entitled "To My CEO," M.H. Schwartz, the general manager of Enterprise Quality Systems Inc., in Silver Spring, Maryland, talks about how top management can provide hands-on leadership actions for Service Quality. The article recommends these actions for top management to show its support of training efforts for Service Quality:

> Visibly and vigorously support your education and training programs. Get the program onto general management meetings' agendas. Discuss the program one-on-one with various executives, managers, supervisors, and front-line people. Review the evaluations and recommendations provided by our surveys of attendees. Personally follow up to make certain that neither the surveys nor any other aspect of the program is a sham. . . . Personally attend early sessions of the courses. Make short visits to classes in session. Express appreciation for the participants' attendance. Let the participants know how you feel about them following up and applying the lessons of the course. Point out, so that participants can plainly see, that they and the company benefit just as much as the customers do. See to it that every manager makes similar visits.[9]

Here are some of the recommendations I make to senior level management when they begin training as a part of a Service Quality initiative:

- Kick off training sessions either in person or by video.
- Go through the training personally.
- Hand out certificates of completion at the end of training sessions.
- Stop by classes in session at breaks or at lunch. Ask participants about the training. Tell them about your experiences.
- Send letters of congratulations to all who have completed the training.
- USE THE SKILLS YOURSELF.

Certainly these actions take planning and valuable time; however, the payback is enormous when employees really do *believe* that you are supporting this whole training effort. These actions clearly and visibly demonstrate your commitment.

#349. Cadillac has a program it calls "Training by Example." Rosetta Riley, director of customer satisfaction at Cadillac, a division of General Motors, said that "leadership means managers must teach, coach, listen, encourage, guide, provide resources, remove impediments, and ensure the effectiveness of processes. 'Training by Example' was key to the cultural change that reinvigorated Cadillac. Members of the executive staff are the first to undergo any training considered critical. Then, no matter what the subject matter—technical skills, statistics, or leadership—the executives teach at least one class in the program."[10]

#350. William J. McGurk, President and CEO of The Savings Bank of Rockville, conducts "service quality" breakfasts for each branch office as a review and reminder of their customer service training efforts. These generally feature one aspect of superior customer service and provide opportunities for general discussion about the bank. The theme of the next round will be "It takes months to win a customer, but only seconds to lose one." He uses anecdotes and stories to prove the point that a small error can create a lot of ill will.

#351. At Standard Insurance, senior level executives do much of the facilitating for the supervisory and management level customer service classes. Current facilitators for "Managing Extraordinary Service" include the Assistant Vice President for Quality, the Senior Vice President for Group Insurance, and the newly appointed president of the company. What a positive message of senior level commitment this involvement sends!

#352. All participants in the Service/Quality training given by Centura Bank receive the following letter from the President of the bank:

Dear _____ ,

Congratulations on completing Achieving Extraordinary Customer Relations, our core service/quality course. I hope you enjoyed the class as much as I did. It really is the foundation of our Service/Quality Initiative. I believe these skills will lead to better relations with internal and external customers resulting in more enjoyment of work for all of us.

I have enclosed a koosh ball to help you remember to listen well, stay unhooked, and create PMCE's (Positive Memorable Customer Experiences). Have fun with it and thanks for your enthusiasm about continuous improvement at Centura.

Above and Beyond,

Bob Mauldin

#353. In a large eastern bank, a senior executive of the company personally writes to employees who receive customer compliment letters. Here are some of the things he says:

Congratulations and thank you (for a customer who received kind service). As you know, a Customer Friendly Environment is one of the Five Cornerstones of Quality Service. From reading the customer's letter, it is apparent that this is the environment you created for her. Keep up the good work. There is nothing any competitor can do when people like you are serving our customers so well.

And in another letter:

In her complimentary letter the customer was clearly impressed with your Responsiveness and Reliability, which are two of the Five Cornerstones of Service Quality. While it's no longer a surprise to have customers write letters about you, it's always a delight to receive them and an honor to be able to thank you on the Bank's behalf for the extra effort and results you consistently put forth. Keep up the superb work. We will certainly succeed in turning the corner to a new era of prosperity with people like you continuing to make the difference with our customers. Congratulations and thank you once again for a job well done.

#354. Commercebank has initiated a top-down approach to customer relations improvement. Guillermo Villar, chairman, Millar Wilson, president, and other board directors were among the first to participate in customer service training. Knowing the effort had top management commitment, employees at all levels participated in a "cascade" of training with enthusiasm!

#355. SaskPower's executive, as well as seniorlevel, management members believe in the benefits of Service Quality training. They show their support by personally attending and introducing each SQ training session. SaskPower is located in Regina, Saskatchewan.

#356. At Bank of Montreal's Quebec Division, all employees—from management to clerical—attending the customer service training course for two days are treated to lunch at one of the finest restaurants of Old Montreal. Bank of Montreal executives feel that the employees should experience a PMCE (Positive Memorable Customer Experience) firsthand, and this also shows how important their commitment to customer service is! Bank of Montreal ensures that the trained employee returns to a reinforcing environment by cascading the training down—from executive vice president to teller.

#357. Edwin Quinones, the President of Coopertiva de Seguros Multiples de Puerto Rico, an insurance company in Puerto Rico, attends the beginning of every customer relations seminar to show his personal involvement at all levels of the company. He discusses the changes being made in the company and his expectations for the participants in the class. He told me he considers customer service training an investment, not a cost!

#358. Republic Mortgage Insurance Company of Winston-Salem, North Carolina, has created a program for senior management (vice presidents, assistant vicepresidents, and some managers) to keep the customer service training skills alive. They call it the "Partnership Program." After attending the customer service training pilots (they were the first group to go through the training), each person was assigned a partner, someone with whom they do not normally work. These partners meet at least once a month for an hour, and their meetings are based on seven concepts, models, or skills from the training. Each month they are asked to review a concept or skill and discuss how they have observed that concept or skill in the workplace or to share changes they have made to reinforce or support that concept or skill. They then write a report about their meeting by the

15th of the month to Martha Carter, Training Service Facilitator, who shares their ideas with the whole group.

#359. Alberta Power presented a one-day Supervisory Information Session the day before supervisors and managers went through training for coaching customer service skills. These sessions were led by various members of senior management, including the chief operating officer, who led about 25 percent of them. The sessions were designed to give information on customer feedback, initiatives in the marketing area, better understanding of the utility's financial status, and the latest information on their customer service initiative. They also provided a question and answer time when a member(s) of senior management answered questions, often tough ones, on any subject.

#360. On the final night of the week-long certification of their customer service facilitators, Alberta Power held a dinner for the new facilitators. This dinner was attended by all members of the company's senior management team, the 10 executives who lead the company. "The message was given loud and clear," said Ron Chapman. "The company IS committed to this new direction—this focus on the customer. Our facilitators, who would be spending two days with every employee, were able to, convincingly, answer the skeptics about management's real commitment. This is not just another 'flavor of the month.'" The facilitators worked only part-time in the facilitation role—usually about 15 percent of the month, including being out of town two or three days, and this wasn't a part of their "job description." To show their support, the company provided regular feedback to their supervisors/managers on their efforts, including participant ratings; brought all their supervisors in for a luncheon midway through their one-year assignment; and at the end of the year, had a dinner to honor their spouses.

Ron went on to say, "One of the strongest messages that communicated commitment to the staff was Alberta Power management's decision to carry on with the initial customer service training of all employees despite an adverse rate decision from the regulatory authorities that resulted in budget cuts throughout the organization. Our history would have indicated that we would have been forced—reluctantly, of course—to 'defer' the training because of the tough economic impact. We didn't."

#361. Iowa Electric Light and Power has an incentive program known as the "Special K Campaign" to reward customer service employees for using the techniques they learned in customer service training. Consultants and collectors observed successfully using the skills receive "Special K Stamps of Approval" that can be redeemed for mini-breakfasts and, finally, a home-cooked breakfast *prepared and served by senior level executives.*

COMMUNICATION CHALLENGE. Are your leaders supporting skills training in your organization? The best support of all is taking part in the training.

COMMIT TO WORK ON THE FRONTLINE WITH CUSTOMERS

Realizing your vision (to become a customer-focused organization): Your executives will spend more time "walking the talk," listening, and learning. The action will be on the front lines and with the customers, and you can expect to find your executives where the action is. Your executives will be much closer to the customers and be far more accurate when they talk about "What customers want." (They) will be much closer to the people really responsible for achieving the mission—the people in teams on the front line.

Kenneth Johnston, *Busting Bureaucracy*

#362. At a southeastern bank the CEO spends one day a month, at a different branch each month, working as a teller or customer service rep. He "surprises" the branch by showing up for work with everyone else. The employees love it—they have to "help" him learn how to do their jobs, and he says it is the hardest day of the month!

#363. "It's a very humbling experience," said Linda Saferite, library director of the City of Scottsdale, Arizona. "I deal with the same frustrations as my staff. It also allows me to test the practical value of library policies and procedures." Linda is referring to the two hours each week she spends at Civic Center and Mustang Libraries' service counters. She checks out books and answers patrons' questions. Since 1987, she has made time to help citizens by "getting down in the trenches." Her front desk experience allows her to work with her library staff and analyze customers' likes and dislikes. While in the public spotlight, she wears a name badge with her title. One citizen commented, "I think it's great you're here!" On a more humorous note, one patron observed—"Gee, things must be tough!"

#364. The chairman and the president of H₂O Plus, a quality bath and skincare company, routinely visit stores to make observations and talk to salespeople and customers. Michael Hanna, Managing Director, told me that the president personally stocked the cosmetic cases at the newest store in Buenos Aires. In fact, the senior executives have a belief that store merchandising should be influenced more by the frontline salespeople than corporate merchandisers. When the president noticed in one store that the Luxury bath line was removed from the other bath products, he asked the salespeople, "How do you think it should be?" They told him it "should be" in the middle of the bath display. He listened to them, and as a result, sales of those products increased substantially!

#365. Kevin Jenkins, the President of Canadian Airlines International, works at least once a month on the frontlines. He puts on a uniform and "gets his hands dirty" doing such things as throwing baggage and checking people in. At the beginning of October he had been out 19 times to work such positions as airport check-in, cargo, customer relations, accounting, dispatch, reservations, in-flight, and ramp (baggage). These activities were reported to the employees in a newsletter article titled "Senior Management Leads the Journey." The newsletter also said:

> Good communication is critical in any quality improvement effort. You have seen senior management commitment to communication in the form of departmental newsletters (such as Contact, Insight, Airwaves, Baselink, and InfoCargo), the establishment of Canadian World videos and InfoToday daily information bulletin. For the past two years Mr. Jenkins and the senior management team have held employee sessions at each major base across the country answering employee questions. Also the company invested in an employee opinion survey that has helped prioritize and focus employee concerns.

#366. Several years ago Darryl Hartley-Leonard, the President of Hyatt Hotels, started what he called "Hyatt In Touch Day." On this day he closes Hyatt's corporate headquarters and dispatches his executives around the empire to work in hotels on the firing line. Hartley-Leonard becomes "Darryl the Doorman," unloading car trunks and hailing taxis or doing some other frontline job such as opening doors, checking in guests, or mixing drinks. "Hyatt In Touch Day reminds the corporate office that the field hotel people make the money for us," he says. "We don't make a dime here. The field deserves our respect."[11]

#367. It was Customer Day 1992, a day that saw United Airline's officers working shoulder-to-shoulder with employees at the airport and on-board aircraft, reports the *United Times*. Led by President and CEO Jack Pope, the officers travelled to 36 different airports on United's system to get a close-up view of service in the Friendly Skies. "The best way to understand a service business like ours is to get as close to the customer as possible," explains Pope. "That means spending time on the front lines of our operation, especially during the heat of the summer travel season."

In an office tucked away in United's San Francisco cargo warehouse, a VP of Cargo matched airway bills with other freight documents. Behind the ticket counter at Narita, a VP of Reservations moved baggage onto conveyor belts. At Houston's Hobby Airport a VP of Reservations placed the blocks under the wheels of a B-737 after it was guided to the gate. Other officers worked in Customer Service, Ramp Service, Maintenance, cleaning cabins, and even the flight kitchen. The efforts of the officers were well-received by the employees who worked with them. "I'm glad they're working around the system," said a Houston Customer Service Rep. "This way they can experience the challenges we face day in and day out and really understand our jobs."

In recent months United's officers have become more active in customer service. Some of them participated in the "Day in the Life of a Travel Agent" program, and many regularly call and write disserviced customers to help win them back to United.

COMMUNICATION CHALLENGE. Do your senior managers work on the frontline with customers? If not, why not issue them an invitation?

VISIT CUSTOMERS

Managers should spend part of their time regularly working with customers. Not selling, but visiting them, talking with them, and asking about their needs. Sometimes managers are so busy managing, they forget about customers. Service 1st Corporation surveyed over 80 companies of all sizes about their service practices and found that 66 percent of senior managers spend less than 25 percent of their time with customers.

Jeffrey E. Disend, *How to Provide Excellent Service in Any Organization*

#368. At Seafirst Bank, executives are encouraged to get out of the office and visit branches. Chairman Luke Helms personally visits 10 locations per week.

#369. At The Savings Bank of Rockville, the Marketing Director coordinates a bi-monthly branch visit program where Senior Officers visit each branch for two hours on a busy day to meet with customers, ask questions, and receive comments. These visits are posted in advance at each location.

#370. At Drake University in Des Moines, Iowa, the president of the university and his wife host a reception in their home during the summer orientation sessions for all new students and their parents, the university's "customers."

#371. One of the 10 points in Fresno, California, based Buckner Corporation's 10-Point Customer Satisfaction Plan is: All executive staff members are required to make at least three visits per fiscal year to a customer's business.

#372. Gary Wheaton/First Chicago Bank has found a unique way for its managers to meet its customers. Office by office, the bank president and the senior managers spend time out in the drive-ups washing customers' windshields while they are waiting in line!

#373. United Airlines has organized a program in which all the officers of the airline will, over a period of several days, travel around the country to visit customers. They will meet with senior people in major corporations to talk with them about United's service and how the airline can better meet their corporate needs.

COMMUNICATION CHALLENGE. Do your senior managers visit customers? If so, how often? If not, why not suggest a plan?

REFLECT KEY VALUES IN DAY-TO-DAY BEHAVIOR

The challenge is not just finding ways to say the words, but more authentic ways to live the words, to WALK THE TALK.
                              Karl Albrecht and Ron Zemke, *Service America*

Business Level

Supporting your organization's beliefs and values on the Business level is extremely important, for it indicates you are willing to "put your time and money where your mouth is"—to take action, to learn, to make changes, to adapt to a new culture, and even to sacrifice to show your commitment.

#374. At Cuyahoga Savings the top 16 executives meet monthly for an all-day session on customer service improvements. Chet Kermode, Senior Vice President, shared that they do the following kinds of activities:

- Use videos for discussion and interaction.
- Read recent books in the field and report how they are implementing ideas in the book.
- Captain a QST (Quality Service Team) that is assigned a quality problem and reports back to the whole group on recommended solutions.
- Role play moments of truth with customers and critique one another.
- Review recent market research.
- Report on customer feedback score trends from regular surveys of both internal and external customers.
- Plan organization-wide training.

#375. Ben and Jerry's ice cream has adopted a 7-to-1 salary ratio. From top to bottom, no one can make more than seven times as much as anyone else makes. This decision involves a commitment by top level management to balance profits at all levels of the organization, reinforcing the value of every employee.[12]

#376. All members of the Service/Quality Steering Committee, the Task Force Leaders, and the Executive Group of Centura Bank in Rocky Mount, North Carolina, recently agreed to do two things:

1. To read the book *Busting Bureaucracy* by Ken Johnston. They discussed the six principles of the bureaucratic organizing form and the negative byproducts it causes.
2. To visit Cummins Diesel Company plant, because they have a great reputation for quality.

Willard Ross, Senior Vice President and Service/Quality Leader, has attended an S/Q forum with S/Q leaders of five other banks to exchange ideas. He recently visited the Bank of Stanley to exchange ideas with them. This open forum has resulted in better communication within the industry as well as shared improvements.

COMMUNICATION CHALLENGE. What can you do to foster learning that supports your organizational commitment?

Human Level

According to Tom Peters,

> If YOU care, THEY will care. If busy leaders consistently demonstrate that they care about employees, then the odds of employees caring about customers goes up dramatically. It's as simple as that, though it takes a lifetime of dedication and awareness to pull it off. Sure, I've said it before. But it needs repeating, and repeating, and repeating again.... Consultants and gurus routinely offer seven-step methods for achieving this and that—for example, customer-first culture—at seven figure prices. But they ignore the main issue, which is care, concern, and the small human gesture.[13]

AT THAT POINT THE BOSS RANG FOR THE VICE PRESIDENT IN CHARGE OF "POSITIVE SELF IMAGING".

Source: © Kaset International.

#377. At a very stressful time for her employees, Peggy Castlen, an officer of the Life Insurance Division of Nationwide Insurance in Columbus, Ohio, gave each of them a roll of Life Savers tied with a bow.

#378. At another time, the Life counselors had been working with a number of unassigned employees to help them find other jobs within Nationwide. This project had a definite time frame, and the counselors were involved on both the Business and the Human levels with these employees. On the last day, even after many hours of coaching and support, several of the people had not been able to be placed by Nationwide, and the counselors were feeling pretty down. Peggy Castlen, the same manager who gave them the Life Savers, brought them each hot water, herbal tea bags, and soothing recorded music.

#379. One manager with whom I worked gave each of his employees five "Helping Hands" cut out of paper for Christmas. Each one of these hands entitled them to one hour of his time during the year—to do anything they requested. That year he had sorted mail, delivered packages, answered the telephones, manned the front desk, collated and stapled papers, and even mowed a front yard! He said the real fun was in hearing the employees talk about all the things they were going to have him do. Some who did the most talking did not even redeem their full five hours—they had more fun planning than actually doing! The "gift" created a special bonding between the manager and his employees as well as giving him a feel for a lot of the work they did.

#380. A large manufacturing company that makes lawn mowers, tractors, and other pieces of equipment has been successful in employee and customer relationships by really working at communicating commitment. The president hosts picnics where he and his family cook and serve the food. When some deep tragedies struck several employees within a three-month period, he invited his minister to the plant to counsel and help employees through the grieving process.

#381. John Darrington, the City Manager of the City of Gillette, Wyoming, has a form letter that begins "Dear John," followed by blank lines. The "Dear John" letter was developed as part of the Excellence in Government Program, which was implemented in 1985. These forms are available in the Excellence Center and in each work area of the company. The letters say "for John's eyes only" on the outside and are for employees who want to communicate with him in a strictly confidential way, bypassing the normal chain of command. At the bottom of the letter there are boxes to check for the follow-up they would like from him. The idea is very popular with employees, and this is what John Darrington has to say about them:

The letters that are confidential generally have eight to ten staples around the outside to make sure no one has peeked at the contents! "Dear John" letters deal with a variety of topics. One of the first ones I received in Gillette had to do with a nuisance item for a police officer. The automatic shutoff on the hot water in the police station restroom would not stay on long enough for him to wash his hands. He had brought it to the attention of the custodians several times and nothing was done; therefore he sent me a "Dear John." I have also received "Dear John" letters from city employees about bidding policies, work place problems, and even seeking recognition from some employee whose work has gone unnoticed. I believe the "Dear John" letters are an effective means of handling nagging or persistent problems where traditional avenues of resolution have failed, and the employee does not want to make

Date   , 19

Dear John,

_____

_____

_____

_____

_____

_____

_____

_____

_____

_____

_____

*Signed ,*_____

Publish in Newsletter ( )   Do Not Publish In Newletter ( )

Verbal Response ( )   Written Response ( )

Forward to Excellence Committee ( )   Strictly Confidential ( )

Source: City of Gillette, Wyoming.

a big thing out of it by going to the Grievance Committee. Also it keeps the Administrator aware of what is happening in the "trenches."

COMMUNICATION CHALLENGE. What are you doing on a Human level to communicate your commitment?

SUPPORT COMMUNITY SERVICE PROJECTS AND SOCIETAL RESPONSIBILITY

Today more than ever before customers are demanding that organizations take some societal responsibility to contribute to their communities, to protect the environment, to give something back to the world in some way.

#382. A recent pamphlet on National Consumer's Week called "Operation Wise Buy" suggests some ideas for organizations interested in helping consumers:

- Have utilities sponsor a safety fair for school age children highlighting product safety, home safety, and car safety.
- Have hospitals or other healthcare facilities and insurance companies sponsor a health fair with information on how consumers can choose a health care provider and insurance companies.
- Have government organizations create consumer games that test awareness and understanding of "environmentally friendly" advertising terms, such as recyclable, biodegradable, and ozone friendly.
- Have financial institutions develop a money management workshop targeted to several special interest groups, for example, high school seniors, consumers with various cultural backgrounds, physically or mentally challenged consumers, senior citizens, and low income consumers. Program ideas include information on criteria needs for consumers to qualify for mortgage loans.
- Another idea for financial institutions is to conduct a multi-media public service campaign promoting the responsible use of credit.
- Other organizations may distribute information on cost-effective alternatives for achieving physical fitness. Develop a guide to fitness and recreation centers that are available free or at a reduced cost to consumers.
- For younger kids, you may want to develop a poster contest that encourages consumers to use fairy tale or nursery rhyme characters to help them relate to the concept of being smart consumers. For example, the nursery rhyme "Jack Sprat" could be used to encourage children to eat healthy foods.[14]

#383. The National Association of Female Executives Women's Foundation is starting a program to match NAFE members in

New York with young women from the inner city "in an effort to encourage mentorship and foster the continuation of future generations of professional women," according to Wendy Reid Crisp, NAFE's national director. "The aim is to instill a sense of self-esteem in these girls and to intervene at a time in their lives when we can really make a difference," says Brenda Ginsberg, NAFE's marketing director, who, along with 50 executive women, is spearheading the program called ESTEEM TEAMS. The plan begins by pairing professional women and girls between the ages of 11 and 13 one-on-one, then combining each of these pairs with four others to form teams. This will provide each young woman with not only a mentor who will give her guidance and tutoring, but also a network of her peers and four other executive women. Besides regular one-on-one and team meetings, each mentor will invite her team to her home or office once a year, and an annual retreat for the entire group of teams will be held.[15]

LIFE SUPPORT PROGRAM

Source: Clark Public Utilities.

#384. Clark Public Utilities in Vancouver, Washington, recently began a "Life Support Program." Many people consider electricity to be a basic necessity, but for some customers it's a matter of life or death. The representatives from several departments met to determine a plan, and the group decided to place some visual identification of these customers on their electric meters to prevent a mistaken disconnection. The first step was to maintain *one* list of people on life-support equipment in *one* place. Then Customer Assistance Representatives contacted each customer by phone or paid them a visit at home "to update information on their medical condition, equipment used, and the type of emergency back-up system they have," said Nancy Youngs. "And we also kept our eyes and ears open for any other needs these customers might have." In addition, a notice was run in the bill insert UPDATE asking all customers on life-support to contact the utility. Now the Dispatch Center will know the substations and feeder lines that serve some of the most critical life-support systems so that these customers will get priority for power restoration during an outage. "We will also be prepared to deliver generators to some of them, if need be," said Technical Superintendent Harlow. All of these steps have made the utility ready to respond to its most dependent customers!

#385. The City of Scottsdale, Arizona, recently received national recognition for two of its programs. At the 59th Annual Conference of Mayors, "Partnerships With and For the Elderly," the home-delivered meals program, was acknowledged for providing needed nutrition to homebound residents of Scottsdale. The Senior Center's brokerage concept was also recognized. This program houses several human service agencies at the center, which gives citizens a "one stop shop" for services such as nutrition and tax counseling. In the same issue of the newsletter announcing these awards I read the following: "ANY VOLUNTEERS? Interested in reading to children at the Family Emergency Services Center—a homeless shelter in Mesa? Call (extension number given)."

#386. Cuyahoga Savings has helped to feed, clothe, and house homeless families through University Settlement as well as providing rooms and scheduling appointments during the recent income tax season for the AARP Tax Counseling for the Elderly Program, which provided free tax service to over 50 senior taxpayers. (The savings bank is continuing both programs this year.) Volunteer counselors, trained in cooperation with the IRS, performed this service.

#387. First Chicago Bank has a strong commitment to the community. Recently, employee volunteers spent one week in the Uptown area of Chicago cooking breakfast at Inspiration Cafe, a restaurant for the homeless. Even a division president was involved in serving food to the people. (He planned to return to help cook the dinner on Saturday night as well.) WLS-TV filmed some of this endeavor. Another community activity of First Chicago is the presentation of a financial workshop it has created for people in low and moderate economic areas. They found that many residents were intimidated by banks and did not know how to use banks or even how to write checks. Instead, they were using currency exchanges and paying high percentages for service. So, this free workshop was designed to teach them about banking, budgeting, and such things as how to change their credit rating. At one of the workshops, a division president spent a whole evening talking with the participants, which impressed them greatly and helped to change their image about banks and people who work there. Bank employees also put together a reference book for the attendees to take with them.

#388. Because tour groups were dismayed by the desperate economic plight of the Russian people when they visited the country and kept asking what they could do, General Tours introduced "Feed a Friend." This program invites tour participants to pack their luggage with humanitarian aid. "Since January, General Tours travelers have been heading to Russia toting boxes filled with such nonperishable all-American fare as cereal, peanut butter and jelly, and canned hams. And the stop at a St. Petersburg or Moscow school, where the packages are given to children to take home to their families, is now a staple of the itinerary."[16]

#389. Since April 1988, Greenville Utilities Commission has been a part of the nationwide Gatekeeper Program to assist the isolated elderly. In the normal course of their jobs, Meter Readers and Meter Service Workers look for signs and symptoms in older people that may indicate a problem—mail piling up, uncut lawns, unattended pets, confusion, etc.

Recently one of the Meter Service Workers was flagged down by an elderly lady (about 90 years old and on crutches) who asked if he could find out why her refrigerator was without power. He investigated and found that the problem was in the circuit. He also noticed that there was virtually no food in the refrigerator. He was able to temporarily restore power to her refrigerator, but more importantly, as a part of the Gatekeeper Program, he contacted his supervisor, who then called the Pitt County Council on Aging, the Gatekeeper agency that follows up on reported problems. The Council on Aging put the lady on its list for meal delivery and sent someone out to permanently repair the circuit for the refrigerator.

Dave Frasier, the Director of Customer Relations at GUC, told the following story from a past employment experience:

Part of the job for field people and inspectors of the Water Division is to test the water when leaks are reported in people's yards to determine if it is from the ground or if it is treated water from a broken pipe. After testing the water in the yard of an elderly lady, the service person determined that it was, in fact, treated water leaking from the service line. He notified her that her water would be cut off because of the leak until the line could be repaired. The service person did everything "according to the book." However, the company learned much later that the elderly lady was so upset that she didn't know whom to call or whom to trust or what to do without water that she cried for several days, had a breakdown, and died of a heart attack. In reviewing the incident, if only the service person had taken a little extra time, even though it wasn't in his normal routine, advised her whom to call and reassured her of the time involved and perhaps suggested some options for her to get water, she might still be alive. He could have responded to her on the HUMAN level. This is what the Gatekeeper program helps us all to remember!

#390. One of the individual goals of the "Goal Rush" incentive program at Clark Public Utilities, Vancouver, Washington, is "To have all employees participate for six hours in one or more authorized outreach activities outside of normal working hours." Some of the opportunities are:

- A Tree Stuffing Party—Ten thousand Douglas Fir trees will be stuffed into plastic bags, brochures will be attached, and then bags will be bundled for distribution to Boy Scouts, who will deliver them to residences as they pick up Christmas trees for recycling.
- "Stream Team Salmon Creek"—A variety of projects, including litter pick-up, farm fencing, stream-bank plantings, and brush pruning, will be carried out along Salmon Creek and its tributaries.
- Clark County Home & Garden Idea Fair, Clark County Fairgrounds—The utility is sponsoring this major event and will have several booths to staff and other opportunities to assist with clinics, demonstrations, and workshops.

#391. Hy-Vee Grocery Store in Harlan, Iowa, has a strong community support program. Earlier this year they worked with a group of parents called "People Who Care" to sponsor a Drug and Alcohol Prevention party for the teenagers of the community. The store contacted a radio D.J., brought in sand to cover their parking lot, and had a beach party/sandlot dance, promoting the idea that you can have a good time without alcohol! They and some of their vendors also supply all the food to sponsor a "Little League Feed." Anyone in the community can attend for a small fee, and all the proceeds go to the local Little League.

#392. As a part of Operation Feed, supported by corporations all over the country, Nationwide Insurance's home office in Columbus, Ohio, has a program called the "Food Pantry Project."

Along with the sponsorship of the local Kroger grocery stores, which sell canned goods to Nationwide at their cost, each department competes to see which one can collect the most food. Not only are they helping the hungry, but they are also having fun, and there are even prizes donated. For example, some employees volunteered their time to teach others "Lotus 1-2-3." To get into the class, each person had to purchase $5 of food. Other employees offered golf lessons for food donations; an optometrist gave eye exams to get commitment from employees to participate. The Nationaires, a company singing group, sold their albums at a discount price and used the money to purchase food. Some departments had pizza parties and charged $1 extra as a donation to the "Food Pantry." One even had a pie throw, using senior managers as "targets," and the money collected from ticket sales went for food. At the regional office in Syracuse, New York, they auctioned managers to the highest bidder to be used for two hours in any way that the group wanted, as long as it was business related. They "bid" with cans of food, the highest bid being 150 cans! All the food that is collected is delivered by Kroger to a distribution center where it is given to the homeless, missions, and churches.

#393. Darryl Hartley-Leonard, President of Hyatt Hotels, has committed to attacking pressing problems in every North American city where its 104 hotels and resorts are located. Crediting an idea created by a regional vice president, Hartley-Leonard began the Hyatt F.O.R.C.E. (Family of Responsible and Caring Employees). Every manager receives four paid days off a year to volunteer. About 1,000 Hyatt employees are involved in the community each month. They do such things as coordinating children's recreation at a sexual and physical abuse victim's center in Scottsdale, translating cookbooks and restaurant menus into braille at the Lighthouse for the Blind in New Orleans, and sweeping the streets in San Francisco every Wednesday. As part of a pilot program, the Hyatt Regency San Francisco took a homeless person off the street and trained him for a hotel job. "This sends a message to all of our employees—that Hyatt is socially conscious—and people want to work for a company with that attitude," Hartley-Leonard says.[17]

#394. Thrifty Auto Rental in Tulsa, Oklahoma, did a study several years ago to determine the value of discounts to seniors. Eleven percent of respondents said a discount would be a "very important" factor in choosing a Thrifty rental car. A second question was posed: If in lieu of a 10% discount, an equivalent amount of money from sales went into a pool to buy vans for senior citizens, would that influence the buying decision? Over 41% said yes. Thrifty thereupon launched a very successful program called, "Give a Friend a Lift."[18]

#395. Gary Wheaton/First Chicago Bank is the first bank in Illinois to participate in a recycling program for checks. Customers can have their choice of either getting their actual cancelled checks back or receiving images of their checks on a special form that includes 18 checks to the page. Their actual checks then become a part of an environmental recycling program.

#396. Clark Public Utilities has a "Community Care program," or ComCare for short, to meet the needs of customers with special or unique circumstances, such as the elderly, low-income nonelderly, and those who are temporarily disadvantaged. ComCare uses Clark Public Utilities' contact with customers in need to make sure they know about assistance that is available to them. Help from the ComCare Representative is available to any customer who wants to pay their bill, but is experiencing difficulty doing so. The Comcare Representative will gladly take time with customers who have special needs, including elderly and handicapped customers and also those who are experiencing difficulties due to health problems, loss of a family wage earner, family breakup, or other crisis situation. Assistance includes such things as directing the customer to available sources of financial assistance for paying utility bills, helping them understand their bill, providing advice on budgeting, showing customers how to reduce energy use by arranging a walk-through home energy audit, making arrangements for applying for any available home weatherization programs, and offering help with other basic needs, including locating food, financial assistance, employment, affordable housing, and medical assistance. The goal of this program is to resolve problems prior to disconnection of service. The utility also has a Guarantee of Service plan, discussed in Chapter 3, #60, which requires only a minimal payment each month for those with difficulties.

#397. United Airlines kicked off its first companywide Green Week in April to promote environmental awareness and the importance of the world's natural resources. Employees at locations across the United States, including Boston, Chicago, Denver, Portland, Seattle, and San Francisco, set up environmental awareness displays and met with environmental experts and vendors to share information and discuss responsible ways to recycle, reduce, and reuse materials. Other Green Week events included scrap metal and aluminum can drives in Seattle and Boston; clothing drives in Chicago, Detroit, and Portland; and tree plantings in Chicago, Detroit, and San Francisco. Washington Dulles' recycling newsletter published a special Green Week issue offering employees information on recycling at work and at home.

#398. ARC International Ltd., a company that provides organizational effectiveness training and services to U.S. organizations, established the One World One People Foundation in 1991 in conjunction with the publication of its book *ONE WORLD ONE*

CHILD. The foundation, located in Englewood, Colorado, is committed to enhancing the quality of children's lives. Robert White, the founder of ARC, writes in informational materials for donors:

> Through our own personal experience in raising two adopted children, one a crack baby and the other a victim of physical abuse, we have experienced firsthand the destructive effects of abuse and neglect upon our children. If we are to have a chance to fulfill the vision of a world that works for all of its people and halt this cycle of abuse and neglect, we must begin by nurturing our children and healing the child within all of us.
>
> We intend to use ONE WORLD ONE CHILD as a fund raising vehicle to support non-profit organizations that deal with the root causes of abuse and neglect and are intervening to halt this destructive cycle. ALL profits from the sale of ONE WORLD ONE CHILD will flow to the foundation which, in turn, will provide financial and technical support to those non-profit organizations committed to enhancing the quality of children's lives. ONE WORLD ONE CHILD is a beginning, a step forward to reverse this cycle of abuse and neglect to reach a place where children are proclaimed, honored, and respected for the gift that they are.

#399. Dr. Jeff Alexander, a children's dentist in Oakland, California, had a marvelous idea to create interaction between children and seniors. As he was doing some volunteer work in a convalescent home one day, he noticed how many bedridden, yet fully alert, people there were there. He began to think about the children in his office and some of the questions they asked. The next time he returned he asked one of the bedridden women if she would like to be the "tooth fairy." She was thrilled, so he began having his "customers" call her whenever they had a tooth removed. In fact, he placed the number of the "tooth fairy" right next to the phones in his office for *any* of the children to call. When he returned to the convalescent home, he was barraged with folks who wanted to be "the fairy." So, the home put up a monthly schedule on the bulletin board and men or women, whoever wanted to be the "tooth fairy" for an hour, could volunteer. It became the first tooth fairy network!

COMMUNICATION CHALLENGE. What is your organization doing to discharge its societal responsibility? Remember, these programs can be fun for your employees as well as a meaningful way to communicate your commitment.

ACTION PAGE

Chapter Twelve

Summary
Flying Free

I hope you have enjoyed reading this book and imagining how you could adapt some of these ideas to your own organization as much as I have enjoyed putting it together. Here are some of the things I have learned in the process:

1. Creativity is all around us. Just look at the *variety* of organizations and individuals whose ideas I have used. I rarely sat next to someone on an airplane without gaining an idea or two! What I discovered is that often we are so accustomed to the way we do things in our organization, we don't realize how innovatiove our ideas may be. (Remember the Way It Is model?)

2. This compilation of ideas is only a beginning. I got ideas from the people I happened to know or meet in my travels, organizations I'd worked with at some time, Kaset customers, places I've experienced, things I've read, or from folks who heard me speak. Because my experience is limited, so are the ideas presented. I will be waiting to hear other ideas from you.

3. It is much more fun to work in a creative, committed environment. The people who shared their ideas with me were excited, enthusiastic, and committed to their organizations with a loyalty, a pride, and a zest that were contagious.

In his book *The Creative Corporation*, Karl Albrecht writes: "We are going to need organizations that are culturally equipped to adapt. They must have internal processes that are creative, generative, and productive rather than controlled, confining, and normative. In short, we must UNSHACKLE THE HUMAN BRAIN and exploit its productive potential."

I hope this book has begun the process of "unshackling your brain"—that you have been stimulated to leave your comfortable cocoon of routine communication to experience the creative potential available in all areas of communication within your organization. As you can see, many individuals and organizations of all kinds are challenging the limitations of "conventional" communication methods to share their values and beliefs. You can, too! And as you do so, your commitment, either as an individual or as an organization, will be understood in a new and powerful way.

I challenge you to begin with the ideas you've noted in your action plan—implement one this month, one next month, and continue this plan for the next 12 months in your workplace or organization. I have added a 12-Month Action Planner for you at the end of this book. As you begin to use some of the creative ideas of others, I hope your own creative spirit will begin to emerge, and that after several months you will start to generate your *very own* creative communication techniques.

My request to you is that you will consider taking time to let me know what you're doing, by letter, fax, or phone, so that I may share your metamorphosis with others. There is a beautiful freedom that comes from loosening up your thinking, and that spirit can permeate your organization with a new zest for continuous improvement, dazzling customer service, and more fun in the workplace!

I end with a challenge that is implicit in a poem that Rick Phillips presented to participants at a recent ASTD presentation:

The Comfort Zone

I used to have a comfort zone where I knew I couldn't fail.
The same four walls and busy work were really more like jail.
I longed, so much, to do the things I'd never done before,
But I stayed inside my comfort zone and paced the same old floor.

I said it didn't matter that I wasn't doing much.
I said I didn't care for things like diamonds, cars, and such.
I claimed to be so busy with the things inside the zone;
But deep inside I longed for some victory of my own.

I couldn't let my life go by just watching others win!
I held my breath and stepped outside to let the change begin!
I took a step and with new strength I'd never felt before,
I kissed my comfort zone good-by and closed and locked the door.

If you are in a comfort zone afraid to venture out,
Remember that all winners at one time were filled with doubt.
A step or two and words of praise can make your dreams come true.
Greet your future with a smile, success is there for you!

Author Unknown

Take the risk and leave your comfort zone, that boring cocoon, behind. May the butterfly, not the caterpillar, represent your new way of communicating your commitment!

12-MONTH ACTION PLANNER

JANUARY:

FEBRUARY:

MARCH:

APRIL:

MAY:

JUNE:

JULY:

AUGUST:

SEPTEMBER:

OCTOBER:

NOVEMBER:

DECEMBER:

Appendix

Additional Statements of Purpose

MISSION STATEMENTS

Customer service employees helped write this mission statement for a well-known financial institution: "To provide investors with prompt, accurate, sparkling, world-class service. Accurate means more friendly, caring and flexible than anyone else, in any business."

The First New Hampshire Bank's Mission Statement, which is posted throughout the organization, reads:

> There is something about First New Hampshire Banks that attracts and retains the public: "excellence in the customer's eyes"—namely, First New Hampshire Banks is the most courteous, most helpful, most understanding, most caring in professionally determining and competently fulfilling our customer's individual goals and objectives.

CalFarm Insurance Company has the following Customer Service Mission Statement: "DO IT ONCE! DO IT RIGHT! DO IT NOW!"

1. CalFarm Insurance Company strives to be a caring, responsive organization, providing quality service to all customers.
2. CalFarm Insurance Company recognizes that the customer is our most important asset. The customer is EVERYONE for whom we provide service: consumer, agent and fellow employee.
3. CalFarm employees are dedicated to the concept that service begins with each individual maintaining a courteous, professional and positive attitude.
4. Quality service means DOING IT RIGHT AND DOING IT PROMPTLY and doing our best to satisfy the customer.

VISION STATEMENTS, PHILOSOPHIES, AND VALUES

Cuyahoga Savings sends "AN IMPORTANT MESSAGE TO OUR CUYAHOGA SAVINGS CUSTOMER." YOU ARE:

* the most important person in our business.
* not dependent upon us—we are dependent upon you.

- not an interruption of our work—you are the purpose of it.
- doing us a favor when you call or visit. We are not doing you a favor by providing exceptional customer service.
- part of our business—not an outsider.
- a flesh and blood human being with feelings and emotions like our own. You deserve to be treated with kindness, compassion, and respect.
- deserving of the most courteous and attentive treatment we can give.
- the man or woman behind our paychecks.
- the life-blood of our business. Without customers, we would have to close our doors.

The Savings Bank of Rockville has a "CUSTOMER CREED":

- The Customer is our reason for being here.
- It takes months to find a customer; seconds to lose one.
- Always be courteous and polite during each customer contact.
- Always do more than is expected when you handle a customer's problem.
- Never promise more than we can deliver.
- Continually look for ways to improve quality and add value to products our customers purchase.

As a kickoff for their Quality effort at Standard Insurance, all of the Home Office management staff were taken to the local Japanese Garden for three separate one-day retreats to share the Quality vision and to explore Leadership topics. During the retreat each manager was given the opportunity to sign his or her name to a large blowup of the Quality Service Vision Statement (Commitment). Then they framed the poster-board and hung it in the foyer of their new training facility for all employees to see as they come through training classes, a constant reminder of the organization's beliefs and values.

Ken Blanchard has spoken about how Florida Power and Light used employee groups chosen by their peers to create a vision of what kind of an organization they wanted to be. The company took these specially chosen employees off their jobs for six months, and at the end of that time, the employees had determined four characteristics they felt their organization should achieve:

1. Be customer-driven.
2. Be cost-effective.
3. Be fast and flexible.
4. Have a philosophy of continuous improvement.

Rosenbluth Travel in Philadelphia, Pennsylvania, operates on the following hierarchy of concerns—people, service, profits, in that order. Hal Rosenbluth, in *The Customer Comes Second*, says, "The company's focus is on its people. Our people then focus on serving our clients. Profits are the results. Human beings must be the pillars of a company. They provide an unshakable foundation."[1]

This is the Vision, Mission, and Cooperative Strategy of Coopertiva de Seguros Multiples de Puerto Rico, San Juan, Puerto Rico, which is printed throughout the company in both Spanish and English:

CSM Vision Statement

- To be the best alternative that guarantees its insurance commitments based on its extraordinary service.
- To have an extraordinary working environment which promotes personal, family, professional, and economic development of our employees.
- To be seen as a company that transcends financial services and hopes to promote the social and cultural development of our country.

Dr. Jeff Alexander, the founder of The Youthful Tooth, a children's dental practice in Oakland, California, felt his employees needed a sense of vision that included what sort of service or product they offered and what they would receive from it. The vision he has created is:

1. "We will offer children the ability to discover the natural powers of healing in a fun and happy place."
2. "We will receive in return (a) a sense of making a difference, (b) financial abundance, and (c) a lot of fun."

Whenever a new employee is hired, he or she receives a welcome package that contains an explanation of the vision. This vision is exemplified in both the physical environment as well as in the emotional relationships. "Dr. Jeff" and his employees look at both the systems (Business level) and the people (Human level) to be sure that they support the vision. For example, if employees aren't willing to have fun, they are asked to leave.

Endnotes

CHAPTER ONE

1. Dr. Arthur DeKruyter, from a sermon at Christ Church, Oak Brook, Illinois, August 1992.
2. *American Heritage Dictionary* (Boston, MA: Houghton Mifflin Co., 1985), p. 298.
3. Louis Harris and Associates for John Hancock Financial Services, "The State of Quality Customer Service in America 1990," pp. 1 and 11.
4. Roger Von Oech, *A Whack on the Side of the Head*, reprinted by permission of Warner Books/New York, copyright 1983, p. 17.
5. Ibid., pp. 14 and 19.
6. Kaset International, *Motivating for Extraordinary Service*, p. 5.
7. Kaset International, *Achieving Extraordinary Customer Relations*, p. 9.
8. Karl Albrecht and Ron Zemke, *Service America!* (Homewood, IL: Dow Jones-Irwin, 1985), pp. 33–34.
9. Kaset International, *Achieving Extraordinary Customer Relations*, p. 18.
10. Charles Garfield, *Peak Performers*. By permission of William Morrow & Company, Inc., New York; Copyright 1986 by Garfield Enterprises, Inc., p. 107.
11. Ned Herrmann, *The Creative Brain*, reprinted with permission, Appendix E (Lake Lure, NC: Brain Books, 1988).

CHAPTER TWO

1. David Erdman, from a speech "Service Quality As the Driving Force Behind Organizational Transformation," Kaset International Executive Conference, 1992, p. 10.
2. This material is from a survey reported in *Foreman Facts*, Labor Relations Institute of New York, December 1946. Discussed in *Personnel* magazine by Laurence Lindahl in January 1949. Updated in 1988 by Valerie Wilson, Achievers International.
3. Ibid.
4. David Erdman, p. 10.

CHAPTER THREE

1. Sherry Sweetnam, President, Sweetnam Communications, Eden Prairie, Minnesota, 1992.

2. Juan Gutierrez, "Improving Service Quality: A Checklist for Success," *Roundtable*, Spring 1992, pp. 46–47.

3. Kaset International and Performance Research Associates, Inc., *Managing Extraordinary Service*, p. 29.

4. Peter Lichtgarn, *The Corporate Communicator's Quick Reference* (Homewood, IL: Business One Irwin, 1990), p. 60.

5. Ron McCann and Joe Vitale, *The Joy of Service* (Stafford, TX: Service Information Source Publications, 1989), pp. 80, 82.

6. Ibid.

7. David Armstrong, *Managing By Storying Around*, used by permission of Doubleday, a division of Bantam Doubleday Dell Publishing Group, Inc., copyright 1992 by David Armstrong, p. 11.

8. "Andy Warhol Would Have Been Proud . . . ," *Customer Service Newsletter, Special Sample Issue 1991.*

9. "Service Guarantees Prove a Potent Marketing Tool," *The Service Edge*, May 1992; reprinted with permission, *Inc.* magazine, copyright 1992 by Goldhirsh Group, Inc., p. 4.

10. Ingrid Eisenstadter, "It's in the Cards," reprinted with permission, *Executive Female* magazine, November/December 1990, pp. 44–45.

CHAPTER FOUR

1. Lichtgarn, p. 62.

2. "Lights, Camera, Quality," reprinted with permission, *Technical Trainer/Skills Trainer*, Winter 1992 (from *Across the Board* magazine, October 1991), p. 4.

3. "Videotape Brings to Life Customer Needs, Problems," *The Service Edge*, August 1992, reprinted with permission of the *Pryor Report*, vol. 8, no. 8 (April 1992), p. 4.

4. "Focus on AMP, Inc.," used with permission, *The Service Edge*, August 1992, p. 3.

5. Ibid.

6. "Voice Response System Improves Caller Access," used with permission, *The Service Edge*, April 1992, p. 5.

7. Jim Meyer, "You'll Get the Picture," *ABA Journal*, November 1992, p. 99.

8. Joan Brightman, "Use Technology to: Meet Face to Face Without Getting on that Plane," reprinted with permission, *Executive Female*, May/June 1992, pp. 14–15.

9. "Interactive Video Links University Classrooms," *Training*, August 1992, p. 15.

10. Meyer, p. 99.

11. Joel Gruber, "Voice Processing: A Fine Line Between Customer Friendly and Customer Deadly," used with permission, *The Service Edge*, March 1992, p. 7.

12. Ibid., p. 7.

13. Ron Zemke, "If Voice Mail Beckons, Approach with Caution," used with permission of Ron Zemke, *The Service Edge*, April 1992, p. 8.

14. Bob Greene, "After Hours in the Electronic Office," *The Chicago Tribune*, Tempo Section, Monday, January 27, 1992, p. 1.

15. "Focus on Seafirst Bank," used with permission, *The Service Edge*, June 1992, p. 5.

CHAPTER FIVE

1. Stephen Covey, *Principle-Centered Leadership* (New York: Simon & Schuster, 1990), pp. 112, 113.

2. Ken Johnston, *Busting Bureaucracy* (Homewood, IL: Business One Irwin, 1993), p. 47.

3. Armstrong, pp. 242–43.

4. Hal Rosenbluth and Diane McFerrin, *The Customer Comes Second*, by permission of William Morrow & Company, Inc., copyright 1992 by Hal Rosenbluth and Diane McFerrin, pp. 18–20.

5. "John Hancock Employees Become Customers," used with permission, *The Service Edge*, November 1991, p. 3.

6. Armstrong, p. 143.

7. "Focus on Servicemaster," used with permission, *The Service Edge*, February 1992, p. 3.

8. "Taking Stock, Moving Ahead," *Technical Trainer/Skills Trainer*, Spring/Summer 1992, p. 3.

9. Alexandra Lang, "in-touch," Kaset International, Summer 1992, pp. 4–5.

10. "More Firms Link Pay, Cash Bonuses to Service to Sustain Long-term Change," used with permission, *The Service Edge*, May 1992, p. 2.

11. Rosenbluth, p. 151.

12. Chris Lee, "After the Cuts," *Training*, July 1992, p. 22.

13. Max De Pree, *Leadership Jazz*, used by permission of Doubleday, a division of Bantam Doubleday Dell Publishing Group, Inc., copyright 1992 by Max Depree, pp. 132–33.

14. Dr. Patrick C. Coggins, Stetson University, Deland, Florida, 1992.

15. Bob Filipczak, "25 Years of Diversity at UPS," *Training*, August 1992, p. 43.

16. DePree, p. 37.

CHAPTER SIX

1. Shannon Johnston, co-founder of Kaset International, Tampa, Florida, 1992.

CHAPTER SEVEN

1. Editors, "All Work and No Play...Isn't Even Good for Work," *Psychology Today,* March 1989, p. 34.

2. David J. Abramis, "Finding the Fun at Work," *Psychology Today,* March 1989, p. 38.

3. "All Work and No Play," p. 35.

4. Armstrong, p. 165.

5. "Flag Serves as Barometer of Service Success, Failure," used with permission, *The Service Edge,* October 1991, p. 4.

6. Rosenbluth, pp. 148, 150.

7. "Mindscapes...Landscapes," Benchmark Communications, Inc., 1991/92, p. 2.

8. Editors, "From Rocky Road to Joy," *Training & Development Journal,* copyright January 1992, the American Society for Training and Development, reprinted with permission, p. 83.

9. Alexandra Lang, "in-touch," Kaset International, Summer 1992, p. 8.

10. "Extended Hours," used with permission, *The Service Edge,* February 1992, p. 2.

CHAPTER EIGHT

1. Chip Bell and Ron Zemke, *Managing Knock Your Socks Off Service* (New York: Amacom, 1992), pp. 113–116.

2. "Customer Surveys: Creating Actionable Questions Is Only Part of the Battle," used with permission, *The Service Edge,* July 1992, p. 2.

3. "Focus on AMP, Inc.," used with permission, *The Service Edge,* August 1992, p. 3.

4. "Personal Attention Boosts Public Transit Ridership," *The Service Edge,* June 1992, p. 4. Used with permission of the *Minneapolis Star Tribune.*

5. "Customer Surveys," used with permission, *The Service Edge,* July 1992, p. 2.

6. Alexandra Lang, "in-touch," Kaset International, Summer 1992, pp. 6–7.

7. Nancy R. Austin, "Wacky Management Ideas That Work," *Working Woman,* November 1991, p. 42.

8. Alexandra Lang, "in-touch," Kaset International, Summer 1992, p. 9.

9. Kaset International and Performance Research Associates, Inc., *Managing Extraordinary Service,* p. 64.

10. "Focus on Seafirst Bank," *The Service Edge,* June 1992, p. 5.

11. "More Firms Link Pay," *The Service Edge,* May 1992, p. 1.

12. "Point System Helps to Elevate Service Focus," used with permission, *The Service Edge,* December 1991, p. 5.

13. *Managing Extraordinary Service,* pp. 17–18.

14. Austin, p. 42.

15. "Focus on Seafirst Bank," *The Service Edge*, June 1992, p. 5.

16. "Focus on Apple Computer," used with permission, *The Service Edge*, March 1992, p. 3.

17. Ron Zemke, "When Good Things Happen to Small Customers," used with permission of Ron Zemke, *The Service Edge*, December 1991, p. 8.

18. Ron Zemke, "Questions Readers Ask," used with permission of Ron Zemke, *The Service Edge*, February 1992, p. 5.

19. "$5 Incentive Provides Valued Customer Feedback," *The Service Edge*, February 1992, reprinted with permission, *Inc.* magazine, copyright by Goldhirsh Group, Inc., p. 4.

CHAPTER NINE

1. "Recognition Is Top Employee Motivator: Study," *National Underwriter*, no. 52 (December 30, 1991), p. 95.

2. Ibid.

3. Fran Solomon, Ritch Davidson, and Jeff Randall, "Celebrate! The Power of Reward and Recognition," Playfair, Inc., Berkeley, CA.

4. Ibid.

5. De Pree, pp. 65, 68–69, 74–75.

6. Michael LeBoeuf, *The Greatest Management Principle in the World*, reprinted by permission of The Putnam Publishing Group, copyright 1985 by Michael LeBoeuf, p. 7–8.

7. Ibid.

8. Armstrong, pp. 55–56.

9. De Pree, pp. 54–55.

CHAPTER TEN

1. *Managing Extraordinary Service*, p. 49.

2. Chip Bell, Performance Research Associates, Inc., Dallas, TX, 1992.

3. Armstrong, pp. 37–39.

4. "Complaining Customers Choose Their Own Amends," used with permission, *The Service Edge*, December 1991, p. 4.

5. Ron Zemke, "When Good Things Happen . . . ," used with permission of Ron Zemke, *The Service Edge*, December 1991, p. 8.

CHAPTER ELEVEN

1. Alan Zaremba, "Turn the Beat Around," *Total Quality Observer*, September 1992, p. 7.

2. James Mapes, "Foresight First," *Sky*, September 1992, pp. 96, 100, 102, 103.

3. Ibid., p. 102.

4. Garfield, pp. 85–86.

5. Kaset International, *Motivating for Extraordinary Service*, p. 6.

6. Joseph Shaute, "Ready, Fire, Aim: Achieving Managerial Support for TQM," *The Quality Observer*, April 1992, p. 11.

7. Rosenbluth, p. 26.

8. Michael Mescon and Timothy Mescon, "Saluting the Champions," *Sky*, February 1989, p. 112.

9. M. H. Schwartz, "To My CEO," *Quality Progress*, July 1992, p. 82.

10. "ASTD's 1991 Technical and Skills Training Conference, Keynote Speakers Focus on Thinking Skills and Employee Involvement," used with permission, *Technical Trainer/Skills Trainer*, Winter 1992, pp. 6–7.

11. Chris Barnett, "Darryl Hartley-Leonard," *VISaVIS*, June 1992, p. 61.

12. Editors, "From Rocky Road to Joy," *Training & Development Journal*, p. 83.

13. Tom Peters, "Managers: Show Your Workers You Care About Them and They'll Care About Customers," *The Service Edge*, June 1992, from Tom Peters's syndicated column "On Excellence," reprinted with permission, copyright 1992, all rights reserved, p. 7.

14. "Operation Wise Buy," National Consumer's Week 1992, produced by National Futures Association in cooperation with the U.S. Office of Consumer Affairs. Translation services in Spanish and Chinese provided by AT&T American Transtech.

15. Dorian Burden, "The Importance of Being a Mentor," used with permission, *Executive Female*, July/August 1992, pp. 47–48.

16. Lydia Preston, "Russian Aid," *National Geographic Traveller*, vol. IX, no. 5, September/October 1992, p. 12.

17. Barnett, p. 60.

18. "Serving Older Customers Well Means Rethinking Some Time-Honored Assumptions," interview with David Wolfe, used with permission, *The Service Edge*, August 1992, p. 7.

APPENDIX

1. Rosenbluth, p. 39.

Bibliography

Albrecht, Karl. *Service Within*. Homewood, IL: Business One Irwin, 1990.

Albrecht, Karl. *The Creative Corporation*. Homewood, IL: Dow Jones-Irwin, 1987.

Armstrong, David. *Managing by Storying Around*. New York: Doubleday Currency, 1992.

Bell, Chip; Zemke, Ron. *Managing Knock Your Socks Off Service*. New York: Amacom, 1992.

Covey, Stephen R. *Principle-Centered Leadership*. New York: Simon & Schuster, 1990.

De Pree, Max. *Leadership Jazz*. New York: Doubleday Currency, 1992.

Garfield, Charles. *Peak Performers*. New York: William Morrow and Co., Inc., 1986.

Herrmann, Ned. *The Creative Brain*. Lake Lure, NC: Brain Books, 1988.

Johnston, Kenneth. *Busting Bureaucracy*. Homewood, IL: Business One Irwin, 1993.

Le Boeuf, Michael. *The Greatest Management Principle in the World*. New York: G. P. Putnam's Sons, 1985.

Lichtgarn, Peter. *The Corporate Communicator's Quick Reference*. Homewood, IL: Business One Irwin, 1993.

McCann, Ron; Vitale, Joe. *The Joy of Service*. Stafford, TX: Service Information Source Publications, 1989.

Peters, Tom; Austin, Nancy. *A Passion for Excellence*. New York: Random House, 1985.

Rosenbluth, Hal F.; McFerrin Peters, Diane. *The Customer Comes Second*. New York: William Morrow and Company, Inc., 1992.

The State of Quality Customer Service in America: 1990, Conducted by Louis Harris and Associates; Sponsored by John Hancock Financial Services: Boston, MA, November 1990. For copies, contact:

Department of Consumer Affairs
John Hancock Financial Services
P.O. Box 111, C-1
Boston, MA 02117

Von Oech, Roger. *A Whack on The Side of The Head*. New York: Warner Books, Inc., 1990.

Nonprofit Organizations:

One World One People Foundation, 5445 DTC Parkway, Suite 720, Englewood, CO 80111-0526. (303) 220-8777, Fax: (303) 220-0526 or contact Spoma Mattson (800) 292-2272.

Index